# PANAMA CANAL B

D0115385

---

**DOCUMENTATION**

Passenger Name _____

Ship Name _____

Date of Voyage _____

Stateroom _____

*A ship passes Gold Hill in Culebra Cut. The same view during construction is shown on opposite page.*

# PANAMA CANAL
## By Cruise Ship

Fifth Edition

## ANNE VIPOND

*YOUR PORTHOLE COMPANION*

**OCEAN CRUISE GUIDES**
*Guidebooks to the world of cruising*

*Vancouver, Canada   Pt. Roberts, USA*

Published by: Ocean Cruise Guides Ltd.
Canada:                                USA:
325 English Bluff Road                 PO Box 2041
Delta, BC V4M 2M9                      Pt. Roberts, WA 98281-2041

Editors: Duart Snow, Richard Rogers, Mel-Lynda Andersen
Contributing Editor: Michael DeFreitas.
Artwork by Alan H. Nakano.
Cartography: Reid Jopson, Doug Quiring, Cartesia, OCG.
Design: Ocean Cruise Guides
Publisher: William Kelly
**Visit our web site: www.oceancruiseguides.com**

**Printed in China**

**Library and Archives Canada Cataloguing in Publication Data**
ISBN: 978-1-927747-04-9
ISSN: 1921-8060

Vipond, Anne, 1957-
Panama Canal by cruise ship : the complete guide to cruising the Panama Canal / Anne Vipond. -- 5th edition

Includes index.
"Your Porthole Companion".
ISBN 978-1-927747-04-9

1. Cruise ships--Panama--Panama Canal--Guidebooks. 2. Cruise ships--Caribbean Area--Guidebooks. 3. Cruise ships--Mexico--Guidebooks. 4. Panama Canal (Panama)--Guidebooks. 5. Caribbean Area--Guidebooks. 6. Mexico--Guidebooks. I. Title.

F1569.C2V56 2014          917.28704'54          C2001-911144-4

*Red Dart Frog*

# Contents

# PART TWO

# THE VOYAGE & THE PORTS

The Panama Canal changed the face of the earth. Upon its completion, the world's two great oceans were joined and a safe maritime route, sought after for centuries, was created. The story of how this passage was conceived, constructed and completed is not only one of mankind's greatest engineering feats, but a saga of human drama – infused with hope, despair, defeat and, ultimately, victory. Above all, the Panama Canal was a success story. Built by the United States, it was completed under budget, in both time and money, and has operated successfully ever since.

The Panama Canal has been compared to the Great Pyramids of Giza. Both were monumental projects, magnificent for their sheer size and triumph of engineering rather than their artistic merit, and both reflect the times in which they were built. The Pyramids are a testament to the supreme power of Ancient Egypt's almighty pharaohs, whereas the Panama Canal is a 20th-century icon to hard work, modern technology and democratic ideals. Built not for one supreme ruler of an empire, but for the benefit of the entire world, the canal was constructed without slave labor by workers who were fiercely proud of the Herculean project they were part of. This monument for the world is not a passive structure symbolizing kingly power, but a massive machine that is constantly harnessing and releasing thousands of cubic tons of water as it lifts and lowers 10-storey-high ships in its locks. Operating night and day, the canal was cut through bedrock of the Continental Divide, enabling ocean liners to travel between the Atlantic and Pacific in a mere eight hours.

For cruise passengers, these are likely the most exciting eight hours ever spent on board a ship. From the moment the ship enters the first set of locks until its release into another ocean, the voyage is momentous – not only for what can be seen and enjoyed while underway but for the historic journey the canal represents. During its construction, the canal was like a battlefield, with thousands dying from disease and accidents. But those who sacrificed their lives to this courageous undertaking have given the world one of its proudest and most unifying accomplishments.

*Anne Vipond*

**A ship eases through the single lift lock at Pedro Miguel.**

# PART I

*GENERAL INFORMATION*

## Choosing Your Cruise

The highlight of a Panama Canal cruise is, of course, the canal itself. There are, however, numerous itineraries covering the Panama Canal. These include 10-day round-trip cruises from Fort Lauderdale, 19-day round-trip cruises from Los Angeles, and two- to three-week cruises between Florida and the West Coast.

It used to be that canal cruises were offered only in spring and fall when cruise ships migrate between the Caribbean and Alaska. Called repositioning cruises (in reference to the

**CARIBBEAN CRUISE DISTANCES**

FROM MIAMI TO:

| | |
|---|---|
| Nassau | 190 miles |
| San Juan | 1100 miles |
| St. Thomas | 1180 miles |
| Jamaica | 810 miles |
| Curacao | 1320 miles |
| Panama Canal | 1430 miles |

ships positioning themselves in the Caribbean for the winter and in Alaskan waters for the summer) these itineraries remain the ideal Panama Canal cruise in terms of visiting numerous ports of call – the idyllic islands of the Caribbean, the tropical rainforests and Mayan ruins of Central America, the beach resorts of the Mexican Riviera, and the exciting coastal cities of California. However, for people looking for a shorter mid-winter cruise, there are now regular Panama Canal transits available from November through March, including 15-day cruises between Fort Lauderdale and San Diego or Los Angeles, and 11-day roundtrip cruises out

*Shipboard view of the watertight miter gates of Pedro Miguel locks – one of many engineering marvels of the Panama Canal.*

of Fort Lauderdale which feature a partial transit of the canal.

Partial transits of the canal from the Caribbean side provide passengers with the experience of being raised in the Gatun Locks, cruising around one of the largest man-made lakes in the world, then being lowered back into the Caribbean. Colon is the Panama port of call for ships entering the canal from the Caribbean, while ships approaching from the Pacific side sometimes dock at Fort Amador (near Panama City). Passengers arriving at either of these Panama ports can take shore excursions throughout the entire Canal Area, including those to the Gatun Locks and the old Spanish forts. Most ships making a full transit of the canal (an eight-hour daytime transit from one ocean to the other) do not stop in Panama. One exception is Princess Cruises, which includes a port call at Fort Amador on the Pacific side.

On the Caribbean side, base ports for canal cruises are Florida's Fort Lauderdale and Miami, and Puerto Rico's San Juan. On the Pacific side, the cruise lines use Costa Rica's Puerto Caldera, San Diego, Los Angeles, San Francisco, Seattle and Vancouver as ports of embarkation and disembarkation.

The best time to take a Panama Canal cruise is during the dry season, which is from mid-December to mid-April. However, even during the wet season, the rainfall is not steady but comes in sporadic downpours. The temperature remains fairly constant throughout the year in the tropics, but the humidity climbs in the summer months, which is when most cruise ships are elsewhere in the world.

Most of the major cruise lines send ships through the Panama Canal. These vessels range from

10-storey-high megaships carrying 2,000+ passengers to small luxury ships carrying only 200 passengers. Many of the new ships have been built with an abundance of private balconies adjoining the outside staterooms and these are proving to be very popular with passengers on a Panama Canal cruise, for everyone wants to be out on deck when the ship is lifted and lowered in each set of locks.

Mexican Riviera cruises are also available from San Diego and Los Angeles. These are roundtrip itineraries that visit several ports in Mexico but do not venture beyond to Central America and the Panama Canal. A seven-day roundtrip cruise from LA or San Diego will typically call at Cabo San Lucas, Mazatlan and Puerto Vallarta.

## Choosing a Cruise Line

Choosing a cruise line used to depend a great deal on your budget and, although that is still true, the competitiveness of the cruise business has resulted in a much narrower price band among the premium and contemporary lines. In fact, the average base price of a cruise is comparable to that of twenty years ago. On large ships,

*(Above) Royal Caribbean's Radiance of the Seas is a Panamax megaship with over 2,000 passengers. (Below) Seabourn's small luxury ships carry about 200 passengers.*

the accommodations are (in order of escalating price): inside stateroom; outside stateroom with window; outside stateroom with balcony; outside suite with large balcony. Some ships also have family staterooms and interconnecting staterooms.

When selecting a stateroom, bear in mind that those located on the lower decks in the middle of the ship will experience less movement than those on the higher decks at either end of the ship – an important consideration if you are susceptible to seasickness. Another thing to consider is your stateroom's location in relation to the ship's facilities. Do you

*Relaxing days at sea are a chance to enjoy a ship's upper decks by the pool.*

want to be a short walk away from the casual restaurant or is it more important that you are close to the health spa, or – if you have small children – the play room? If you have preferences for cabin location, be sure to discuss these with your cruise agent when booking. If your budget permits, an outside cabin – especially one with a verandah – is preferable for enjoying the scenery and orienting yourself at a new port. Cruise lines often reward passengers who book early with upgrades to a more expensive stateroom.

When choosing a cruise line, it's best to use a qualified cruise agent. Look for an agency displaying the CLIA logo, indicating its agents have received training from the Florida-based Cruise Lines International Association. CLIA-certified cruise agents are an excellent source of information, with personal knowledge of ships and itineraries. A certified cruise agent can provide detail about the choices of itineraries

and cabin categories, and will be able to get you the best deals available – both early-bird specials and last-minute promotions.

Buying a cruise through the Internet is an option, but the results may not be wholly satisfactory. For example, cabins available in a specific price category will be limited and those available may not be in desirable locations of the ship. At the very least, a travel agent can use their experience with a cruise line to find a cabin you want on the itinerary you want. Most cruise lines encourage their customers to book through a travel agent.

For a brief description of the various lines and ships currently offering Panama Canal cruises – and Mexican Riviera cruises – see the Cruise Lines Glossary at the back of this book.

Cruise lines that offer the ultimate in comfort, cuisine and attentive service are the **luxury** brands and they are the most expensive ships to cruise on. These finely appointed ships are small to mid-sized ships and carry relatively few passengers in spacious staterooms, often with private verandahs. The onboard facilities and entertainment cater mostly to adults, dining is open seating and the dress code tends to be casually elegant. All-inclusive fares are another feature of most luxury brands.

Next in rank are the **upper-premium** lines (also called deluxe and upmarket). These lines usually operate spacious, mid-sized ships with a country-club atmosphere and port-intensive itineraries. They appeal to seasoned cruisers who are more interested in destinations than onboard diversions.

Ships of the **premium** brands range in size from mid-sized to large, and offer above-average food, service and amenities, including a high number of outside cabins with balconies. These lines appeal to all age groups, with facilities for children and a broad range of activities and entertainment. Premium brands have a fairly high ratio of public space aboard the ship for each passenger, and dining options usually include both traditional and open sittings in the main dining room, where formal nights remain a popular event with passengers .

Ships of the **contemporary** lines are usually large but have less space per passenger, and provide average food and service, although some represent excellent value, with staterooms, meals and entertainment comparable to the premium lines. These megaships appeal to families and young couples because of their extensive recreational facilities, range of activities for children and upbeat atmosphere. The overall ambience is casual, but formal nights in the main dining room remain a popular feature on many of these ships.

The size of cruise ships has increased dramatically over the last few decades. The *Titanic*, which held 2,400 passengers and was a huge ship for its time, was about 46,000 tons. Today there are numerous ships over 100,000 tons carrying 3,000+ passengers (too large to transit the Canal) and their massive size allows for such onboard amenities as putting greens, water slides and shopping malls. The largest size of ship able to transit the Panama Canal is about 90,000 tons, but this will change upon completion of a new third lane and larger locks (slated to open in 2015) when the term Panamax will no longer apply.

*Holland America's 55,000-ton Veendam is a mid-sized ship carrying 1,260 passengers.*

## Land Tours

A cruise is a perfect opportunity to combine a vacation at sea with a land-based holiday. If time allows, fly to your port of embarkation at least a day before the cruise begins, thus avoiding the stress of making same-day travel connections. Better yet, stay two or three nights at your base port to recover from jet lag, relax and have time to enjoy the local sights. Cities such as Fort Lauderdale, Miami, San Juan, Acapulco, San Diego, Los Angeles, San Francisco, Seattle and Vancouver are all tourist destinations in themselves and warrant a brief stay either at the beginning or end of a canal cruise. The major

*Snorkeling excursions are offered at the Caribbean ports.*

cruise lines offer hotel packages at their turn-around ports, and several offer extended land tours.

Some intriguing tours include the rail journey along Mexico's breathtaking Copper Canyon, weaving through the rugged mountains of the Sierra Madre. Costa Rican land tours often include an overnight stay in the capital of San Jose and a day or two spent visiting rainforests and viewing volcanoes.

## Shore Excursions

*(See Part Two for specific shoreside excursions and options at each port of call.)*

The cruise lines offer organized shore excursions for the convenience of their passengers and these are described on their websites. On-board presentations are also given during the cruise by the ship's shore excursion staff..

Most cruise lines accept advance on-line bookings of shore excursions, and accept bookings (and cancellations) throughout the cruise. There is a charge for these excursions but they are usually fairly priced and the tour operators used are reliable and monitored by the cruise company to ensure they maintain the level of service promised to passengers, with the added advantage that the ship will wait for any of its overdue excursions.

Ship-organized shore excursions cover the whole range of possible activities and are attractive for their convenience. You are transported to and from the ship, any needed equipment is provided, and you know ahead of time the cost and length of the tour. They are especially useful for sports activities such as golf, kayaking and scuba diving.

However, independent-minded passengers need not feel that pre-booked shore excursions are their only option when exploring various ports of call. If the ship docks right beside a town or city center, a person can simply set off on foot to do some sightseeing and shopping. Beaches are often within walking distance or a short taxi ride away and most are open to tourists, although it's not unusual for there to be a small admission charge. Beachfront hotels often rent lounge chairs, beach umbrellas, watersports equipment and the use of lockers and change facilities to the public.

Many Caribbean and Mexican Riviera resorts let non-guests use their tennis courts for a fee, and the ship's shore excursion office can usually provide resort information and recommendations for each port of call.

For independent sightseeing, renting a car is an option on most Caribbean islands. However, driving is often on the left, the roads can be narrow and winding, and a temporary driver's licence is usually required in addition to the rental fee, bringing the total cost above that of hiring a taxi for a few hours. However, it's fun to strike out on your own, and the roads are often quiet once you get away from the port area. Be sure to give yourself plenty of time to get back to the ship.

Hiring a taxi is another option. The cruise line will likely provide you with a port information sheet containing some sample fares, which are often set by the local taxi association and posted near the cruise ship pier. At some ports a taxi director is stationed at the cruise terminal to quote fares and direct passengers to qualified drivers. Other ports provide pierside information booths. Customized tours can be negotiated, so don't hesitate to chat with a few drivers before striking a deal. Always agree beforehand on the price of the tour and exactly which stops are included. Most drivers are a wealth of information and represent an opportunity to learn more about the local people while seeing the port of call's natural and historical sights.

*Excursions by boat are popular at Cabo San Lucas and other Mexican ports of call.*

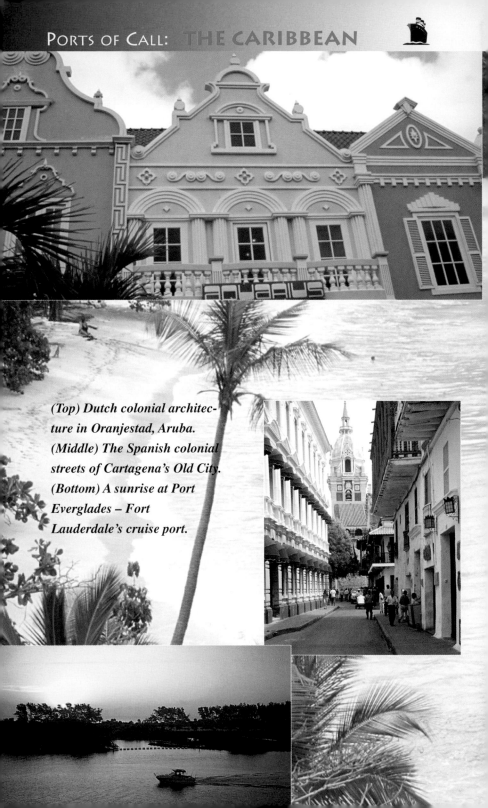

*(Top) Dutch colonial architecture in Oranjestad, Aruba.*
*(Middle) The Spanish colonial streets of Cartagena's Old City.*
*(Bottom) A sunrise at Port Everglades – Fort Lauderdale's cruise port.*

*(Top) Private island stops are sometimes part of a Panama Canal itinerary.*
*(Middle) Flowers that flourish in the tropics include the exquisite hibiscus.*
*(Bottom) George Town on Grand Cayman Island is a popular port of call with its boat tours and easy access to famous Seven Mile Beach.*

*(Above) The remains of the old French Canal near the Atlantic entrance.*
*(Left) Miraflores Locks; Ancon Hill in background.*
*(Below right) Embera children at Gatun Lake.*
*(Bottom) Children on a ship watch their progress through Gatun Locks.*

*(Top) Mangroves line an estuary of the Tarcoles River, Costa Rica.*
*(Right) Enjoying the view of beautiful, island-dotted Lake Nicaragua.*
*(Bottom) The great Maya site of Tikal, situated in the jungles of Guatemala.*

*(Top) El Arco, Cabo San Lucas. (Middle) A dancer performs a festive folk number in Mazatlan. (Bottom) The tranquil fishing port of Zihuatenejo.*

*(Top) One of Acapulco's famous cliff divers. (Middle) The Arches grace the waterfront at Puerto Vallarta. (Bottom) The fishing village of Santa Cruz is now part of Huatulco, a growing eco-tourism resort.*

## Documentation

A valid passport is the best proof of citizenship a traveler can carry, and is required for entering Costa Rica and other Central American countries included in a Panama Canal cruise. Should you be taking a Mexican Riviera cruise, be aware that American citizens returning to their country by air must have a passport, and Canadian citizens arriving by air into the United Sates must carry a passport. Under the Western Hemisphere Travel Initiative (WHTI), American and Canadian citizens entering the U.S. at land and sea ports of entry without a passport must carry a WHTI-compliant document.

Before your departure, leave a detailed travel itinerary with a friend or family member in case someone needs to contact you while you're away. Be sure to include the name of your ship, its phone number and the applicable ocean code, as well as your stateroom number – all of which will be included in your cruise documents. With this information, a person can call the international telephone operator and place a satellite call to your ship in an emergency. Connecting by cell phone is not certain – there's a good chance your cell phone will not work at most Caribbean and Panama stops.

As a precaution, you should photocopy the identification page of your passport, your driver's licence and any credit cards you will be taking on your trip. Keep one copy of this photocopied information with you, separate from your passport and wallet, and leave another one at home.

With regard to travel insurance, a comprehensive policy can be bought when you book your cruise – one that covers trip cancellation, delayed departure, medical expenses, personal accident and liability, lost baggage and money, and legal expenses.

## Currency

Each country visited on a Panama Canal cruise has its own legal tender, but American currency is accepted everywhere in the Caribbean, Central America and Mexico, as are major credit cards and travelers cheques. It's best to have several credit cards, and married couples should arrange for at least one set of separate cards (without joint signing privileges) in case one spouse loses his or her wallet and all of the couple's joint cards have to be cancelled.

*Costa Rica's beautiful paper money.*

Taxi fares are usually paid in cash, and it's prudent to carry enough to cover the fare back to your ship in the event you somehow miss your tour bus. It's also a good idea to carry a handful of small US bills for tips and minor purchases rather than receive large amounts of local currency in change. Travelers cheques should be cashed on board the ship unless you are planning a large purchase.

## Health Precautions

No vaccinations are required for a Canal cruise but you may want to consult your doctor in this regard. Mosquito-transmitted diseases, such as dengue fever, do exist in the tropics and some precautions should be taken if embarking on a rainforest hike, such as wearing a long-sleeved cotton shirt and slacks, and applying insect repellent to exposed skin.

To avoid traveler's diarrhea, it's best to drink bottled water when ashore, avoid eating food from street vendors or open-air stands, and never eat a piece of unfamiliar fruit you see hanging from a tree.

The overall standards of cleanliness on board cruise ships are extremely high. However, contagious viruses (such as the Norwalk stomach virus – a brief but severe gastrointestinal illness) are spread by person-to-person contact. To avoid contracting such a virus, practise frequent and thorough handwashing with warm soapy water.

All large ships have a fully equipped medical center with a doctor and nurses. Passengers needing medical attention are billed at private rates which are added to their shipboard account. This invoice can be submitted to your insurance company upon your return home. You may already have supplementary health insurance through a credit card, automobile club policy or employment health plan, but you should check these carefully. Whatever policy you choose for your trip, carry details of it with you and documents showing that you are covered by a plan. If you plan on doing any scuba diving, be sure to bring your diving certification.

Modern cruise ships use stabilizers to reduce any rolling motion when underway, so seasickness is not a widespread or prolonged problem with most passengers. However, there are a number of remedies for people susceptible to this affliction. One is to wear special wrist bands, the balls of which rest on an acupressure point. Another option is to chew meclizine tablets (often available at the ship's front office) or take Dramamine, an over-the-counter antihistamine. It's best to take these pills ahead of time, before you feel too nauseous, and they may make you feel drowsy. Fresh air is one of the best antidotes to motion sickness, so stepping out on deck is often all that's needed to counter any queasiness. Other simple remedies include sipping on ginger ale and nibbling on dry crackers and an apple. Should you become concerned about your condition, simply visit the medical center on board for professional attention.

## What to Pack

Trunks of new clothes aren't a necessity for a cruise. Pack casual attire for daytime wear – both on board the ship and in port. Swimwear is unacceptable when you're away from the beach, so dress modestly when visiting the local towns of the Caribbean, Central America and Mexico, especially if you plan to enter any of the churches. Cool, loose cottons are best. Take a wide-brimmed straw or cotton hat and a comfortable pair of rubber-soled shoes for walking on cobblestone streets or trekking along forest trails. Also, take along a light, waterproof windbreaker for rain forest hikes. A light sweater or sweat top will come in handy when the air conditioning in restaurants, stores and museums is much cooler than the temperature outside. Sunscreen is also important, one with a protection factor of 15 or

*Good walking shoes are imperative for getting around at the ports of call, where cobblestone streets are common.*

higher, to shield your skin from the sun's burning rays. Apply generously before going outside and reapply frequently if you are spending time at the beach, even when the sky is overcast.

Your evening wear should include something suitable for the formal nights held on board most ships. Women wear gowns or cocktail dresses and men favor suits. For casual evenings, the women wear dresses, skirts or slacks, and the men wear open-necked shirts and sports jackets. Some ships have coin-operated launderettes with an iron and ironing board, or you can pay a small fee to have your laundry done by the ship's staff, as well as steam pressing and dry cleaning.

Basic toiletries, such as soap and shampoo, are usually provided, and a hair dryer may or may not be installed in the bathroom, something you can determine at the time of booking. The on-board shops usually carry toiletries as well. Beach towels are supplied, upon request, for use on shore, and it's not necessary to pack snorkeling or diving gear, or golf clubs, because this equipment is included in ship-organized shore excursions or can be rented. For boat excursions, deck shoes or light-colored rubber-soled sneakers are needed. A pair of small, lightweight binoculars is especially useful for viewing wildlife in the rainforests.

Keep prescribed medication in original, labeled containers and carry a doctor's prescription for any controlled drug. If you wear prescription eyeglasses, consider packing a spare pair. And keep

all valuables (travelers cheques, camera, expensive jewelry) in your carry-on luggage, as well as all prescription medicines and documentation (passport, tickets, insurance policy). It's also prudent to pack in your carry-on bag any other essentials you would need in the event your luggage is late arriving. And, be sure to leave room for souvenirs.

## Connecting With Home

Text messaging and e-mail have pretty much replaced phone calls as the most convenient and inexpensive way to reach someone while you're away. Many of the ships provide satellite-based broadband service that allows you to use your wireless internet devices while at sea. The service, however, remains slow and sending large picture files to friends and family can be expensive. Efforts are underway to improve internet connection speeds on ships within the next few years.

Most ships have an internet cafe on board and offer flat-rate use (about $10 for 15 minutes, sometimes less). Passengers log on with their shipboard card, issued at boarding, and within seconds (hopefully!) are online. At the end of the session, the ship's system shows how much time the passenger was online and the total cost.

On many ships, passengers can use their own laptop computers or tablets to plug into the ship's connection, which can be slow (feels like about 56kps) due its reliance on satellites.

Although cell phones are the easiest way to call home, roaming charges can quickly add up (although even this is now declining). One option is to purchase a local pre-paid SIM card.

Calls can also be made through the ship's radio office or by placing a direct satellite telephone call, which is expensive (about $10 per minute). Non-urgent calls can be placed from a land-based phone at the ports of call.

*Internet cafes aboard ships are a good way to contact home.*

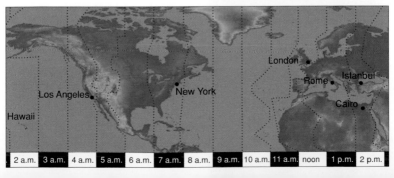

Hawaii | Los Angeles | New York | London | Rome | Istanbul | Cairo

2 a.m. | 3 a.m. | 4 a.m. | 5 a.m. | 6 a.m. | 7 a.m. | 8 a.m. | 9 a.m. | 10 a.m. | 11 a.m. | noon | 1 p.m. | 2 p.m.

## Vacation Photos

Digital images have largely replaced film, but the goal of capturing your holiday highlights with pictures remains the same. Flash card memory storage increases every year and a 8 or 16 GB card will be all most people need. However, because flash memory is so inexpensive, a backup flash card makes good sense. The ship's photo department can also transfer your photo files to a DVD or CD or can print out any photos you want. Shoot at a fine setting for print-quality reproduction. Most avid photographers pack an extra battery pack and these can be recharged in your stateroom.

The ship's photo gallery is also a good place to purchase images of yourself, friends and family members as you disembark at each port of call. These make nice mementos of your cruise. On formal nights, when everyone is looking their best, the ship's photographers are set up to take formal portraits that are displayed the next day in the photo gallery. There is no obligation to purchase

these prints but they are popular because it's a convenient and relatively inexpensive way to obtain a professional portrait.

## Shopping

The Caribbean, Mexico and Central America are well-known for their excellent and colorful handicrafts, which include pottery, wood carvings and hand-woven textiles. Sold at open-air markets, where bartering is common, items to look for are covered in each destination's respective chapter. The Caribbean is also famous for its 'free ports' where the selection and savings on luxury goods are among the world's best. With few local manufacturing industries to protect, most Caribbean countries charge no duty on imports, nor is there sales tax, resulting in savings of up to 50%. These savings are passed on to visitors who, in turn, are allowed a duty-free allowance on goods they take home.

Before you embark on your cruise, you may want to visit your local customs office and register valuables you plan to take with you (i.e. cameras, jewelry) so there is no problem re-importing them duty- and tax-free. In addition to goods bought at duty-free prices are those that are duty exempt. Any item purchased in its country of manufacture, such as locally made handicrafts, is duty exempt. Loose gems are also duty exempt.

Your ship's port lecturer will offer valuable advice on shopping at each port of call. Although recommended merchants often pay a promotional fee to the cruise line, they must guarantee products they are selling to the line's passengers. If you are considering an expensive purchase, it's prudent to shop at stores known or recommended by the cruise line. Good buys in the Caribbean include large single diamonds and tennis bracelets. The world's finest emeralds are mined in Colombia and sold throughout the Caribbean at quite low prices. Shops on board the large ships also carry leading brands of liquor, perfume, watches, jewelry, crystal and china at duty-free prices.

Special permits are required to bring home restricted animal products made from certain species, including sea turtles, most crocodiles, and all corals. To determine what you can and cannot legally bring back into your country, contact the federal department handling environmental matters.

*(Above) A Guatemalan girl displays her merchandise. (Below) Negotiating with street vendors in Mexico.*

## Watching your language

Spanish being the mother tongue of the Latin American countries visited on a Panama Canal cruise, here is a smattering of Spanish to help you communicate with your hosts:

**Common Phrases**
Good morning   Buenos dias
Good afternoon   Buenas tardes
Good night   Buenas noches
Please   Por favor
Thank you   Gracias
How much does it cost?   Cuanto cuesta?

**Spanish Place Words**
bahia – bay
lago – lake
rio – river
sierra or cordillera – mountains
malecon – sea wall /promenade
zocalo – central plaza
ciudad – city

A Panama Canal cruise is more than just a fascinating voyage through the 'big ditch'. It can include cruising the coasts of Central America and Mexico, and the intriguing islands of the Caribbean. Whatever your itinerary, there are many opportunities to ponder the complex workings of a modern cruise ship. Ships, however, have always been complex. Few people appreciate how difficult it was in the era of sail to beat against the wind from Portobelo to Florida. This 1,500-mile voyage could take months and required knowledge of currents, winds and sail settings to take advantage of changing conditions. Today, a voyage across the Caribbean on a large ship takes only a matter of days.

The complexities of ships prompted mariners to develop their own colorful vocabulary adapted with lyrical precision to describe each task. As quoted in *Smythe's Sailor's Word-Book*,

*Excellent jazz is served up on many premium brand ships.*

"How could the whereabouts of an aching tooth be better pointed out to an operative dentist than Jack's, 'Tis the aftermost grinder aloft, on the starboard quarter.'"

In the 15th century, when commerce with distant lands became increasingly profitable, trading countries began improving ship design. This resulted in stronger, faster ships with better sailing characteristics. But sea travel for passengers was usually a wretched affair until a huge wave of immigration to America in the late 19th century resulted in increased competition.

To attract passengers, ships became more elegant with opulent public areas and more cabin facilities. When grand transatlantic ocean liners were introduced in the late 19th century, elegance, fine service and superb cuisine became part of the experience, at least in first class. Graceful and inspiring, these ships usually had an extended bow, rounded stern and raked funnels. Design aspects have changed since then of course, but today's cruise ships retain the ocean liner tradition of attractive lines and elegant interiors.

## How Ships Move

Ships are pushed through the water by the turning of propellers, two of which are usually used on cruise ships. A propeller is like a screw threading its way through the sea, pushing water away from its pitched blades. Props can be 15 to 20 feet in diameter on large cruise ships and normally turn at 100 to 150 revolutions per minute. It takes a lot of horsepower – about 50,000 on a large ship – to make these propellers push a ship along. The bridge crew can tap into any amount of engine power by moving small levers which adjust the angle (or pitch) of the propeller blades to determine the speed of the ship. In addition to propelling the ship, the engines generate hot water and electrical power. Cruise ships normally travel at about 10 to 20 knots

between ports, depending on distances to be covered from port to port. Distances at sea are measured in nautical miles (1 nautical mile = 1.15 statute miles = 1.85 kilometers).

The amount of soot smoke from today's ships is a fraction of that produced by earlier ships. Today, all ships use diesel engines to transmit power by supplying electricity either to motors that smoothly turn the prop shafts or to motors mounted on pods hung from the stern of the ship, like huge outboard motors, which can swivel 360 degrees.

The majority of cruise ships currently sailing North American waters were built in the last decade or two. These new ships have been dubbed 'floating resorts' for their extensive onboard facilities, from swimming pools and health spas to show lounges and casinos. Cabins, formerly equipped with portholes, now are fitted with picture windows or sliding glass doors that open onto private verandas.

Modern cruise ships are quite different from those of the Golden Age of ocean liners, which ended on a high note with the launch of the SS *France* (which became the

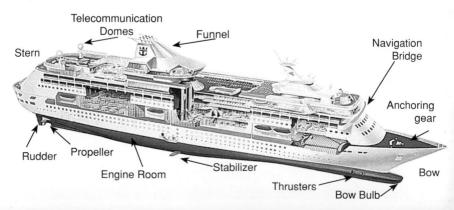

Telecommunication Domes — Funnel — Stern — Navigation Bridge — Anchoring gear — Rudder — Propeller — Engine Room — Stabilizer — Thrusters — Bow Bulb — Bow

*Norway*) in 1960 and the *Queen Elizabeth II* in 1969. These ships were designed for the rigors of regular year-round ocean crossings and some of the worst weather imaginable. Constructed with heavy riveted plating, their design features included a deep draft (more stability in rough seas) and a low profile (less windage, more maneuverability in storms).

Ships built today are generally taller, shallower, lighter and powered by smaller, more compact engines. Although their steel hulls are thinner and welded together in numerous sections, modern ships are as strong as the older ocean liners because of advances in construction technology and metallurgy.

## The Engine Room

Located many decks below the passenger cabins is the engine room – a labyrinth of tunnels, catwalks and bulkheads connecting and supporting the machinery that generates the vast amount of power needed to operate a ship.

A large, proficient crew keeps everything running smoothly, but its size is a far cry from the hundreds once needed to operate coal-burning steam engines that were used before the advent of diesel fuel.

Recent technical advancements below the ship's waterline include the bow bulb, stabilizers and thrusters. The bow bulb is located just below the waterline and displaces the same amount of water that would be pushed out of the way by the ship's bow. This virtually eliminates a bow wave, resulting in some fuel saving because less energy is needed to push the ship forward. Stabilizers are small, wing-like appendages that protrude amidships below the waterline and act to dampen the ship's roll in beam seas. These are normally not needed during an Alaskan cruise. Thrusters are

*A ship's bow bulb, the protruding red shape at bottom of the ship, reduces fuel consumption.*

port-like openings with small propellers at the bow and sometimes at the stern, located just below the waterline. They push the front or rear of the ship as it is approaching or leaving a dock and they greatly reduce the need for tugboat assistance.

## The Bridge

The bridge (located at the bow or front of the ship) is an elevated, enclosed platform bridging (or crossing) the width of the ship with an unobstructed view ahead and to either side. It is from the ship's bridge that the highest-ranking officer, the captain, oversees the operation of the ship. The bridge is manned 24 hours a day by two officers working four hours on, eight hours off, in a three-watch system. They all report to the captain, and their various duties include recording all course changes, keeping lookout and making sure the junior officer has a fresh pot of coffee going. The captain does not usually have a set watch but will be on the bridge whenever the ship is entering or leaving port, or transiting a pass. Other conditions that would bring the captain to the bridge would be poor weather or when there are numerous vessels in the area, such as commercial fishboats.

An array of instrumentation provides the ship's officers with pertinent information. The electronic Global Positioning System (GPS) uses a system of satellite signals to provide a fix of where the ship is, accurate to within a few feet. This position is displayed in a series of numbers indicating the latitude and longitude, which is compared with a chart (usually an electronic chart) to determine the ship's location.

Radar is used most intensely in foggy conditions or at night. Radar's electronic signals can survey the ocean for many miles, and anything solid – such as land or other boats – appears

*A young passenger sizes up the ship's bridge.*

on its screen. Radar is also used for plotting the course of other ships and for alerting the crew of a potential collision situation. Depth sounders track the bottom of the seabed to ensure the ship's course agrees with the depth of water shown on the official chart.

The helm on modern ships is a surprisingly small wheel. An automatic telemotor transmission connects the wheel to the steering mechanism at the stern of the ship. Ships also use an 'autopilot' which works through an electronic compass to steer a set course, and is used when cruising in open water.

Other instruments monitor engine speed, power, angle of list, speed through water, speed over ground and time arrival estimations. Along intricate sections of coastline, large ships must

*Pilot and captain navigate a ship through the Panama Canal.*

have a pilot on board to provide navigational advice to the ship's officers. These pilots have local knowledge of every back eddy, stray current and dangerous reef in their territory.

## Pilotage Challenges

In the Panama Canal, the main hazard is the waterway itself. The pilot must instruct the helmsperson exactly when to turn and by how much. The canal, in places, is less that 600 feet wide and for canal authorities, there are few things worse than a grounded ship. Ships maintain a speed of about eight knots (about nine miles per hour) through the Canal to ensure maneuverability. While in the locks, a ship is held by six to eight electric locomotives (called mules) to hold it securely in place. Double gates in the locks ensure that even the largest ship cannot breach the locks.

Because the Panama Canal is a high-level lock system, with a dam controlling all rivers flowing into Gatun Lake, currents are minimal. Ships sometimes encounter strong wind across the lake, but not enough to affect navigation. Wind conditions can be a hazard at Pacific Ocean ports which are otherwise unencumbered.

The Caribbean poses a number of challenges for cruise ship officers, not the least of which are hurricanes from June to November. However, weather information has become very accurate and ship's officers are aware of approaching storms well in advance. If necessary, they take evasive action and alter course for other ports. Ships are usually safer at sea than near land, where wind strengths often accelerate and there is the danger of a ship being blown onto a reef or incurring damage while moored to a dock.

Pinpoint navigation is lesson number one for all junior officers on cruise ships, who must always be aware of the ship's exact position and of any nearby hazards, such as reefs or strong ocean currents. Specifically, currents are strong in the Straits of Florida (between Florida and Cuba) where the Gulf Stream flows north at speeds up to five mph. If undetected, a current can slowly push a ship off course and into danger. During the days of the Spanish Main in the Caribbean, many galleons came to ruin from currents pushing them onto sandbars or reefs.

## Ship Safety

The cruise lines treat passenger safety as a top priority. The International Maritime Organization maintains high standards for safety at sea, including regular fire and lifeboat drills, as well as frequent ship inspections for cleanliness and seaworthiness.

Cruise ships must adhere to a law requiring that a lifeboat drill take place within 24 hours of embarkation, and most ships hold this mandatory drill before leaving port. All passengers must participate and you will be asked to proceed to your lifeboat station or designated gathering place (directions will be displayed somewhere in your cabin). Ship's staff are on hand to guide you through

*A tender pulls alongside a ship lying to anchor.*

the safety drill so you will know what to do in the unlikely event of an emergency. Life jackets are stowed in your stateroom.

On the ship's bridge, a large area of instrumentation is devoted to the monitoring of numerous fire alarms placed throughout the ship. If an alarm sounds, it rings on the bridge and is illuminated on a ship's diagram so that its location is immediately known and the officers can promptly secure the area to prevent the blaze from spreading. Next to ship navigation, the threat of a fire is the most serious concern for the ship's officers, and deck crews regularly practise fire safety drills.

## Tendering

At some ports, the ship will anchor rather than dock. In such instances, passengers are tendered ashore in the ship's launches. Passengers on organized shore excursions will be taken ashore first. If you're heading ashore independently, wait an hour or so to board a tender, when the line-ups are much shorter or even non-existent.

*(Above) The Front Desk is usually located in the atrium area of the ship. (Left) The hotel manager oversees a large, highly trained staff.*

## Hotel Staff

The Purser's Office/Front Desk is the pleasure center of the ship. And since a cruise is meant to be an extremely enjoyable experience, it is fitting the Hotel Manager's rank is second only to that of the Captain. In terms of staff, the Hotel Manager (or Passenger Services Director) has by far the largest. It is his responsibility to make sure beds are made, meals are served, wines are poured, entertainment is provided and tour buses arrive on time – all while keeping a smile on his face. Hotel managers generally have many years' experience on ships working in various departments before rising to this position, and usually have graduated from a university or college program in management. Often they train in the hotel or food industries, where they learn the logistics of feeding hundreds of people at a sitting.

The Hotel Manager's management staff includes a Purser, Food Services Manager, Beverage Manager, Chief Housekeeper, Cruise Director and Shore Excursion Manager. All ship's staff wear a uniform and even if a hotel officer doesn't recognize a staff member, he will know at a glance that person's duties by their uniform's color and the distinguishing bars on the sleeves. The hotel staff on cruise ships come from countries around the world.

## Life Aboard

Cruise ship cabins – also called staterooms – vary in size, from standard inside cabins to outside suites complete with a verandah. Whatever the size of your accommodation, it will be clean and comfortable. A telephone and television are standard features in stateroom, and stor-

age space includes closets and drawers ample enough to hold your clothes and miscellaneous items. Valuables can be left in your stateroom safe or in a safety deposit box at the front office, also called the purser's office.

Both casual and formal **dining** are offered on the large ships, with breakfast and lunch served in the buffet-style lido restaurant or at an open seating in the main dining room. Dinner is served at two sittings in the main dining room and, when booking your cruise, you will be asked to indicate your preference for first or second sitting at dinner. Luxury cruise lines usually have one open seating for dinner, while several of the premium and contemporary lines offer both the traditional fixed sittings as well

*(Above) A ship's specialty restaurant. (Below) An outside suite with verandah.*

as open seating in their main dining room.

Most ships also offer alternative dining – small specialty restaurants that require a reservation and for which there is usually a surcharge (about $20-$30 per person). Room service is also available, free of charge, for all meals and in-between snacks.

## Things to Do

There are so many things to do on a modern cruise ship, you would have to spend a few months onboard to participate in every activity and enjoy all of the ship's facilities. A daily newsletter, deliv-

ered to your stateroom, will keep you informed of all the ship's happenings. If exercise is a priority, you can swim in the pool, work out in the gym, jog around the promenade deck, join the aerobics and dance classes, or join in the ping pong and volleyball tournaments. Perhaps you just want to soak in the jacuzzi, relax in the sauna or treat yourself to a massage and facial at the spa.

Stop by the library if you're looking for a good book, a board game or an informal hand of bridge with your fellow passengers. Check your newsletter to see which films are scheduled for the movie theater or just settle into a deck chair, breathing the fresh sea air. Your days on the ship can be as busy or as relaxed as you want. You can stay up late every night, enjoying the varied entertainment in the ship's lounges, or you can retire early and rise at dawn to watch the ship pull into port. When the ship is in port, you can remain onboard if you wish or you can head ashore, returning to the ship as many times as you like before it leaves for the next port. Ships are punctual about departing, so be sure to get back to the ship at least a half hour before it is scheduled to leave.

Children and teenagers are welcome on most cruise ships, which offer an ideal environment for a family vacation. Youth facilities on the large ships usually include a playroom for children and a disco-type club for teenagers. Supervised activities are offered on a daily basis, overseen by staff with degrees in education, recreation or a related field. Each cruise line has a minimum age for participation (usually three years old), and some also offer private babysitting. Youth facilities and programs vary from line to line, and from ship to ship.

## Extra Expenses

There are very few additional expenses once you board a cruise ship. Your cabin and meals (including 24-hour room service) are paid for, as are any stage shows, lectures, movies,

*(Above) A lone jogger on the sports deck. (Left) Birthdays and anniversaries are celebrated with a complimentary cake.*

lounge acts, exercise classes and other activities held in the ship's public areas. If you make use of the personal services offered on board – such as dry cleaning or a spa treatment – these are not covered in the basic price of a cruise. Neither are any drinks you might order in a lounge (although you can certainly sit there and enjoy the ambience without ordering a drink). You will also be charged for any wine or alcoholic beverages you order with your meals. Optional shore excursions are another additional cost.

**Tipping** is extra and each cruise line provides its own guidelines on what various service staff should be tipped. A general amount for gratuities (in US dollars) is $3.50 per day per passenger for both your cabin steward and dining room waiter, $2 per day for your assistant waiter, and $1 per day for dining room management. A 15 percent service charge is automatically added to wine and beverage bills. Gratuities were traditionally given the last night at sea and preferably in American cash, but most cruise lines now offer a service that automatically bills a daily amount for gratuities to your shipboard account (about $10 per person). However, if you prefer to personally hand out your tips, you simply notify the front desk at the beginning of your cruise and these automatic tipping charges will be removed from your account. Most ships are cashless societies in which passengers sign for incidental expenses which are itemized on a final statement and settled at the front office by credit card or cash.

*(Above) A couple enjoys a romantic moment at the ship's rail. (Below) Dinner and champagne in the main dining room.*

## Plate Tectonics

The islands of the Caribbean and the Pacific coast of Central America all lie along the boundaries of the Caribbean plate – one of 20 or so crustal plates comprising the earth's surface. The boundaries of these plates are marked by fault lines (fractures in the earth's crust), and when the spreading ocean floors of the Atlantic and Pacific Plates are driven beneath an adjoining plate, such as the Caribbean Plate, a deepsea trench is created by a process called subduction.

A subduction zone lies at both ends of the Caribbean Plate, its eastern edge marked by an arc of volcanic islands (the Lesser Antilles) and underwater volcanoes (called sea mounts), its western boundary marked by another string of volcanic peaks lining the Pacific coastline of Central America. Here the deepsea Middle America Trench extends north along the coast of Mexico, terminating at a latitude parallel with Mexico City. From this point north, the boundaries of the oceanic Pacific Plate and the continental North American Plate come together. For several hundred miles between Los Angeles and San Francisco these two plates are moving horizontally past each other along a transform fault called the San Andreas Fault. Movement along this fault is slow and steady in some places, sporadic in others where friction prevents the plate edges from sliding smoothly.

The tectonic tug of war that created today's land masses began when the Earth's newly formed crust first divided into plates. As the large plates rubbed against each other, pieces chipped off and became terranes. These fragments could move more freely than the large plates and the earth's crust became a sort of jigsaw puzzle as pieces slowly moved from one location to another. Over the last few hundred million years, terranes off the Pacific Plate have been pushed, as if on a conveyor belt, up the west side of the North American Plate. Baja California and the site of Los Angeles were once part of the North American Plate until they were snagged by the Pacific Plate and are now being carried north. If the terrane upon which Los Angeles sits continues moving north at an average rate of two inches per year, it will reach the northern Gulf of Alaska in 76 million years.

## Earthquakes

Earthquakes are generated by blocks of rock grinding past one another along fault lines. Their relative movements can be vertical, horizontal or oblique, and are usually measured in inches per year, except when a sudden release of stress along a fault triggers an earthquake. An earthquake begins with tremors, followed by more violent shocks which gradually diminish. The origin (focus of a quake) is underground or underwater, and the epicenter is a point on the surface directly above the focus. The magnitude and intensity of the seismic waves that travel in all directions outward from

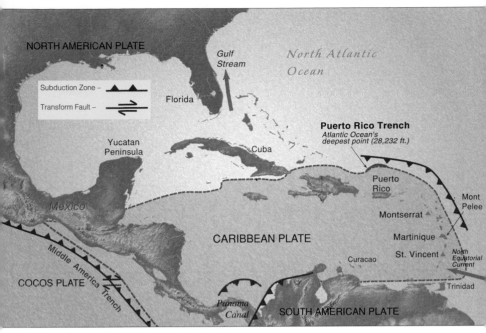

NORTH AMERICAN PLATE

Gulf
Stream

*North Atlantic*
*Ocean*

Subduction Zone –
Transform Fault –

Florida

Yucatan
Peninsula

Cuba

**Puerto Rico Trench**
*Atlantic Ocean's*
*deepest point (28,232 ft.)*

*Mexico*

Puerto
Rico

Montserrat

Mont
Pelee

Martinique

CARIBBEAN PLATE

St. Vincent

Curacao

*North*
*Equatorial*
*Current*

Middle America Trench

COCOS PLATE

Trinidad

*Panama*
*Canal*

SOUTH AMERICAN PLATE

the epicenter are determined by scales, such as the Richter scale, which measures ground motion to determine the amount of energy released at the quake's origin. A reading of less than 4.5 on the Richter scale indicates an earthquake causing light damage; a reading of more than 7 indicates a severe earthquake of devastating force. The nature of the epicenter's underlying rock and soil affects ground movements and the extent of damage.

The great San Francisco earthquake of 1906 registered 7.8 on the Richter scale, and was triggered by the sudden slippage of about six meters of rock along the San Andreas Fault. In 1971, movement of the San Fernando fault near Los Angeles rocked the ground for 10 seconds, thrusting parts of mountains upward 8 feet (2.4 m). Other California loca-

tions hit by severe earthquakes this past century include Santa Cruz in 1989 and two near Los Angeles, in 1992 and 1994. In 1972, the capital of Nicaragua, Managua, was almost totally destroyed by a severe earthquake, and in 1976 an earthquake registering a magnitude of 7.6 struck Guatemala and killed close to 23,000 people. Seismologists can predict where and how a potential earthquake will occur, but they cannot tell us when the next one will strike.

## Tsunamis

A tsunami – meaning harbor wave in Japanese – is often referred to as a tidal wave. However, tsunamis are not caused by tidal action (although a high tide can increase their onshore damage) but by sea floor earthquakes or underwater landslides. Up to 100 miles in length but with heights of only a few feet, tsunamis can travel thousands of miles across the open ocean at speeds exceeding 500 miles per hour. Their movement is undetected by ships at sea, but when they approach a shelving coastline they build into a series of waves of disastrous proportion. Anywhere from 10 to 40 minutes can pass between crests and the highest wave may occur several hours after the first wave. The sudden withdrawal of water from a shoreline could be the trough of an approaching tsunami, so people who venture onto these newly exposed beaches risk being engulfed by the wave's huge crest. A tsunami warning system is in place for the Pacific Ocean, where almost two-thirds of all tsunamis occur. In Central America, a total of 49 tsunamis have been documented between 1539 and 1999. Nine of these were destructive, the worst striking the Nicaragua coast in 1992, when a massive wave several hundred meters wide and 9.5 meters high crashed onto shore and killed 170 people.

**Tides**, controlled by the moon, are usually minimal near the equator. However, the shape and orientation of the Gulf of Panama, facing due south, forms a large catch basin for north-flowing currents, thus creating large tidal variations at the Pacific end of the Canal. While the tidal range on the Atlantic side is measured in mere inches, the tide can rise over twenty feet on the Pacific side. To compensate for these large tides,

the outermost locks at Miraflores can lift ships as little as 18 feet or as much as 38 feet, depending on the size of the tide.

## Volcanic Eruptions

Volcanoes form around an aperture in the earth's crust, through which gases, lava (molten rock) and solid fragments are ejected. A volcano's crater, its floor often covered with steam vents, is formed when the cone collapses during an eruption. A dormant volcano quickly loses its conical shape to erosion, so any mountain that is cone-shaped can be considered a potentially active volcano.

A line of active volcanoes will form above a subduction zone – where one crustal plate is slowly sliding beneath another – and this is the situation along the Pacific coast of Central America and southern Mexico, where recent eruptions of note include Guatemala's Santa Maria (1902), and Mexico's Paricutin (1943) and El Chichon (1982). In 2001, two more of Mexico's volcanoes erupted, namely Volcan de Fuego and Popocatepetl, the latter blanketing two cities southeast of Mexico City in ash. More active volcanoes are found further up the Pacific coast in the Cascade range of mountains which extends from northern California, (where Lassen Peak erupted in 1914), into southern British Columbia, and includes Washington State's Mount St. Helens which erupted in 1980.

Numerous volcanoes in the Lesser Antilles are also active, including Montserrat's Soufriere

*The 1902 eruption of Mount Pelee on Martinique killed all but one of St. Pierre's residents.*

Hills volcano which, after standing dormant for nearly 400 years, roared back to life in 1995, leaving the southern two-thirds of this once verdant island in ash-covered ruins.

The Caribbean's most violent eruption in recent times was that of Martinique's Mount Pelee on May 8, 1902. Gases within the volcano reached such a critical pressure that masses of solid and liquid rock erupted into the air and a superheated cloud of burning gas and fine ash swept down the mountainside, blanketing the nearby town of St. Pierre and destroying all life in its path. Torrential rain, caused by the condensation of steam, often accompanies such an explosion.

La Soufriere volcano on the nearby island of St. Vincent, also erupted in 1902, shortly after Mount Pelee's cataclysmic explosion, as did Santa Maria volcano in Guatemala.

## Rock Formations

The earth's layers of rock have formed in a variety of ways, including the cooling and hardening of magmas, and by metamorphism, in which intense pressures and temperatures transform the rock at great depths. The oldest of the earth's rocks have endured four billion years of tectonic activity, their changes recorded in the fossil sequence and disruptions of rock layers.

During construction of the Panama Canal, especially in the cut across the Continental Divide, engineers had to deal with complex rock formations. Culebra Hill proved to be an ancient volcanic core of solid basalt (lava hardened into igneous rock) while the soil in the valley being dug for the canal was an unstable mix of granite, sedimentary rock, shales and many forms of clay which, when wet, would flow like a glacier down the newly exposed slopes and bury months of excavation work in just a few days.

As workers modified the area's existing soil mechanics, sections of the canal floor, newly relieved of pressure, would rise as much as ten feet within minutes. On one occasion the head engineer thought a steam shovel was sinking before his eyes, but it was actually the valley floor lifting him upward six feet, "so smoothly and so little jar as to make the movement scarcely appreciable."

At one point, alarmed workers reported vents of smoke and boiling water escaping from cracks in the earth along the valley floor. The fear was that they were digging into a volcano, but a hastily summoned geologist calmed the men with the explanation they were seeing the oxidation of pyrite, a common mineral that is burned in making sulfuric acid. Geologists believe the entire Isthmus is slowly rising as the Cocos Plate is driven beneath the Caribbean Plate, presenting the possibility that some day the entire canal may have to be dug again!

## Tropical Weather

The lands and waters lying between the Tropic of Cancer and the Tropic of Capricorn are referred to as the tropics, or the torrid zone. The sun's rays are more direct in the tropics than areas in higher latitudes, so the temperature remains high year round, although this is moderated by varying wind conditions and changes in elevation, with tropical highlands experiencing a more temperate climate than the lowlands. The seasons in the steamy tropics are defined by rainfall. During the wet season, from spring through fall, the trade winds draw moisture from the oceans and carry this to land where it falls in torrential downpours. The people of Central America rely on this weather pattern for their food production, and if the rains do not come and drought conditions persist for several months, the region's bean and corn crops soon die in the parched conditions, forcing residents to scavenge for mangoes and bananas. Prolonged droughts can also impair operations in the Canal, as they have in 1983 and 2001, by lowering its water level and forcing authorities to limit the draft of some cargo ships.

## Hurricanes

When summer tropical storms collect over an ocean, they create a deepening low pressure center which can develop into a cyclone – referred to as a hurricane if it develops over the North Atlantic and a typhoon if it occurs over the West Pacific Ocean. Hurricanes occasionally form off the west coast of Mexico, but the majority of hurricanes develop over the North Atlantic from June to November when the northward shift of the sun increases the temperatures of the Atlantic Ocean and of the air mass lying between Africa and North America. In an average year, more than 100 disturbances (low-pressure systems) with hurricane potential are observed in the Atlantic Ocean; on average only 10 of these reach the tropical-storm stage and about six mature into hurricanes which sweep across the Caribbean Sea, Gulf of Mexico or eastern seaboard of the United States.

The wind speed, which exceeds 74 mph in a hurricane, is caused by heavy, cool air rushing to fill a low-pressure area where the warmer, lighter air is rising. If the low-pressure area is large and the pressure gradient (the rate of pressure change over distance) between it and adjacent pools of air is steep, it will attract larger amounts of cooler air. As the cooler air spins around the eye of the low-pressure system, it can begin to tighten the eye, making it smaller in diameter. This begins a cycle of increasing winds and an increase of air flowing upward. The warm, rising air loses heat and, as a result, water is condensed to form massive nimbostratus clouds. Heavy torrential rain is always a precursor of an approaching hurricane.

Although a hurricane's greatest wind strength (usually between 100 and 200 mph) is at the wall or edge of its eye, where the winds cause very heavy seas and spray that reduces visibility to almost nil, the eye itself is very calm with little wind and a warmer air

*August and September are usually the worst months for hurricanes in the Caribbean.*

temperature. A hurricane can have a diameter of 500 miles or more, but the strength or intensity of a hurricane is unrelated to its overall size and very strong hurricanes usually have relatively small eyes – less than 10 miles in diameter.

Hurricanes are assigned different categories depending on their storm surge, wind speed and other factors that provide a measure of the storm's destructive power. The United States National Oceanic and Atmospheric Administration (NOAA) uses five categories, beginning with category one. A hurricane of this strength will produce winds of 75 to 95 mph that can damage unanchored mobile homes and vegetation. A category-five hurricane is potentially catastrophic, packing winds in excess of 155 mph. Such winds can rip roofs off buildings, some of which may be completely

blown away, and residential areas within 10 miles of the shoreline are evacuated.

In the previous century, there were just two category-five hurricanes – one in 1935 that hit the Florida Keys especially hard, and Hurricane Camille in 1969. Hurricane Andrew in 1992 was the third-strongest storm in history to hit the Caribbean and Florida, with sustained winds of 145 mph and gusts over 175 mph. One of the deadliest hurricanes to hit Central America was Hurricane Mitch in 1998, its five-day rampage through the region claiming 10,000 lives and dumping several feet of rain which triggered huge floods and mudslides in Nicaragua, Honduras, El Salvador and Guatemala.

The prediction and surveillance of hurricanes has improved dramatically in the last 40 years. The National Hurricane Center in Miami provides accurate hurricane forecasts, and warning stations have been established throughout the West Indies. Weather systems in the Atlantic are monitored 24 hours a day with highly advanced radar and satellites for detecting and tracking storms long before they hit land, and reconnaissance planes measure the approaching storm's wind strength. Residents of the region are warned of an approaching hurricane several days in advance – time enough to nail plywood over the windows or retreat to public shelters, built of solid concrete, to wait out the storm.

Officers of cruise ships receive hurricane information from the National Hurricane Center and from NOAA. A cruise ship will sometimes forego a port if the captain decides conditions warrant such action. The ship will either head to another port, or spend a day at sea, keeping well away from the track of the hurricane.

*Hurricane Katrina heads for New Orleans in August 2005.*

## The Creation of the Panama Canal

Panama has always been defined by its geography – namely the short distance across it from sea to sea. Viewed as a barrier to seagoing trade, the isthmus nonetheless became a crossroads of commerce as people and goods travelled across this narrow neck of land, first on foot with pack mules, then by train. Spanish conquistadores, British buccaneers, American entrepreneurs – their legendary exploits in the jungles of Panama have given this part of the world an aura of adventure and adversity that endures to this day.

## Spanish America

When Christopher Columbus, the son of an Italian wool weaver, made his momentous voyage to the New World in 1492, the nation backing his audacious plan of reaching the Far East by sailing due west was Spain. Columbus did not reach the Far East, but his arrival in the West Indies marked the beginning of Spain's rise to world superpower. The 16th cen-

*As long ago as 1524, King Charles V of Spain ordered a survey of the Isthmus of Panama.*

tury would be Spain's 'Golden Century', with fleets on every sea and an empire encompassing nearly all of South America and Central America, as well as parts of North America and the Philippines. The Spanish conquistadores who landed on the shores of the New World proceeded to conquer vast regions in the name of crown, country and a Christian god. In an era of unscrupulous pilfering, these daring adventurers were known for their courage and cunning, as well as their ruthless ambition. Yet, the conquistador who first sighted the Pacific Ocean, on a late September day in 1513, was unlike the others. Vasco Nunez de Balboa rarely displayed the rapacity that was characteristic of his fellow conquistadores, and his friendship with the local natives enabled him to successfully undertake an epic march across the Isthmus of Panama.

Accompanied by 1,000 natives and 190 Spaniards, including Francisco Pizarro (the future conqueror of Peru), Balboa led the expedition through a jungle wilderness that would, over time, claim thousands of lives. Although the Isthmus is only 40 miles wide, anyone unfamiliar with the swampy terrain risked getting lost amid the twisting rivers and rain-soaked hills where the dense vegetation, the stifling heat and the clouds of mosquitoes could make the journey hellish.

Balboa was fortunate. His guides knew the way and 24 days after departing Darien (the colony he founded on the Gulf of Uraba), Balboa reached the crest of the divide and saw the Pacific Ocean – the great sea his native guides had told him about. A few days later, after descending to the Pacific coast, Balboa stood at the ocean's edge and, in the name of King Ferdinand of Spain, claimed possession not only of the 'Great South Sea' but all shores washed by it.

Balboa's historic discovery and triumphant return to Darien, replete with treasures he had gathered at the Pearl Islands in the Gulf of Panama, earned him the Spanish king's favor and the title Admiral of the South Sea. In 1524, King Charles V of Spain ordered a coastal survey of the region in search of a maritime passage from the Caribbean to the Pacific, but none existed.

An overland route spanning the Isthmus of Panama was established along an existing trail where a road of sorts was constructed. Wide enough for two carts to pass, this road ran between Nombre de Dios on the Atlantic side and Panama (today called Old Panama) on the Pacific side. These Spanish-built towns contained royal storehouses and stone stables for the mules of the treasure trains.

Near the end of the 16th century, Nombre de Dios was abandoned in favor of Portobelo as an Atlantic port. By this time,

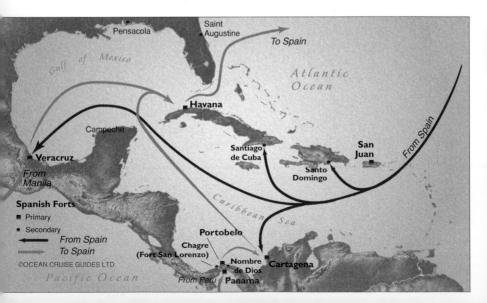

the volume of trade along the trans-isthmian route had made it the richest mule track in the world. Pizarro's conquest of the Incas had provided access to the gold mines of Peru, and shipments would arrive at Panama for overland transport to Portobelo.

From the mid-1500s to the mid-1700s, two armed convoys were sent annually from Spain to collect the precious cargo. The New Spain flotilla sailed in April for Veracruz to load silver from Central Mexico and treasures from the Orient. The Tierra Firme fleet would sail in August to Cartagena and wait for the gold and silver to arrive from Portobelo. Both fleets would rendezvous in Havana to reprovision for the long trip home. The majority of Spanish ships made the journey safely back to Seville, but some foundered on reefs or were caught in storms. Others fell prey to pirates.

The treasure fleets of the Spanish Main soon attracted the unwanted attention of pirates and privateers who hid out on abandoned Caribbean islands deemed 'useless' by Spanish settlers for their lack of gold. Piracy was called privateering when it received tacit approval from the British, French or Dutch crowns in the form of licensing or commissions. This subtle distinction gave captains latitude to pursue innocuous activities, such as collecting livestock on Caribbean islands, when the real purpose was to pillage Spanish towns and ships. The captains would return home to divide their spoils with the crown while receiving the royal pardon. The exploits of Francis Drake, the greatest privateer of all time, fired the imagination of all of Europe when he captured an entire year's production of Peruvian silver in 1572.

*Fort San Felipe was built to protect the walled city of Cartagena, an important port for Spain's treasure fleets.*

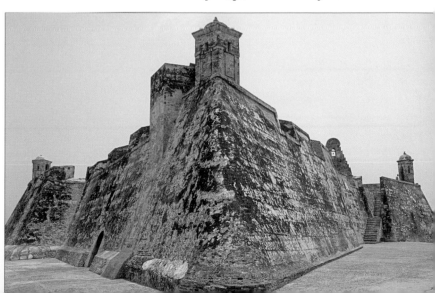

Sir Francis Drake.
*From an Original in the Sydenham Family.*

*Sir Francis Drake (above) and Sir Henry Morgan (below) were two of England's most celebrated privateers, famous for their exploits along the Spanish Main.*

Sᵣ HEN: MORGAN
*Part. 2. Chap 4.*

With only two ships and 73 men, he took Nombre de Dios and captured three mule trains transporting 30 tons of silver. This voyage brought Drake wealth and fame, and inspired generations of adventurers to seek their fortune in the Caribbean, among them the great Dutch naval hero Piet Heyn who, in 1628, captured the entire Mexican treasure fleet near Cuba, and Henry Morgan, whose great success in taking Portobelo in 1666 was followed by his spectacular capture and destruction of Panama in 1671.

Centuries of war with rival naval powers slowly weakened the once-powerful nation of Spain and by the early 1800s, the mighty Spanish Empire was crumbling. Most of Spain's colonies in Latin America had attained independence by 1825, including Panama which became part of Greater Colombia. The last remnants of Spain's vast colonial empire were lost in 1898 during the Spanish American War, when Cuba, Puerto Rico, Guam and the Philippines all shed the Spanish yoke and entered America's growing sphere of international power.

## The Canal Question

Gold was discovered near San Francisco in 1848, and over the next two years more than 40,000 prospectors rushed to California to strike it rich. There were three routes for getting there from the east coast – across the continent, around Cape Horn, or over the Isthmus of Panama. The latter soon drew its first steamer full

of Americans who landed at the marshy mouth of the Chagres River to set off through a wilderness the likes of which none had before experienced. They and others who followed would later write home of the heavy rains and stifling heat, the muck and the slime, the swarms of mosquitoes and sand flies, the poisonous snakes and scorpions.

The men who staggered, rain-soaked and hungry, into Panama City to board a steamer for California had ascended the Chagres by native canoe, then continued overland on mule or by foot where the jungle had reclaimed any trace of the Spanish wagon trails, and the winding foot paths were overshadowed by a thick canopy of tropical trees that grew to 100 feet. Mind you, not all of the stampeders had a wretched time crossing the Isthmus. Those who traversed it

*The remains of Old Panama were abandoned after its sacking by Henry Morgan who left with 200 pack mules laden with riches.*

in the dry season (mid-December to mid-April), when the rains abate, were often overwhelmed by the primeval beauty of the jungle. Monkeys chattered from tree tops and the hypnotic chant of cicadas became synonymous with the tropical rainforest's sultry atmosphere. The emerald green of the luxuriant foliage, the profusion of brilliant flowers and blue butterflies, the great gorges and broad mangrove swamps – all evoked a Garden of Eden atmosphere that could not fail to enchant an intrepid adventurer.

The Panama route was not the only option for crossing Central

America. Many opted for the Nicaragua route, which entailed riding a boat up the San Juan River and a steamer across Lake Nicaragua before boarding a stagecoach for the final overland leg to the Pacific. This route, although longer than the one at Panama, was closer to the United States and became the popular choice for a future canal.

The 'canal question' was of increasing concern to the United States, where the American public's widespread belief in their country's inevitable expansion across the North American continent was referred to as 'manifest destiny'. In keeping with this expansionist sentiment was the Monroe Doctrine which, as enun-ciated by President James Monroe in his 1823 message to Congress, was a foreign policy based on the principle that European nations should refrain from any further colonization or intervention in the Americas. Rivalry between the United States and Great Britain was resolved by a treaty guaranteeing that neither country would have exclusive rights or threaten the neutrality of a potential interoceanic canal. Meanwhile, the countries of Latin America viewed the Monroe Doctrine with suspicion and dislike, seeing it as validation for American imperialism in the region.

In tandem with the tremendous growth of the United States was the Industrial Revolution, orig-

**New York to San Francisco:**
Via Cape Horn: 13,135 nautical miles
Via Panama Canal: 5,262
Distance Saved = 7,873

inating in England in the mid-1700s. The steam engine was its most important invention, and by 1814 the steam locomotive was being used to power early rail travel, followed by the first steamship crossing of the Atlantic in 1819. This rapid industrialization spread to the United States, and by 1869 the American frontier had disappeared as railways were built from coast to coast and people flocked in huge numbers to the growing cities.

A wealthy New York merchant named William Henry Aspinwall, owner of a steamship line, led an American venture to build a railroad across the Isthmus of Panama. This one-track, broad-gauge line, built between 1848 and 1855, was the world's first transcontinental railroad – and it was exactly 47.5 miles long. With Aspinwall's steamships operating on both coasts, the railway was the land link needed to transport passengers and mail between New York and California. The profits made by the Panama Railroad Company, with its monopoly on the Panama transit, were spectacular. Its success also accentuated the need for a maritime route connecting the east and west coasts of the United States, and in 1870 the first thorough survey of the region was carried out by the United States Navy, followed by six other expeditions.

The results of these surveys were presented at an international congress hosted by the Societe de Geographie in Paris in 1879, its purpose ostensibly being to determine the most feasible route for a Central American canal. A year earlier, a French syndicate had sent a young lieutenant, distantly related to Napoleon Bonaparte, on an expedition to Colombia to explore the Panama route. His survey was cursory, carried out by an assistant, while he spent most of his time travelling by horseback to Bogota to negotiate a concession from the government of Colombia. When he presented his plan in support of a Panama route to the congress in Paris, his lack of thoroughness was in contrast to the detailed surveys of the American delegation, which supported a Nicaragua route. Yet the congress voted in favor of a sea-level canal at Panama, mainly because of the persuasive powers of one man whose name was known throughout the world. He was Ferdinand de Lesseps.

## The French Effort

The latter half of the 19th century, often referred to as the Victorian Age, was one of unbridled optimism and belief in modern science and engineering. And no man better epitomized this outlook than did Vicomte Ferdinand de Lesseps. Born in 1805 in Versailles to a distinguished family of diplomats and adventurers, de Lesseps exuded charm, charisma and an unwavering belief in his ability to succeed. Handsome, athletic, a natural leader and patron of the arts, de Lesseps began his career as a French diplomat. He became a national hero when he successfully planned and oversaw construction of the Suez Canal, which opened in 1869. Not only did this remarkable achievement restore glory to post-Napoleonic France, it made money for thousands of ordinary French citizens who had invested in the project.

De Lesseps, hailed as The Great Engineer, was actually more of an entrepreneur extraordinaire with his vision, his unrelenting energy, his powers of persuasion, his suave diplomacy (some might call it duplicity), all of which contributed to his success at Suez. Basking in the public's adoration, de Lesseps maintained a high profile as president of the Suez Canal Company. He cut an elegant figure in Paris with his fashionable

*The Panama Rail Road's Barbacoas Bridge. Built of heavy wrought iron on massive stone piers, it was no match for the Chagres River and was destroyed just weeks before de Lesseps' first visit to Panama.*

young wife and brood of children, and when he wasn't delivering speeches or granting interviews, his fertile mind was planning new and fantastic schemes – such as creating an inland sea in the Sahara – which seemed to belong in a novel by Jules Verne, who was a friend and fellow member of the prestigious Societe de Geographie.

The self-confidence that had always propelled de Lesseps was now edging toward hubris as he cast his sights on Central America and the inevitable construction of an interoceanic canal. At an age when most men sought the comforts of a well-earned retirement, de Lesseps was still enjoying the drive and vigor of a man in his prime. In 1875, the year Great Britain gained financial control of the Suez Canal, de Lesseps first expressed publicly his interest in building a Central American canal. Opposed to this grandiose project was his 38-year-old son

Charles, one of five children de Lesseps had with his first wife who died of scarlet fever in 1853. "You succeeded at Suez by a miracle," said Charles, who was his father's right-hand man. "Should not one be satisfied with accomplishing one miracle in a lifetime?"

Another who opposed the canal being proposed by de Lesseps was President Rutherford Hayes who declared in a message to Congress that America's policy concerning any isthmian canal was that it be under American control. The specter of French interests building a canal in Central America was, in the minds of many, in conflict with the Monroe Doctrine. The French government reassured the United States that it was in no way involved with the de Lesseps enterprise. It was de Lesseps, however, who skillfully refuted this view when he barnstormed America by train in March 1880.

Treated like a head of state and feted everywhere he went, de Lesseps won widespread public approval but could not interest a single New York capitalist in his scheme. The funds needed to finance a canal would come, as they had for Suez, from share offerings to the French public.

In retrospect, it was clear that the French effort to build a canal at Panama was doomed from the start. There was no single reason, but several, including financial problems and a lack of medical knowledge concerning the mosquito-transmitted diseases of malaria and yellow fever. In addition, railway and hydraulic engineering had not yet made some of the advances necessary for the volume of excavating, dam building and lock construction required for such a massive project. The French success at Suez, ironically, contributed to failure at Panama. From the beginning,

*France's Ferdinand de Lesseps was determined to build La Grande Tranchee (The Great Trench) across the Isthmus of Panama.*

de Lesseps insisted on building a sea-level canal at Panama, as he had done so successfully at Suez. But Panama was not Suez, even though the comparisons were inevitable, beginning with de Lesseps' declaration that "Panama will be easier to make, easier to complete, and easier to keep than Suez."

It was not the similarities between the two projects that were noteworthy, but the differences. Suez was built in a hot, dry desert; Panama was a tropical jungle. The terrain at Suez was flat; in Panama it was rugged. At Suez the digging was through sand; at Panama it was through slippery clay lying atop rock stratum. Furthermore, there had been no river to harness at Suez, unlike Panama's mighty Chagres, which was fed by 17 tributaries and stood directly in the canal's path.

The French engineers who worked on the Panama project were of the highest calibre. In the late 1800s, France was considered to have the best-trained corps of civil and military engineers of any country. Their approach to their work was thoroughly scientific, based on sound mathematics and abstract computations, but these engineers had no training in improvisation – an approach they somewhat disparagingly applied to American engineering. Their inability to improvise, and to discard much of what they had learned in Suez, was the downfall of French engineering in Panama. With no prior experience in the tropics, these men of science waged a war with nature and lost. It was, however, a valiant effort,

and their work paved the way for the Americans who followed.

In January 1881, the first shipload of French engineers arrived at Panama. Using a local force of laborers, they set about clearing the jungle along the canal line, and building barracks and hospitals. Survey parties mapped the canal route and made test borings. The canal company bought the Grand Hotel in Panama City and set up headquarters. It soon became apparent, however, that control of the Panama Railroad was vital for transporting people, supplies and equipment back and forth across the Isthmus, so the canal company bought the railroad at three times its market value. This purchase did not affect an 1846 treaty between Colombia and the United States, which guaranteed an American military presence to maintain both Colombian sovereignty on the Isthmus and uninterrupted traffic on the rail line.

No sooner had the canal company set up operations when yellow fever struck. It arrived with the start of the rains, as it always did, which began in May and lasted until mid-December. By June, the first canal employee had died. Some 20,000 more would die before the French abandoned their efforts in Panama, earning the Isthmus its reputation of a death trap. The region was feared long before the French arrived, its climate considered a killer by the early explorers and privateers. In 1698, a large group of Scottish settlers, attempting to establish a colony on Caledonia Bay, was decimated by disease. In more recent memory, scores of laborers who had worked on the Panama Railroad were stricken with infectious diseases and died. Those who recovered from malaria often suffered such severe melancholia they would commit suicide.

Everyone knew that Panama was deadly. What they didn't know was why. There were many theories of course. One was that malaria was caused by a poisonous marsh gas released into the air by rotting vegetation. Yellow fever was also believed to be airborne, its source supposedly being human and animal waste, sewage and the carcasses of dead animals. It was treated as a plague and its victims were thought to be contagious. Of the two diseases, yellow fever was the most feared. Malaria could be treated with quinine, but there was little to be done for patients with yellow fever, except pray it was a mild case from which the victim would recover and henceforth be immune. Those struck with a severe case of yellow fever suffered a horrific death. It began with fever, chills, headaches, back pains and extreme physical weakness. By the third day jaundice would appear, at which time the symptoms receded, only to return with a vengeance. Internal hemorrhaging is common in the final stage, with the vomitus containing blood, before the patient lapses into delirium and coma, then death. Malaria was no picnic either. Bouts of chills caused uncontrollable shivering, and a fever was accompanied by an unquenchable thirst, these symptoms lasting several hours and reoccurring every three or four days. Survivors were left physically and mentally debilitated, and susceptible to recurrence of the disease.

Canal workers stricken with fever were reluctant to go the hospital, where the mortality rate was

*The French canal company set up headquarters in Panama City's former Grand Hotel in 1881. Digging began a year later, marked by the blasting of dynamite and the popping of champagne corks.*

roughly 75% despite the efforts of trained French doctors and nurses working in modern facilities. The cruel irony of the situation was that the hospitals themselves and their manicured gardens were a perfect breeding ground for yellow fever. The Aedes mosquito, which transmits yellow fever, lays its eggs in still, fresh water, and they found plenty of this on the hospital grounds where no screens covered the windows, and the legs of patients' beds and pots of flowers were set in pottery dishes filled with water to protect them from ants. The Anopheles mosquito,

*French housing and landscaped grounds in Cristobal brought civilization to the jungle but didn't eradicate the disease-transmitting mosquitoes that killed workers by the hundreds.*

which transmits malaria, thrives in the shaded streams and swamps of the jungle. Only by eliminating the breeding grounds of mosquitoes and segregating stricken patients, can malaria and yellow fever be eradicated.

As the death toll on the Isthmus mounted, moral decadence was blamed for the grim situation. As in any frontier town, the most popular pastimes were drinking, gambling and prostitution. Bar room brawls were commonplace and the empty wine bottles piling up in Colon were used (bottom-side up) to pave Bottle Alley behind Front Street. The three most profitable businesses on the Isthmus were said to be gambling houses, brothels and coffin makers. The clientele – technicians, tradesmen and laborers – hailed from a variety of countries, including Germany, Switzerland, Russia, Italy, Holland, Belgium and England, as well as Jamaica,

Cuba and Venezuela. Americans, who ran the Panama Railroad, also came to Panama to work for the French canal company as mechanics, contractors and laborers, the latter arriving from New Orleans and other Gulf ports.

The cosmopolitan nature of the local populace extended to the equipment, which arrived from various countries – often in parts – and were not always compatible. This lack of standardization made the chief engineer's job a daunting one. In 1882, the year digging began, the General Agent – the top official in Panama – resigned, citing "the disorder of details", as did his successor. Amid this confusion, an earthquake struck on September 7, in the early hours of the morning, the worst in recorded history for the Isthmus. The twin towers of the cathedral at Panama City toppled to the ground and much of the rail line was damaged. Then, a few months later, the canal company's general contractor – a prestigious French firm – resigned, stating that work could proceed more efficiently using smaller, specialized contractors.

In early 1883, Charles de Lesseps and a new General Agent named Jules Dingler (pronounced Danglay) arrived from Paris to restore order and morale. Highly organized, Dingler prepared the first master plan for the canal and was soon issuing contracts for every conceivable piece of machinery needed – dredges, steam shovels, picks, shovels, wheelbarrows – as well as for hundreds of laborers, mostly from the West Indies. The wages at Panama were good and the company had no trouble recruiting willing workers. The company's contracts were also lucrative and there were plenty of bidders in Europe, Great Britain and the United States who were eager to get a piece of the Panama pie.

In the fall of 1883, Dingler returned from a trip to France with his wife, son, daughter and her fiance. By the end of the following year, they had all died of yellow fever. Somehow Dingler managed to carry on his duties despite his grief, inspiring the young engineers in his employ with his dignity, courage and determination to succeed. The setbacks were, however, discouraging. The amount of excavation required was proving to be much more than originally anticipated, and the wet weather was blamed for the landslides that plagued the freshly exposed slopes of the Culebra Cut. The fill being removed itself became a source of slides. It was hauled by rail cars to adjacent valleys where pile upon pile formed an unstable, terraced slope of mud that would give way in a torrential downpour and bury the train track below. It was an inefficient system, in which time was continually wasted digging out from yet another slide, but it was indicative of how the contractors – seeking the quickest, most economical solution – operated.

To add to the growing list of problems the French canal company was facing in Panama, the region's politics were as unstable as the slide-plagued slopes of Culebra Cut, and in March

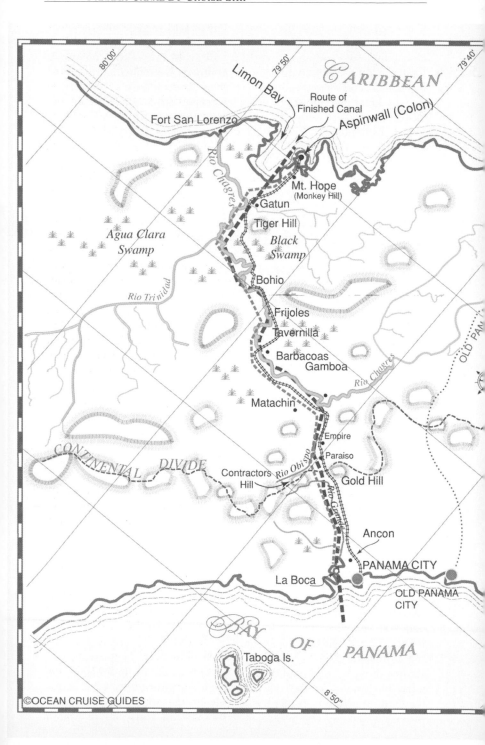

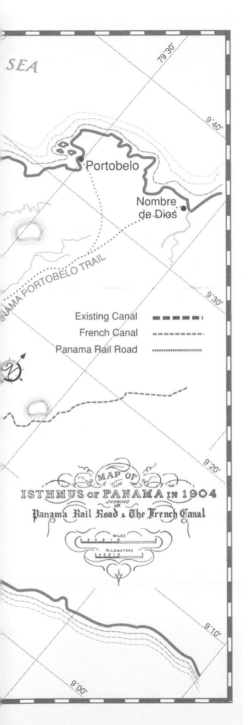

SEA

Portobelo

Nombre de Dios

ANAMA PORTOBELO TRAIL

Existing Canal
French Canal
Panama Rail Road

79°30'

9°40'

9°30'

9°20'

9°10'

9°00'

MAP OF
ISTHMUS of PANAMA in 1904
SHOWING THE
Panama Rail Road & The French Canal

MILES

KILOMETERS

1885 two simultaneous uprisings, one led by a Haitian mulatto in Colon, the other by an ambitious Colombian politician in Panama City, resulted in the deaths of at least one hundred people (more than half of them executed by government troops). Colon was burned to the ground – which proved to be a quick way to rid the town of its filth and squalor.

By August, an exhausted and short-tempered Dingler resigned and returned to Paris, leaving forever the country that had claimed his entire family. His temporary replacement was a 26-year-old engineer named Philippe Bunau-Varilla. Small and slightly built, Bunau-Varilla was a man of high energy and pleasing personality who had risen rapidly in the ranks since arriving at Panama. Acutely aware of the health risks, he regarded Panama not so much as a death trap but a great adventure, a place where a man could prove his courage and competence.

Panama had become a battlefield on several fronts, and the stench of death and defeat could no longer be ignored. Back in Paris, the company's share prices were slipping and unpaid bills were mounting. To raise more funds and restore morale among canal workers, de Lesseps embarked, at the age of 80, on his second trip to Panama. His charismatic presence had the desired effect, and the French continued their advance at Panama. The next blow came from an influential report released in May 1886, in which abandoning the canal was not recommended, but government financial support in the form of a bond lottery was. The need for modifications of the canal plans was also stressed, which could mean only one thing – switching from a sea-level passage to one with locks, a concept de Lesseps had opposed from the start. France's great hero was starting to look like a stubborn old man as he steadfastly refused to alter his plans. Meanwhile, the company continued to borrow heavily.

A year passed, and digging continued. Then, amid ongoing rumors of pending collapse and bankruptcy, Bunau-Varilla, who had resigned from the canal company to work for one of its main contractors, came up with a incredible plan that would allow de Lesseps to save face. The contractors would build a lock canal adjacent to the sea-level canal route and use it instead of rail tracks to transport excavating equipment and carry away fill. In other words, build two canals.

Gustave Eiffel, designer of the Eiffel Tower which was then under construction, was hired to design and build the locks, but his high profile was not enough to stop the downward slide of the canal company's share prices. A government lottery was the company's only hope and in April 1888 the necessary bill was approved and share prices rebounded. This was a shortlived turn of fortune, however, for the lottery failed to sell enough bonds to keep the company solvent. De Lesseps, fighting to the end, tried to muster his followers with yet another battle cry to press on with construction of his canal, but the

company's board of directors conceded defeat and the man who had seemed ageless now lapsed into a slow decline. To the shock of the company's investors, many of whom had invested their life savings, they had lost everything. The worst, however, was yet to come.

Nearly three years passed before the real scandal broke. An anti-Semitic journalist named Edouard Drumont began investigating and writing about the collapse of the canal company. Anxious to prove that Jewish financiers were the real culprits, he questioned the French government's failure to audit the company's books. As Drumont began turning over rocks, strange things began crawling out. An official investigation was launched into the possible misuse of funds and the willful deception of the public. Few realized how far it would go.

Members of government at the highest level came under suspicion of receiving pay-offs for voting in favor of the lottery bond bill, and two powerful financiers – Baron Jacques de Reinach and Cornelius Herz – were revealed as the major players. The de Lesseps, who had feared their company's financial lifelines would be severed if they refused to co-operate, had paid huge sums of money to de Reinach who was supposed to pay off the press but who was, as revealed in the criminal investigation, also paying off members of government as well as Herz, who was blackmailing de Reinach. The details of the intrigue were never revealed in a court of law for de Reinach committed suicide in the early days of the investigation and Herz fled to England where he died of kidney failure while under house arrest in a Bournemouth hotel.

The scapegoats for the scandal, which deeply shocked the French public, were Ferdinand and Charles de Lesseps. The elder de Lesseps was not made to stand trial due to his age and failing health, but his son faced two sets of charges – one of fraud and maladministration, another of corruption (i.e. bribery) of public officials. Madame de Lesseps took her ailing husband to their country estate to protect him from the events unfolding in Paris, but when he eventually learned that his son had been arrested and was in prison awaiting trial, the elder de Lesseps was devastated.

All along, Ferdinand de Lesseps claimed that an Isthmian canal would benefit the world, and his motives reflected the motto of the Ecole Polytechnique: For country, science, and glory. Millions of francs had changed hands, but neither de Lesseps nor his son Charles had personally profited in spite of having ample opportunity to pad their own pockets. De Lesseps had in fact invested more than he made from the Company, losing a consider-

*The French had great expectations of the giant bucket excavators but these were far less efficient than the American 95-ton Bucyrus steam shovels which could handle three to five times more in a day.*

able sum which included part of his wife's savings. As for Charles, he was found guilty of both sets of charges but served only a light sentence. He maintained his dignity throughout the ordeal and for the remainder of his life never talked of Panama.

## An American Canal

Three weeks after his 89th birthday, Ferdinand de Lesseps quietly died in bed at his country home. The year was 1894 and Theodore Roosevelt, still in his thirties, was on the ascent.

Born into a prominent New York family, raised by nannies and educated by private tutors, Roosevelt travelled widely with his parents before graduating from Harvard and studying law at Columbia. He was an intellectual, an outdoorsman, a conservationist, a reformist, an expansionist and a fighter.

A man of boundless vitality and enthusiasm, Roosevelt as president would capture the imagination of the American people with his pithy phrases and adamant defence of the rights of the "little man" versus the powerful industrialists. He stood 5' 8" but he was stocky and appeared to be much larger. And he exuded confidence, in his walk, in his talk. Suffering frail health as a child, he led a life of vigorous pursuits, returning home a hero from the Spanish-American war in Cuba where his famous Rough Riders regiment was victorious.

Above all else, Roosevelt believed in military muscle and the importance of sea power if America was to achieve world supremacy – a point sharply illustrated during the Spanish-American war when it took an American battleship two months to reach Cuba, sailing from San Francisco via Cape Horn. It was obvious that a Central American canal must be built. And it must be American built and under American control. And the place to build it, most Americans agreed, was Nicaragua.

Nicaragua had a shining reputation. Not only was it closer than Panama to American shores, Nicaragua was viewed as politically stable and disease-free. The proposed inter-oceanic route would follow a navigable river and the sparkling waters of Lake Nicaragua before reverting to a man-made canal on its Pacific side. Volumes of data from American surveys supported the Nicaragua route, as did the Nicaragua Canal Commission, a presidential study of the best potential route for the canal. And, perhaps most important in the minds of the American public, Nicaragua would be a fresh start, far removed from the "junk heap of Panama" – as veteran Senator John Tyler Morgan of Alabama liked to refer to the abandoned French canal.

In 1899 a second study was ordered by President William McKinley, called the Isthmian Canal Commission but widely referred to as the Walker Commission, for the name of the Admiral who headed its board of eminent engineers. When the Commission's report was

*President Theodore Roosevelt believed in sea power and was determined to build a canal in Panama, thus joining America's two coastlines and guaranteeing the country's security. He, perhaps more than anyone, made the Panama Canal happen.*

released in November 1901, it contained some surprising recommendations. Based on two years of field work, including trips to Panama and to Paris to view the French canal company's records and plans, the board maintained that Nicaragua was still the most feasible route.

However, the deciding factor was not an engineering one, but the high price tag the French had put on their canal holdings. Within weeks of the study's release, the new canal company slashed its asking price from $109,000,000 to $40,000,000, and a month later the Walker Commission reversed its decision, unanimously supporting Panama as the best choice for an American canal.

How this remarkable about-face occurred was due in large part to the behind-the-scenes

*Philippe Bunau-Varilla, who first came to Panama as a 26-year-old engineer, played an important role in the creation of the Republic of Panama.*

efforts of two highly effective lobbyists – Philippe Bunau-Varilla and William Nelson Cromwell. Bunau-Varilla, a chief engineer with the original canal company at Panama, was the organizer of the new company that had taken over the canal rights. He and others, including Gustave Eiffel, were penalty shareholders in the new company, which meant they would have faced fraud charges for the profits they had made from the original canal project had they refused to invest in the new venture. Cromwell, an American, was a high-powered corporate lawyer hired in 1894 by the new canal company to represent its interests, i.e. sell its canal holdings to the United States government.

*There were, at one point, five possible routes across the Isthmus as shown below. Panama and Nicaragua were the popular choices.*

These two men, working independently and openly disdainful of each other, proceeded to unleash their powers of persuasion and logic on the key American officials who would play a role in deciding where an American canal would be built. Cromwell was simply earning his $80,000 commission, while Buneau-Varilla's motives were more complex. As a shareholder in the new canal company he certainly had a vested interest in selling its holdings to the United States government, yet he convincingly claimed he was on a mission to resurrect the Panama Canal and restore French glory. The impeccably polite little Frenchman struck Americans as being slightly eccentric with his huge black moustache waxed at the ends into sharp points, but he had a steel-trap mind, a riveting personality and was zealous in his quest to redeem French pride, using whatever means were necessary to achieve his goal.

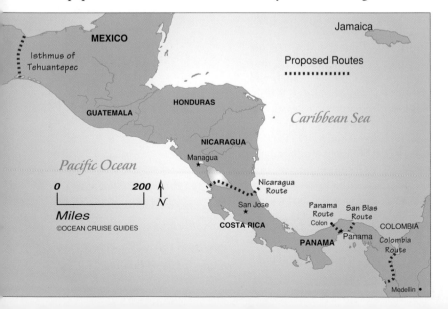

In early 1901, Bunau-Varilla had embarked on a three-month tour of the United States, delivering speeches and making friends in high places. All along he had focused his efforts on the key players, convincing Ohio Senator Mark Hanna, a powerful industrialist and dominant force within the Republican party, that Panama was the superior canal route. Bunau-Varilla even paid a visit to the home of the irascible John Tyler Morgan, a vociferous opponent of the Panama route, and their brief meeting almost ended in a punch-up when, baited by Morgan, Buneau-Varilla came close to striking the elderly Senator.

Then, in the fall of 1901, shortly before the Walker Commission released its report, President McKinley was shot by an anarchist and died eight days later. Theodore Roosevelt, at the age of 42, was now President of the United States. The response was far from muted. Upon hearing the news, Mark Hanna, whose political and financial backing had propelled McKinley to the White House, is reported to have said, "Now look! That damned cowboy is President of the United States." Back in Paris, Bunau-Varilla was aghast, for he had not even bothered trying to meet Roosevelt while he was Vice-President. Bunau-Varilla now hurried back to the United States to try and meet with the new Commander in Chief.

The shift in presidential style was swift and spellbinding. Roosevelt, a Harvard-educated New Yorker who enjoyed horseback riding at his ranch in Dakota Territory, was now the center of his country's attention and he revelled in his new role. He was the first president to call his official residence the White House (instead of the Executive Mansion) into which he moved his large and boisterous family. While distinguished guests arriving for state dinners were gathering in the mansion's public rooms, the President could be found upstairs in the nursery having pillow fights with his children.

Roosevelt's youthful vigor struck a responsive chord with the American people, yet he was a complex man, whose passion for physical pursuits and outdoor activities belied his scholarly mind. An avid reader and progressive thinker, Roosevelt harbored an intense interest in the 'canal question' and was painstakingly familiar with all aspects of potential canal routes, right down to details on topography. And it would soon become apparent that Roosevelt had changed his mind about where the canal should be built. Like most Americans, he had long favored the Nicaragua route. However, the case for Panama was more logical when based on engineering considerations, namely that the Panama route had better harbors, was shorter, required fewer locks (five versus eight), and its potential problems had already been exposed by the failed French effort. Nicaragua on the other hand was an unknown.

In addition, there was the issue of volcanoes – with no fewer than a dozen located in Nicaragua – a point Bunau-Varilla kept making in his speeches but which no one seemed to take very seriously until May 8, 1902, when Mount Pelee on the Caribbean island of Martinique erupted with such force that a superheated cloud of burning gas blanketed the nearby town of St. Pierre and killed all 30,000 residents but one – a prisoner protected by the walls of his jail cell. Days later, Momotombo in Nicaragua erupted, followed by another explosion of Pelee and a volcanic eruption on the Caribbean island of St. Vincent.

While volcanoes were erupting, the Senate hearings got under way. Morgan delivered a vehement speech against Panama, warning that it was only a matter of time before the United States would be compelled to take Panama by force in order to protect the canal, should it be built there. He did not address the engineering aspects of the two routes, only the political pitfalls of Panama. This was in contrast to the contents of Mark Hanna's speech, possibly the best of his career, in which he convincingly listed the reasons for favoring Panama. Backing his argument were statements by dozens of shipmasters and pilots who would be using the canal, all of whom agreed that the shorter the canal, the better, for the less time spent in a canal meant less risk of damage to their ships. Reiterating the points made by the Walker Commission, Hanna stated that a Panama Canal would have fewer curves, would cost less to run and, most importantly, it was the route the engineers

studying the issue recommended – an argument Morgan had scoffed at earlier, declaring that the Walker Commission's preference for Panama had nothing to do with engineering arguments but with the cheap price the U.S. was being offered for the French company's holdings.

The pending vote in the Senate looked like it could go either way. The American press still supported the Nicaragua route and political cartoonists like to poke fun at the pro-Panama forces' "volcano scare". Throughout the hearings, the Nicaraguan embassy in Washington steadfastly denied that Momotombo had just erupted, even though it had. In a final pitch, Bunau-Varilla hit on an idea of sending to each Senator the one-centavo Nicaraguan stamp depicting Momotombo in full eruption. Days later, when the Senate vote was held, Nicaragua received 34 votes, Panama 42. A week later the House passed the Spooner Bill, which authorized the President to build a Panama canal.

## Revolution and Remuneration

When the Spooner Bill was passed by an overwhelming majority in the House on June 26, 1902, the Isthmus of Panama was part of the republic of Colombia, and had been since 1819. That was the year Simon Bolivar became president of Greater Colombia after leading his revolutionary forces across the flooded Apure valley and over the Andes mountains to defeat a surprised Spanish army in north-central Colombia. After three centuries of exploitation under Spanish colonialism, during which the Isthmus of Panama was ruled first by the viceroyalty of Peru, then by the viceroyalty of New Granada, this strategically located neck of land was for the first time part of an independent nation.

In 1830, Venezuela and Ecuador broke away from Greater Colombia and the remaining country would eventually be called the United States of Colombia. The Isthmus of Panama, although physically separated from the rest of Colombia by the dense Darien jungle, was highly prized by the Colombian government as a source of revenue. Its annual share in the earnings of the Panama Railroad was $250,000, and potential profits from a canal promised to be even more lucrative.

Although rich in natural resources, Colombia, like many a former Spanish colony, struggled with self-government. Social and political stability remained elusive, and a revolution in 1885 was followed by the outbreak of a bloody civil war in 1899, which raged until 1904 when internal order was restored. But it was too late for Colombia to save its cherished province of Panama. Through an insurrection supported by the United States and orchestrated by Bunau-Varilla, Panama had gained independence from Colombia. It was one of the strangest revolutions the world has witnessed.

It began back in Washington, where negotiations were tediously slow between Secretary of State John Hay and three successive Colombian foreign ministers. The soft-spoken Hay was a man of letters, trained in law and journalism, who had served as President Lincoln's assistant private secretary and written several books. He had negotiated the Hay-Pauncefort treaty in which Britain relinquished to the U.S. the right to build an isthmian canal in Central America, and his Colombian assignment seemed straightforward enough. But Hay, the experienced and erudite statesman, was dealing not only with Colombian diplomats whose Spanish sense of pride and decorum were at odds with the 'let's get on with it' American approach, but with a cryptic Colombian government which seemed to be continually shifting its position in its instructions from Bogota. The two main issues were Colombian sovereignty and money. Colombia's diplomats in Washington felt they were being bullied by the American administration, which threatened to enter negotiations with Nicaragua if Colombia persisted in delaying a treaty settlement. Dr. Tomas Herran, the multilingual and highly educated Colombian diplomat who cautiously reached an agreement with Hay, spoke in private of Roosevelt's "impetuous and violent disposition" which might predispose him to taking Panama by force. Hay urged restraint to President Roosevelt, who was becoming increasingly impatient with the Colombians whom he referred to as "jack rabbits" and "those bandits in Bogota."

The main stumbling block for Colombia was the $40,000,000 the French canal company was to receive from the United States. Colombia wanted to receive a portion of this payment as commission for allowing the transfer of the canal zone, but the French canal company did not agree and Cromwell was working hard behind the scenes to convince the American government that none of the agreed-upon purchase price should go to Colombia.

Eventually a treaty was drawn up and signed in Washington by Hay and Herran, which granted the United States control of a canal zone six miles wide between Colon and Panama City, and which authorized the French company to sell its Panama holdings to the American government. In return, Colombia would receive a lump sum of $10,000,000 and, after nine years, an annuity of $250,000. The treaty's terms were not popular with Colombians, who believed they should be receiving more financial compensation, and the Colombian Senate refused to ratify it.

While Colombia equivocated, Panama conspired. A small group of prominent Panamanians began planning a revolution, led by 70-year-old Dr. Manuel Amador who, although born and educated in Cartagena, had lived in Panama since the California gold rush of 1848. The leaders of the movement all worked for the Panama Railroad and were in contact with Cromwell. These included Jose Agustin Arango, the railroad's attorney and a Panamanian senator, and the assistant superintendent Herbert Prescott, an American. In August 1903, Dr. Amador boarded a steamer bound for New York to drum up American support for their insurrection.

An intrigue of secret meetings and coded messages unfolded during Amador's stay in New York. Doublecrossed by a Panamanian businessman he had met while playing poker on the sea voyage to New York, Amador found himself getting nowhere with his American contacts until Bunau-Varilla arrived from Paris

*Dr. Manuel Amador was the leader of the U.S.-backed revolution in Panama and became the new country's first president.*

and, with characteristic efficiency, began organizing Amador's revolution down to the minutest details, including the first draft of a Panamanian declaration of independence and a new flag his wife had quickly stitched together.

While Amador waited in New York, Bunau-Varilla hurried by train to Washington where he was able to meet with Roosevelt and engage in an oblique conversation concerning a possible revolution in Panama. By the end of their meeting, Bunau-Varilla was convinced Roosevelt was prepared to support an insurrection. Back in New York, in his final briefing with Amador, Bunau-Varilla insisted the revolution take place on November 3 and provided the text for a telegram to be sent once the junta gained power, confirming Panama's independence and authorizing Bunau-Varilla to sign a canal treaty with the U.S.

When Amador returned to Panama, his cohorts didn't like the new flag and were nervous about staging a revolution based on the assurances of an unknown Frenchman. One influential member of the junta, claiming he was too young to be hanged, threatened to back out unless there was a tangible sign of support from the United States, namely an American man-of-war standing offshore. No one, not even Bunau-Varilla, was entirely sure of Roosevelt's intentions at this point, but a pending revolution in Panama seemed to be that year's worst-kept secret and anyone monitoring the situation would have noticed a small item in *The New York Times* reporting that the U.S. gunboat *Nashville* had sailed on the morning of October 31 from Kingston, Jamaica, its destination believed to be Colombia.

In the end, no fewer than 10 American warships would converge on both sides of the Isthmus, and it was undoubtedly their presence that decided the fate of Panama. In the meantime, it was the Panama Railroad and its superintendent, a 70-year-old American named Colonel James Shaler, who saved the day for the junta when the Colombian warship *Cartagena* arrived at Colon only hours after the *Nashville* showed up on November 2.

Commander Hubbard of the *Nashville* was there under the pretext of maintaining free and uninterrupted transit of the Panama Railroad, so he did nothing to stop General Tobar, the Colombian commander, from landing five hundred troops the next morning.

It was at the railroad wharf that the stonewalling began by Shaler, who had been notified of the troops' pending arrival and had shunted railcars away from the station. General Tobar and his senior officers suspected no hanky-panky when Shaler suggested they board a special car for Panama City, leaving their troops behind in Colon until more railcars were available. Away went Tobar and his officers, heading straight for a trap that was being set in Panama City, where a small garrison of Colombian troops was stationed. These soldiers had not been paid for months and their commanding officer, General Huertas, was known to be sympathetic to the revolutionary movement. So, when approached by Amador and offered a small fortune if he joined the revolution and arrested Tobar, the young general reportedly hesitated for about a second before accepting the offer.

Back in Colon, a confidential telegram arrived for Hubbard, instructing him to prevent the landing of Colombian troops. Meanwhile Shaler was using delay tactics to prevent the movement of these same troops, insisting their fares be paid in full and in cash before they could ride on the railroad. At the other end of the line, Panama City buzzed with anticipation of an uprising slated for 5:00 p.m. in Cathedral Square. General Tobar and his officers, enjoying a fine lunch at Government House, still suspected nothing. But when his troops failed to arrive by mid-afternoon, Tobar began to grow anxious.

*Cathedral Square was renamed Independence Square after Panama revolted against Colombia in 1903 and became a separate republic.*

As a crowd gathered in front of the military barracks, and an unsuspecting Tobar and his officers conferred on a bench near the gate to the seawall, Huertas issued the order. Armed with fixed bayonets, a company of soldiers marched out of the barracks and surrounded the seated general and his officers, demanding their surrender, which they did after beseeching some of the nearby sentries to come to the defense of their country. None came to their aid, and they were marched to the local jail.

While a jubilant crowd celebrated the success of their revolution in Cathedral Square, back in Colon the Colombian troops, under the command of a young colonel named Torres, were still trying to catch a train to Panama City.

At noon the following day, over a drink in the Astor Hotel saloon, a Panamanian named Melendez told Torres what had happened the day before in Panama City. Torres flew into a rage and threatened to burn the town and kill all Americans if the Colombian generals were

not released. No one took this threat idly, and after sequestering the town's American civilians to ensure their safety, Hubbard landed an armed detachment of sailors who barricaded the railroad's stone warehouse. He also moved the *Nashville* closer to shore, its decks cleared for action and its guns trained on the railroad wharf and on the *Cartagena*, which to everyone's surprise suddenly steamed out of the harbor.

A tense few hours followed as the Colombian soldiers surrounded the warehouse, but no shots were fired and Torres eventually marched his troops to Monkey Hill (also called Mount Hope) where they camped for the night. The next day, driven off by mosquitoes, the Colombian troops marched back into town and Torres agreed to evacuate Colon in exchange for $8,000 which was paid in twenty-dollar gold pieces from the railroad company's safe. By evening he and his troops had boarded a Royal Mail steamer bound for Cartagena.

With the dispatch of Colombian troops and the arrival of more American gunboats at Colon and Panama City, all that remained was for the new Republic of Panama to sign a treaty with the U.S. According to the agreement reached between Amador and Bunau-Varilla in New York, the latter would have the diplomatic powers to act on behalf of the new nation, and act he did, in spite of receiving new instructions not to proceed until a small delegation led by President Amador arrived from Panama.

Bunau-Varilla hurriedly revised the treaty Hay had drafted, making the conditions so favorable to the U.S. – including perpetual control of a 10-mile-wide canal zone – it couldn't possibly be rejected in the Senate. When the Panamanian delegation stepped off the train in Washington and were told by Bunau-Varilla that he had just signed a treaty on behalf of the Republic of Panama, one of the delegates responded by striking the Frenchman across the face.

Panama had to be content with the treaty and it was not such a bad deal for a new nation, starting out debt free, with a $10,000,000 surplus in the government coffers, a guaranteed annual revenue from its railroad and canal concessions, and the security of U.S. naval protection. Colombian troops did attempt to regain their lost province with an overland march through the Darien jungle but had to turn back. The loss of national income for Colombia, already burdened by a costly civil war, was crippling.

Panama's swift secession from Colombia was achieved without bloodshed, but Roosevelt was accused of acting impulsively in his "sordid conquest" of Panama. Roosevelt vehemently defended himself, claiming later in his autobiography that it was "by far the most important action I took in foreign affairs" and totally justified in the interests of national defence. Depending on a person's point of view, it had been gunboat diplomacy at its best, or its worst, tarnishing U.S. relations with Latin America for years to come. The mood of the American public was generally in favor of Roosevelt's actions, especially when Colombia made a desperate attempt following the revolution to accept the terms of the Hay-Herran treaty, proof in many peoples' minds that Roosevelt was right when he accused the Colombian government of extortion. The American President had, in his own words, "taken the Isthmus" and it was time now for the U.S. to make the dirt fly and build that damn canal.

## The World's Largest Construction Job

When the United States took possession of the canal works in Panama on May 4, 1904, the scene was, at first glance, one of rot and despair – abandoned and rusted machinery, dilapidated buildings, filthy towns. On closer

*Colon was the scene of high tension when an American and a Colombian warship both arrived in port on the eve of the revolution.*

inspection, however, the amount of excavation already completed by the French was impressive, much of the equipment was salvageable, and many of the buildings could be refurbished.

Nonetheless, organizing the manpower and supplies needed to bring order and efficiency to the Canal Zone was a gargantuan task, made even more daunting by the establishment in Washington of the Isthmian Canal Commission which had to approve all requisitions received from Panama. It was headed by Walker, whose passion was to make sure no graft tainted the American effort in Panama. As a result, the first Chief Engineer appointed to Panama, John Wallace, was as bogged down in red tape as he was in mud. On top of these administrative frustrations was the weight of American public opinion, which wanted to see "the dirt fly" in Panama, prompting Wallace to commence digging right away at Culebra Cut.

There seemed to be no master plan in place, and morale among the workers, already low, plummeted with the outbreak of yellow fever. Panic swept the

Isthmus and people couldn't leave fast enough. Even Wallace fled, under the pretext that he had important business to discuss with Secretary William Taft in Washington. Wallace was fired and a new man was quickly found to turn things around in Panama. That man was John Stevens who, at age 52, was widely considered the best construction engineer in the country. Self-educated, Stevens had learned surveying on the job, working his way from track hand to chief engineer. He was gruff, physically tough and a legend among railroaders for discovering, in the dead of a Montana winter, the Mariah Pass over the Continental Divide. When Stevens met with Roosevelt, the two men hit it off immediately and the new Chief Engineer was told to do whatever was needed in Panama, which the President called a "devil of a mess."

It took Stevens, upon arriving in Panama, less than a week to assess the situation. A hands-on and approachable man, he spent hours walking the Canal Zone, in any kind of weather, observing every detail and asking questions. He said little, just looked and listened.

Then, six days after his arrival, on August 1, 1905, Stevens ordered all digging stopped. He had determined that the equipment left behind by the French was not large or heavy enough, and the undersized railroad so inefficient it was astounding how much had been accomplished. But the first problem to deal with, in Stevens's view, was the overriding atmosphere of fear due to yellow fever and other diseases plaguing Panama. Already at hand was the man best qualified to rid the Isthmus of the dreaded yellow fever, namely Dr. William Gorgas – a leading disease and sanitation expert who had rid Havana of yellow fever when sent there with the Army in 1898. Gorgas had been trying to replicate this suc-

*John Stevens, the second chief engineer to lead the American effort at building a canal in Panama, was the man who turned things around and laid the groundwork for success.*

cess since his arrival in Panama a year earlier but with limited results. Few people, including members of the ICC, believed in the 'mosquito theory'. To spend thousands of dollars chasing mosquitoes seemed a waste of money to General Walker, who had refused to provide the resources Gorgas had repeatedly requested.

Stevens too was skeptical of the mosquito theory, but he had faith in Dr. Gorgas and he threw the weight of the engineering department at the doctor's disposal. Fumigation brigades, armed with buckets, brooms and scrub brushes, marched on Panama City and Colon where every single house was cleaned and fumigated. Sources of standing water, such as cisterns and cesspools were oiled once a week, and both towns were provided with running water, eliminating the need for fresh water containers. The results were immediate. The yellow fever epidemic ended within a month and, although it would take time for Panama to shed its reputation as a death trap, the tide was slowly turning. Malaria was also brought under control as brigades were dispatched to burn brush, dig ditches, drain swamps and clear the areas around the settlements being built along the canal route. The malaria-transmitting Anopheles mosquito is susceptible to strong sunshine and wind, so the cleared areas around the new towns were kept continually clipped and trimmed.

The key to successfully building the canal, Stevens had concluded, was the rail line. Not only was it a lifeline, transporting the needed manpower, machinery and supplies back and forth across the Isthmus, it would be the conveyer belt needed to haul away the huge amounts of dirt to be dug at Culebra Cut. His was not a complicated task, he claimed, but challenging for the massive scale of excavation required. So with a workable plan laid out, the man who had built railroads spanning hundreds of miles of rugged northern terrain, now focused his

*Dr. William Gorgas was a modest but tenacious man who rid the Isthmus of yellow fever. Born in Alabama, he met his future wife during a yellow-fever epidemic in Texas. Both fell ill, then fell in love during their convalescence and were hence immune to yellow fever, allowing the doctor and his wife to live in Panama without fear of the disease.*

talents and tenacity on a narrow, 50-mile-long jungle corridor, and the transformation was nothing less than extraordinary.

Stevens brought in experienced railroad men from across North America and proceeded to completely overhaul the existing rail line, installing heavier rails that were double-tracked and equipped with cars that were four times the size the French had used. He also recruited conductors, engineers and switchmen to operate the new rail line, while thousands of tradesmen and laborers were put to work building towns alongside it. A cold-storage plant was built at the Cristobal terminal and fresh food, arriving by steamship from New York, was distributed via the rail line, as were fresh loaves of bread from the new bakery.

Stevens was not just building a canal but a modern industrial state in the middle of an isolated tropical wilderness, and a complete infrastructure had to be put in place before the Canal itself could be built. This mammoth undertaking required both skilled tradesmen and unskilled laborers, and six months after his arrival Stevens had tripled the size of the labor force. A year later, by the end of 1906, nearly 24,000 men were working on the Isthmus. The labor force came from all parts of the world, but the majority of skilled white workers were American, representing forty different trades and specialties – from carpenters and bricklayers to cooks and plumbers. Many of the unskilled laborers were from the West Indies, specifically Barbados, where men lined up for the chance to go to Panama and earn a dollar day.

In early 1906, Stevens resumed digging at Culebra Cut, where he had devised an ingenious system of rail tracks which kept the steam

*Spraying all ditches and streams with oil was a key method of controlling mosquito larvae in Gorgas's sanitation campaign.*

shovels in constant motion as loaded dirt trains rolled out and a steady stream of empty cars rolled in. There was still no official decision regarding the type of canal he was supposed to be building, but Stevens had made up his own mind after watching the Chagres River flood its banks during the rainy season. He firmly believed a sea-level canal would be a "narrow tortuous ditch" plagued with endless slides and ships running aground in the shallow channel, whereas a lock canal could harness and utilize the floodwaters of the Chagres, creating a freshwater lake that would form a section of the canal and provide water to the locks. Stevens was summoned to Washington to lobby on behalf of a lock canal, and on June 19, 1906, the Senate voted by a narrow margin to build a lock canal.

Everything was now coming together, and in November of that year Roosevelt paid a visit to Panama, the first time a serving president had left the country while in office. Unlike de Lesseps, who twice visited Panama during the dry season, Roosevelt purposely planned his visit during the rainy season so he could experience Panama at its worst. Eager to see everything, Roosevelt set a pace that left Stevens and everyone else exhausted. His infectious enthusiasm was undampened by the driving rain as he cheerfully waved to bystanders from the back of his train and made impromptu speeches whenever the occasion presented itself. At one point, while touring the Cut, he climbed into the driver's seat of a 95-ton steam shovel where he was obviously delighted to be sitting at the controls while the engineer explained how it worked. He was always on the go and often not where the official schedule said he should be. On one occasion, he and his wife were expected at a formal luncheon in the Tivoli Hotel but they instead walked unannounced into one of the employees' mess halls and sat down to a 30-cent lunch.

No sooner did an exuberant Roosevelt return to Washington, confident of success in Panama, when a fly appeared in the ointment. Stevens, who had won Roosevelt's full confidence, was showing signs of cracking under the pressure. Suffering from insomnia, Stevens wrote what was interpreted as a letter of resignation to Roosevelt in late January 1907. Just as the French chief engineers had complained of the "disorder of detail", Stevens now spoke of the tremendous responsibility and strain he was under due to "the immense amount of detail." These complaints were likely not too startling to Roosevelt, but farther along in the letter came the clincher, wherein Stevens refers to the canal, Roosevelt's "future highway of civilization", as "just a ditch" and one of questionable utility at that.

Stevens, who dreaded ocean voyages due to his seasickness, did not share Roosevelt's passion for naval supremacy and seagoing trade, but his personal reasons for resigning were never disclosed. Most observers concluded that the man was, quite simply, worn out. As for Roosevelt, he was profoundly disappointed in Stevens for his lack of commitment and sense of duty. To insure that the next man in charge of building the canal stayed on the job, Roosevelt declared he was turning the work over to the army, to a corps of elite engineers trained at West Point Military Academy, its curriculum patterned after that of France's prestigious Ecole Polytechnique. These were engineering officers instilled with an honored tradition of serving their country. For them, the option of quitting was unthinkable.

The man Roosevelt appointed as chief engineer and chairman of the canal commission was a 48-year-old colonel named George Goethals. Born in New York of Flemish parents, Goethals was a model officer and specialist in coastal defenses. The line of authority in Panama had been streamlined at Stevens's request, and Goethals was now supreme commander of the Canal Zone. It

*President Roosevelt set a non-stop pace during his tour of Panama in 1906, shown in this famous photo at the controls of a steam shovel.*

quickly became apparent that he was a leader of unbending standards. His efficiency and command of details was unsurpassed, but he lacked the warmth and colorful personality of Stevens, whose departure from Panama was marked by a crowd of workers waving and cheering and singing *Auld Lang Syne* as his steamer pulled away from the pier at Cristobal.

Goethals had big shoes to fill and his first months in Panama were lonely, his evenings spent writing long letters home to his son who was in his senior year at West Point. Goethals soon earned the respect if not the affection of the canal workers and, despite his stern manner, was regarded as a benevolent despot by holding, each Sunday morning, a court of appeal in his office where workers could voice their grievances and requests while he listened patiently. His decision on each

matter was final and few questioned his authority.

Goethals also started a weekly community newspaper, called the *Canal Record*, which boosted morale and tied the settlements along the rail line together. Weekly excavation statistics for the teams operating the steam shovels and dredges were published, prompting an ongoing competition to capture that week's record. A healthy rivalry was also inspired by Goethal's reorganization of departments into three geographic units, with army engineers assigned to the Atlantic Division (handling design and construction of the Gatun Locks and Dam) and civilian engineers responsible for the locks and dams of the Pacific Division on the other side. The 32 miles of canal in between were called the Central Division, comprised of both army and civilian engineers, whose major challenge was the nine-mile stretch of Culebra Cut. Stevens had laid the foundations for building the canal, but engineers with expertise in hydraulics and the large-scale use of concrete were now needed to construct the colossal locks and dams, and their work would prove to be outstanding.

The American public, and the world at large, was fascinated with the canal's construction and

*George Goethals, the chief engineer who oversaw completion of the Panama Canal, was widely respected and got the job done.*

tourists arrived by the shipload to view the proceedings. The biggest attraction was Culebra Cut, where men in straw hats and ladies with long skirts and parasols would watch from grassy bluffs the Herculean efforts of men and machines to claw a canyon into the earth's surface. There was much noise down below, but no confusion, only the continuous motion of drilling, blasting, shoveling and dirt hauling. The Cut, called Hell's Gorge by one steam-shovel man, was never silent and always hot and dusty, except when torrential rain turned the dust to mud and threatened to trigger yet another landslide.

While the work went ahead on the canal, a distinct class system emerged on the Isthmus, delineated by race and defined by the pay system which issued wages to the skilled whites in gold currency and to the unskilled blacks in silver currency. Living accommodations also reflected a person's 'gold' or 'silver' status. Simple

barracks were built for the black workers and food was provided in mess kitchens. However, most of the West Indians did not like the food or the regimentation of barracks life, and many opted to live in ramshackle huts in the jungle. Their living conditions appeared deplorable but were in fact better than what many of them had known before coming to Panama.

Those on the gold payroll lived in white clapboard buildings with screened porches and manicured lawns. These buildings were divided into two or four apartments, each fully furnished and fitted out with plumbing, electricity and other conveniences, all at government expense. The size of

*A freighter passes through the Continental Divide between Gold Hill and Contractors Hill. The remains of the Cucaracha Slide are just behind and to the left of the container ship.*

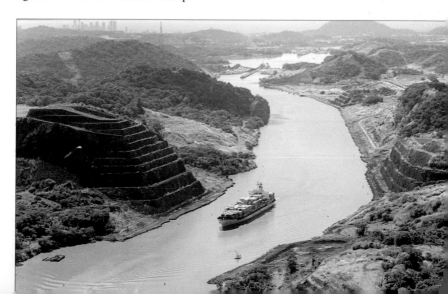

a gold worker's apartment was determined by his salary, which entitled him to one square foot per dollar of monthly pay. To encourage married men to send for their families, wives were also entitled to one square foot per dollar of their husband's monthly pay. The top salaried, married men lived in detached houses, while single men lived in one of the bachelor hotels, usually sharing a room with another man.

The average pay for white workers was $87 per month, plus free housing and medical treatment. A young graduate engineer was paid $250 to start, while a

*Italian laborers pose on a dirt train at Culebra Cut. Workers of all nationalities were brought in to work on the canal.*

steam-shovel engineer received $310. The annual salary paid to Goethals was $15,000, half of what Stevens had made. These were generous salaries, but no one person or company grew rich building the canal. Salaries were set, there were no commissions, and the only work contracted out was the construction of the gates (which was handled by a Pittsburgh bridge builder) and the manufacture of electric motors by General Electric and of steel parts for the lock walls and gates, which kept 50 mills, foundries, machine shops and specialty fabricators busy in Pittsburgh.

As the years went by, 'the work' gained momentum. Everyone took pride in their efforts – they were seeing results and knew they were working together to build something of great significance. They were making history, but

the monumental task they faced no longer felt like a war. In fact, most everyone seemed to be having a good time.

The American families living in the Canal Zone enjoyed a strangely carefree lifestyle, one in which their basic needs and recreational pursuits were taken care of by the Commission. A friendly atmosphere and strong sense of community prevailed, along with an abundance of clubs and fraternities. Baseball fields had been built and leagues organized during Stevens's tenure, and other popular events included Saturday night dances, Sunday afternoon picnics and weekly band concerts.

Life in fact appeared to be too good to some visitors, who saw the place as some sort of socialist utopia where workers were so completely taken care of, critics wondered how they would adjust to the real world when the canal was completed and they returned to the United States. Others were concerned that the Canal Zone would become a breeding ground for political activists sold on socialism. Yet the zone was anything but political, with the people living there having no say in how things were run and their government located 2,000 miles away in Washington.

In 1912 the Gatun Dam was completed, causing water in the Chagres River to back up and overflow its banks, submerging the lower Chagres valley and creating an artificial lake. As the basin slowly filled, animals fled to high ground and native villages were relocated.

Despite setbacks from slides and floods in the Cut, the work proceeded day and night. As dry excavations in the Cut neared completion, Goethals decided to finish the work with dredges doing wet excavation. The rail tracks in the Cut were taken up and all equipment removed. Then, with the workers all assembled at Gamboa at the north end of the Cut, a charge was set off to remove the dike holding back the Chagres River, and its waters flowed into the Cut.

The canal's historic opening day finally arrived on August 15, 1914, two weeks after World War I began in Europe and 10 years after the United States had taken over the project. The Canal was ready for its first official vessel, and although there were numerous dignitaries on hand who were eager to go through on the first boat, Goethals decreed that only Americans who had worked at least seven years on the canal would enjoy that privilege. A group of them and their families boarded the S.S. *Ancon* and entered the canal from the Atlantic. They were lifted up in the locks and transported across Gatun Lake before entering the Cut where their vessel traversed the Continental Divide, passing between Gold Hill and Contractors Hill. By this point most of the men were in tears. The boat was then lowered back down to sea level in the Pedro Miguel and Miraflores locks, where it was set free to sail into the Pacific Ocean. The world's greatest shortcut was finally complete.

*Caribbean bound, a cruise ship enters the last of the Gatun Locks.*

# Afterword

The Panama Canal was an American success story. Built under budget (total cost: $336,650,000) and ahead of schedule, the canal was the 'moon launch' of the early 20th century. The massive locks, which raise and lower up to 40 ships a day, have worked with the precision of Swiss watches, and the canal now handles more vessel traffic annually than was ever envisaged by its builders. To this day, a more efficient means of digging the canal could not be applied. Many of the talented men who worked on this engineering marvel went on to other projects, most notably the building of railroads in South and Central America,

northern Canada and Alaska.

In 1921, after years of seeking redress, Colombia finally recognized the independence of Panama upon receiving financial compensation from the United States in a lump sum payment of $25 million. In 1939, the United States agreed to increase Panama's annuity to $434,000, an amount increased again in 1955 to $1,930,000. The United States also undertook to build a high-level bridge at the Pacific entrance to the canal, completed in 1962 and called the Bridge of the Americas.

There remained, however, ongoing grievances on the part of Panama, which sought greater control over the canal. In 1977 under the Carter administration, a new treaty was signed which ceded the Panama Canal Zone, now called the Canal Area, to Panama under joint U.S.-Panamanian control until the year 2000, at which time Panama would assume full control. A separate treaty guarantees the permanent neutrality of the canal. When Colonel Manuel Noriega, a known drug smuggler who had seized military control of Panama, gained the country's presidency in December 1989 and declared war on the United States, an American military force of more than 25,000 soldiers attacked Panama City and forced Noriega's surrender. Panama's legitimately elected president was sworn into office during the American invasion and Noriega was taken to the United States to face charges of drug trafficking. Found guilty, he remains in a Florida prison.

Politics have always plagued Panama. When the canal was officially handed over to Panama at the close of the 20th century, President Clinton chose not to attend the ceremony, his absence underlying the ambivalence of the American people regarding a U.S. withdrawal. However, despite initial misgivings concerning efficiency and maintenance of the canal, it continues to thrive.

Improvements to operating machinery and in the form of widening, deepening and straightening have increased the canal's capacity. Ports have been expanded and large infrastructure projects have transformed much of the Canal Area. Meanwhile, this rapid growth has drawn the attention of World Monuments Watch, which cites development pressures and lack of regulations as a threat to the region's tropical rainforests. With construction underway for a new third set of locks to accommodate larger ships (see page 214), the canal will continue to grow as an important cruising destination as cruisers come to view this engineering miracle.

*Panama's President Mireya Moscoso and former U.S. President Jimmy Carter at the official handover of the Panama Canal in 1999.*

Long before becoming part of Spanish America, regions of Central America and Mexico were inhabited by various agricultural tribes including the Maya. The Maya were an advanced society with an understanding of astronomy and engineering. They built their pyramidal structures oriented to the spring and fall equinoxes, and one of the world's earliest suspension bridges was built by the Maya in the seventh century in Yaxchilan, near Mexico's border with Guatemala. The Mayans also developed a hieroglyphic script, a numerical system and several calendars, some of which were accurate to within 20 seconds over a year.

They practiced agriculture and formed a hierarchical society based on patrilineal descent, in which kinship played a major role. There was no widespread political organization of the Mayans; each city state had its own internal structure of dynastic status and power. Their civic centers followed a pattern in which pyramidal structures and temples were built around a central plaza. Kilns were used to reduce the region's limestone into lime, which was mixed with white earth and water to create the mortar used in constructing the walls, corbelled arches and roof combs of these massive stone temples which were often decorated with elaborate carvings and ceramic paintings.

A common feature of their civic centers was a ball court with stone hoops. Opposing teams played with a heavy rubber ball which players kept in the air by bouncing it off any part of the body except the hands and feet. It's believed that these games were sometimes used as a peaceful means to settle disputes between leaders, with the loser giving up his land and followers to be assimilated with the winning team's people. Another theory is that the losing team offered a human sacrifice – often the team captain. The Maya civilization reached its height during the Classic Period (AD 300 to 900), then went into a rapid decline during which the population plummeted.

*In poor, rural settlements, the Maya lived in small dwellings made of perishable materials – in contrast to the massive civic centers built of stone.*

With the Spanish conquest came the suppression of Maya culture and the introduction of Spanish art and architecture. The initial structures built by the Spanish, including cathedrals, were military in design and their style was massive and plain. This strain of simple, solid construction prevailed throughout the colonial period, as exemplified by the Spanish missions of California. However, other styles were also introduced, including Moorish elements that had long been a part of Spanish design. Open courts were adorned with a multitude of low arches, and Moorish craftsmanship was reflected in the glazed tiles, lacy wooden carvings, fine pottery and filigreed jewelry.

*High roof combs are an impressive feature of the temples at Tikal, Guatemala. (Below) The Maya site of Copan is renowned for its profusion of carved images.*

When Spanish styles fused with the inventiveness of the New World's native craftsmen, the result was a unique style of art and architecture. And, as Spain's artists made the stylistic transition from Gothic to Renaissance, elaborate design elements were introduced by their colonial counterparts, such as the Plateresque style of contrasting bare walls and ornamental doorways.

The Latin-American adaptation of Churrigueresque, a highly ornate form of Spanish baroque, is best represented by Mexico City's Cathedral of the Three Kings, which has been described as ultrabaroque for its profusion of opulent surface decoration.

Common features of Spanish colonial houses, monasteries and other buildings include overhanging grilled balconies, inner courtyards surrounded by arched

*Examples of Spanish colonial architecture: the 16th-century San Pedro Claver Church (above) and a residential street (below), both in Cartagena.*

arcades, red-tile roofs and glazed tiles set in white or pastel adobe walls. Adobe is a brick or building material made of sun-dried earth and straw. The mountainside town of Taxco, founded in 1529 as a silver-mining community and an important stop between Acapulco and Mexico City during the era of colonial trade, is a prime example of the Spanish colonial town.

In Mexico, where native art was highly developed before the Spanish conquest, the region's art became became a hybrid of native and European styles, especially in its paintings, which achieved a serenity and richness of blues and reds for which they became known as Mexican baroque.

Religious themes eventually gave way to revolutionary ideals and 20th-century Mexican artists enjoyed generous government patronage. Diego Rivera was one of Mexico's greatest painters, his celebrated murals paying homage to the working man. He was married to the artist Frida Kahlo, another Mexican icon, and theirs was a tumultuous but artistically productive relationship.

Mexico's architects have in recent times designed hotels with bold geometric lines and dramatic scale inspired by past architecture, including Aztec pyramids, Mayan temples and Moorish palaces. Some noteworthy examples are Acapulco's Mayan Palace, the Acapulco Princess Hotel, and the Westin Regina Resort in Los Cabos.

The folk arts have not been left behind, and throughout Mexico and Central America the local artisans produce high-quality crafts in styles reflecting both the Spanish influence and the traditions of the Maya, Aztec and other ancients.

*(Above)* **La Popa Monastery's courtyard, in Cartagena, reflects Moorish design. (Below) The Plateresque style of adornment graces the Aduana's facade in Old San Juan.**

*(Above) Tropical tree frogs come in a variety of colors, including this Red Dart Frog. (Below) The massive trunk of this tropical tree is supported by buttress roots.*

The plant and animal life found in the tropics is unsurpassed in abundance, variety and beauty. Covering only 7% of the earth's land mass, tropical rainforests are home to half of the planet's species. Within these dense jungles – where humidity is high, rainfall is plentiful and temperatures are hot year round – the foliage is luxuriant, from ground level to the tops of tall trees where interlaced branches form a dense canopy through which little sunlight can penetrate.

Bromeliads (air plants) sprout from massive tree trunks, and include countless species of orchids thriving high in the forks of trees where they obtain moisture and nutrients from the air. Ferns grow at the tree bases and rapidly growing woody vines ascend to the canopy in search of light.

The brilliantly colored flowers found amid the verdant growth include the poinsettia, an ornamental flowering plant which is a type of spurge. Some spurges produce poisonous saps which the natives used on arrow tips. The tropical hardwoods, such as mahogany, are deciduous but are considered evergreen because, rather than shed all their leaves at once, they do so sporadically throughout the year.

The widespread cutting of tropical rain forests to clear the land for agriculture has become a controversial practice due to the damage this causes to an area's watershed, where rainfall collects in rivers and lakes that depend on the surrounding forest for their survival. Tree roots prevent soil erosion during heavy rains, and when land is cleared for plantations, the absence of a vast forest to absorb the rainwater has detrimental effects on the area's water table. Trees also supply nutrients to the soil and are a vital source of oxygen.

In mountainous regions of the tropics, a montane (mist) forest grows on the upper slopes and ridges, and consists of small trees and ground vegetation of grasses and ferns. At the summits of the higher peaks is an elfin woodland of matted mosses, lichens and ferns which can survive in wet and windy conditions.

**Palm trees** grow throughout the tropics, their flowing crowns of frond leaves swaying in the breeze and providing welcome shade. Palms grow to heights of 100 feet or more, their smooth cylindrical stems marked by ringlike scars left by former leaves. The coco palm, from 60 to 100 feet tall, readily establishes itself on shorelines and small islands because its seeds, enclosed in a large buoyant pod, can float. Its fruit is the coconut, a hard woody shell encased in a brown fibrous husk, and a single coco palm can bear more than 200 nuts annually. A coconut has three round scars at one end, its embryo lying against the largest which is easily punctured to drain the nutritious juice inside. Copra, from which oil is extracted to make soaps, cooking oil and suntan lotion, is produced when a ripened coconut is broken open and dried.

*(Top to bottom) Tropical rainforests contain hidden waterfalls and delicate orchids, while coco palms thrive near beaches.*

*Sloth*

Bananas, coffee and other crops were introduced to the West Indies and Central America for cultivation. **Banana plants** are widely grown, their leafy, palm-like aspect a familiar sight. The overlapping bases of the banana plant form a false trunk, from which emerges the true stem of a mature plant, bearing the male and female flowers. The latter develop into clusters of upturned bananas, called 'hands', with each banana a 'finger'. The plant is cut down for harvesting, since it bears fruit only the once.

The **coffee tree**, a small evergreen brought to Spanish America from Africa, thrives at higher altitudes in the tropics – especially in fertile, well-drained soil of volcanic origin. The tree yields clusters of fragrant white flowers that mature into small red fruits containing two coffee beans each. Some of the world's finest coffee is cultivated in the

*Toucan*

*Iguana*

highlands of Jamaica and Costa Rica where conditions are ideal.

The tropical rainforest is a habitat for hundreds of species of birds and butterflies, including macaws (parrots), quetzals, hummingbirds and **keel-billed toucans**, the latter a perching bird related to the woodpecker but with an enormous, tusk-shaped bill that is often brightly colored. In Costa Rica alone, some 800 species of birds live in its forests and are joined each winter by millions of birds that migrate from northern temperate zones to the tropics.

Animals inhabiting the tropical forest include monkeys, sloths and **jaguars**, these big cats becoming arboreal during flood conditions. **Spider monkeys** are agile acrobats who use their tail as a fifth limb and live in the forest canopy, as do howler monkeys whose bloodcurdling screams can be heard over six miles away. **Sloths** are about the size of a house cat and they hang upside down from branches while they sleep, eat and travel from tree to tree. Related to the sloth

*Spider Monkey*

is the course-haired, collared **anteater**, which is less than two feet long and feeds on ants and termites, licking them up with its sticky tongue. The ring-tailed **coatimundi**, related to the raccoon, ranges from Peru to Mexico where it is often raised as a pet.

*Great Egret*

*Frigate Bird*

*Brown Pelican*

*Crocodile*

The large diverse **iguana** family includes species which live in trees along streams and those that inhabit the desert where they feed on cactus flowers and fruits. A herbivorous lizard, the cold-blooded iguana derives body heat from the sun and basks on rocks and tree tops for much of the day to maintain a body temperature high enough to digest the leaves and fruits it consumes. Peaceful and harmless, iguanas grow to three feet in length and can weigh over 400 pounds. The larger males are gray with a tall crest on the back, while the females retain the bright green body of a young iguana. The female burrows a nest in sandy soil, laying her eggs at the end of a tunnel which she then refills for concealment. When the young iguanas hatch, they dig their way to the surface where they are vulnerable to predators.

**Crocodiles** are large, carnivorous reptiles which live in swamps or on river banks, slipping into the water to hunt for prey with their powerful jaws. The eyes, ears and nostrils are on top of its head, with valves closing on the ears and nostrils when the crocodile submerges. The average length of a crocodile's flat body and tail is about 10 feet but the saltwater variety is often 14 feet long, sometimes growing to 20 feet. The American crocodile lives in both fresh and salt water in South Florida, the West Indies and Central America, and usually does not attack humans without provocation.

**Alligators**, which are found in the southern United States, are generally less aggressive than crocodiles, have wider snouts and, unlike the crocodile, the lower fourth tooth does not protrude when the mouth is closed. Caimans are similar to alligators, growing to lengths of 15 feet, and are found in Central America.

Wading birds, found in coastal mangroves and lagoons, include the **flamingo** – a tall, tropical bird related to the heron. The flamingo feeds in the shallow water of marshes and lagoons where it scoops water into its large bill, the serrated edges of which strain algae and shellfish from the water. The bird's pink color comes from its diet of shrimp and other crustaceans containing the pigment carotene. Flamingos build conical mud nests, one to two feet high and one foot across, with mates taking turns incubating the one or two eggs.

The **Great Egret** (also called Common Egret) is a type of heron that feeds in shallow water on small aquatic life. Threatened at the turn of the century when its white, silky plumage was used to adorn ladies hats, the egret is now a protected species.

The magnificent **frigate bird**, also called man-of-war bird, is the most aerial of the water birds with a wing spread of 7.5 feet – the largest in proportion to its body of any bird. A highly skilled flier, its long tail (deeply forked and scissor-like) is opened only while maneuvering in flight.

The **brown pelican**, in contrast to the frigate bird, is heavy bodied with a long neck and large, flat bill. It too is a graceful flier as well as a skilled swimmer, and

*Flamingo*

*Quetzal*

it will glide in circles in the air before suddenly diving straight into the water to scoop a fish into the large, expandable pouch hanging from its lower jaw. Brown pelicans nest on shore and the young feed from their parent's pouch.

Green Sea Turtle

Queen Angelfish

Moray Eel

Brain Coral

# A Coral Reef Community

Some of the most unusual animal life in the tropics is found beneath the water's surface where coral reefs, formed by living organisms, are home to a fascinating variety of fish and other sea creatures.

Gray Angelfish

Trumpetfish

# Coral Reefs

These underwater habitats are formed by soft, saclike animals called polyps. Smaller than a pea, each polyp secretes an exoskeleton of limestone. A colony forms by polyps budding new polyps, with all the buds remaining connected. These tiny polyps, each living inside its own limestone cavity, feed mainly at night on floating plankton which they trap with their extended tentacles. Microscopic algae grow within the polyp tissues and are collectively responsible for the coral colony's vivid colors. These symbiotic algae, called zooxanthellae, need sunlight and clear water to take up carbon dioxide and photosynthesize, thus providing an internal supply of oxygen and organic nutrients to the polyp.

When coral colonies die, their surfaces are recolonized by new corals or other types of invertebrates, such as sponges or soft corals. Layers of skeletal materials gradually accumulate over time to form a coral reef. Although corals live in temperate as well as tropical waters, coral reefs are found only in tropical waters, within 30 degrees of the equator, where the water temperature remains above 70 degrees Fahrenheit year round.

Coral reefs that extend from shore are called fringing reefs and those separated from shore by a wide lagoon are called barrier reefs. Barrier reefs rise like fortress walls from the sea floor and are habitat for tropical fish and large predators which feed here on the smaller fish. Fringe reefs, often within a few yards of the water's surface, serve as nurseries for hundreds of small tropical fish, as do mangroves which grow along shorelines. Their tangled roots and dense branches are saltwater tolerant, and they help stabilize coastlines by absorbing wave action.

Coral reefs also deflect incoming waves, their porous character allowing the absorption and dissipation of a pounding sea. In bays protected by strategically placed reefs, the steady shifting of particulate debris from the coral colony onto shore results in a beach of fine sand. Adjacent to reefs are seagrass beds, where sturdy stems and roots of underwater plants weave together to form a mat that stabilizes the shallow bottom and provides food for sea turtles, manatees, conchs and reef fishes. Seagrass beds also anchor sediments, helping maintain the water clarity required for a healthy reef which needs sunlight to survive.

Environmental pressures in the form of coastal development, water pollution, over fishing and increased recreational use have all threatened the survival of coral reefs. Excessive nutrients in the water, often caused by sewage and agricultural run-off, can trigger algal blooms that cloud the water and prevent sunlight from penetrating and activating photosynthesis in the corals' symbiotic algae. These unwanted blooms of algae can also attach to the surfaces of corals and grow until portions of the reef are smothered. Protective measures are being taken in the Florida Keys and other areas, which include the installation of mooring buoys so that no anchors are dropped from boats, and prohibiting snorkelers and divers from touching and taking pieces of coral.

Most reef-forming corals belong to the stony or hard group of corals. There are many different types of hard corals, some branch-like, others rounded, their distinctive shapes determined by the budding pattern of the various polyp species. Corals are often named for their appearance and some common hard corals include elkhorn, with its thick stocky branches, and staghorn, which has smaller branches. Other branching colonies include flower, finger, pencil and ivory corals. Pillar and ribbon corals grow upright in clusters, and brain corals grow in rounded shapes. Soft corals also help build the reefs, their feathery forms including sea fans and gorgonians in a variety of vivid colors. Sea anemones, unlike the corals, do not have a skeleton and often look like flowers when their feeding end is open and tentacles are fully extended. Brilliantly colored sponges, another aquatic animal, attach themselves to coral reefs, often in colonies. They vary in shape and size, and show little movement.

The shimmering tropical fish found along coral reefs come in an assortment of shapes, sizes, colors and markings which often change as the juvenile fish matures. Angelfishes are among the most beautiful of the small fish that inhabit shallow reefs, their flattened, disc-like shapes allowing them to slip through nooks and crannies as they feed on sponges and the ectoparasites of other fishes. Butterflyfishes are similar to angelfishes with yellow their dominant color. They travel in pairs, feeding on coral polyps, sea anemones, tubeworms and algae.

*A reef shark looks for prey near a barrier reef.*

*Southern stingrays, common in the Caribbean, live near shore.*

The size of reef fish can vary, the butterflyfishes growing to about 6 inches, the angelfishes ranging from one to two feet in length, and the tiny cherubfish, which prefers deepwater reefs, reaching less than three inches in size. Parrotfishes begin life as drably colored females then turn into males with gaudy green and blue scales. They have molar-like teeth with which they grind algae off the corals, producing sand in the process.

Other members of the coral reef community include the spiny lobster which hides in crevices by day and feeds at night, as does the moray eel - a snake-like fish which is harmless unless provoked. The tiny sea horse (ranging in length from 2 to 8 inches) is usually found swimming upright among the seagrasses, using its tail to hold onto a seaweed when resting. The seahorse, which utters musical sounds during the mating embrace, belongs to the same family as the pipefishes, with which it shares a unique breeding habit in which the female's eggs are forced into a pouch on the male's underside, where they are fertilized and nourished until expelled as miniature versions of the adult.

Coral reefs attract a variety of feeding creatures, including **sharks**, which are heavy fishes with skeletons made of cartilage. A shark must keep moving in order to breathe by taking water in through the mouth and passing it over the gills which form a line of slits down both sides of the fish. There are over 250 species of shark, ranging in size from 2 feet to 50 feet. Abundant in warm waters, not all sharks are predatory and few are interested in humans. Those considered harmless are the Nurse Shark, which grows to 12 feet in length, and the Caribbean reef shark, which grows to about 8 feet on a diet of reef fish, octopus, crabs and lobster. To detect their prey, sharks have electromagnetic senses on their snouts, which is why professional shark feeders wearing stainless-steel mesh suits and gloves can hypnotize a reef shark with a gentle stroke of the hand. Not so placid are the hammerhead and tiger sharks, which are predatory and dangerous to humans.

**Rays** are flat-bodied fish related to the shark. Shaped like a kite with winglike pectoral fins which propel it through the water, a ray also has a long whiplike tail. There are three basic groups of ray: mantas, eagles and stingrays. Mantas are the largest, up to 22 feet in width and 3,000 pounds in weight. Mantas and eagles are active rays whereas stingrays are bottom dwellers, lying like rugs on the sea floor as they dredge up shellfish and other small animals. The stingray's eyes and spiracles (breathing orifices) are on top of the head, its mouth and gill slits on the underside. Southern stingrays are common along Caribbean reefs, the female growing up to six feet in width. They have rows of spines along their tail which contain a poison that can inflict pain and be fatal to humans. Stingrays defend themselves against sharks by lashing with their tails but they rarely attack humans unless provoked or stepped on. They have no teeth, but their jaws are strong for grinding and sucking, which is why snorkelers at Stingray City on Grand Cayman will sometimes receive a hickey from a nuzzling stingray looking for food.

**Turtles** are the world's oldest surviving reptile, in existence since the time of the earliest dinosaurs some 200 million years ago. Equipped with toeless, oarlike legs, these ancient mariners can swim at speeds approaching 20 miles per hour, and some will travel thousands of ocean miles to reach their nesting sites. Pacific loggerhead turtles have been tracked crossing the Pacific Ocean from Yaku Shima in south-

*Sea turtles come ashore to lay their eggs on sandy beaches.*

ern Japan to Baja California. The voyage for these 300-pound swimmers can take two to six years along a line in the ocean where cool water from the north and warm water from the south meets and where buoyant jellyfish, a favorite food of sea turtles, are trapped as the plankton-rich cooler water sinks beneath the warmer water.

Once a source of food for sailors, the green turtle is now protected by law, as are the hawksbill, olive ridley, leatherback and loggerhead, the latter named for its large head (up to 10 inches wide) and powerful jaws used to crush clams and crabs. The green turtle, named for the greenish color of its body fat, is a plant eater and can be seen grazing on seagrasses or sleeping under reef ledges. The hawksbill turtle, named for its narrow, pointed beak with which it pries sponges from coral reefs, was hunted nearly to extinction for its beautiful tortoiseshell, which was used in making jewelry. The leatherback has a rubbery dark shell and is the largest of all turtles, reaching lengths of eight feet and weighing up to 1,100 pounds. The olive ridley is one of the smallest with a shell length of 30 inches or less, and seabirds will sometimes hitch a ride on the back of an olive ridley as it swims across hundreds of miles of Pacific Ocean.

The female nests on beaches where the warm sand incubates her eggs. She drags herself onto shore in the night, selects a site and digs a hole in which 100 or more eggs are laid. After covering them, she returns to the sea having spent one to three hours on shore under cover of darkness. The two-inch-long hatchlings emerge two months later, again in the cool of the night, and crawl into the water. For years, the catching of females while they laid their eggs was a major factor in the marine turtle's decline, for as few as one

in a thousand hatchlings survive to adulthood and it can take up to 50 years for some turtles to reach sexual maturity, their average lifespan being 150 years.

The olive ridley, and its Atlantic cousin the Kemp's ridley, are the only sea turtles that stage *arribidas* (arrivals), during which thousands of females laden with eggs will crawl ashore en masse and jostle for position as they dig their nests in the sand.

Several species of large baleen **whales** frequent the warm waters off Mexico each winter, including the gray whale and the humpback. Baleen whales are filter feeders who eat schooling fish, plankton and other small organisms, which they catch by swimming with their mouths wide open. When the whale closes its massive mouth, it raises its tongue to force the scooped water out the sides where the bristles of its baleen plates trap the food.

*A female humpback and her calf.*

The Pacific coast of Baja California is one of the best places in the world to sight gray whales. Each fall, an estimated 11,000 to 15,000 gray whales migrate south from their feeding ground in the Beaufort Sea to the Baja's warm-water lagoons where the females give birth and nurse their young from January to early April. A fully grown gray whale is 40-45 feet in length and weighs up to 40 tons. Strongly migratory but slow swimmers, gray whales travel near shore on their twice-annual migration between Mexico and the Beaufort Sea.

The Pacific humpback is about the same size as the gray whale, and it also migrates twice a year, spending the summer in Alaskan coastal waters, then heading south to breed and calve in tropical waters. December and January are the birthing months, following a 12-month gestation period. Cows give birth to a single calf weighing about a ton and measuring 12 to 15 feet in length. Calves are born without a blubber layer and nurse on their mother's milk which contains 50 percent butter fat. Humpbacks travel in threesomes - a female, her calf and a male escort. The male earns his position as escort by serenading the female with a repeated pattern of sounds at depths of 60 feet or more. If this doesn't win her, the male will challenge her current escort by smacking him with his fluked tail which packs 8,000 pounds of muscle and, studded with barnacles, is a humpback's most powerful weapon. No two humpback tails are alike and scientists identify each whale by the

*Dolphins are highly intelligent, sociable and athletic.*

pattern on its flukes which are visible when the whale raises its tail high out of the water before making deep dive.

The common **dolphin**, a small toothed whale about eight feet long, is often seen travelling in large groups, riding the bow waves of ships. Wave riding is also a favorite pastime of the acrobatic bottlenosed dolphin, which averages 9 feet in length and weighs about 350 pounds. These playful creatures swim in large groups and can reach speeds up to 30 mph. With a beak holding 200 teeth, the bottlenose feeds on small fish, crustaceans and squid. When pursued by a shark or killer whale, dolphins will try to out swim their predator or, as a group, they will try battering it to death. Bottlenosed dolphins communicate with an extensive array of sounds using the air sacs and valves in their blowhole, and these clicking sounds are used for echolocation (projecting a sound beam and listening to the echo) with which dolphins locate prey and avoid predators. The bottlenose likes inshore waters and is friendly to humans, often approaching close enough to be touched. Tales of dolphins rescuing people from drowning date back to Greek mythology.

In contrast to the gregarious bottlenosed dolphin is the reclusive **manatee**. Also called sirenian or sea cow, this large marine mammal descends from the same primitive group of land mammals as the elephant. The manatee spends its entire life in the water, surfacing to breathe at least every 15 or 20 minutes through nostrils on the upper surface of its snout which close tightly like valves when the animal submerges. Shy and completely harmless, manatees live in warm, shallow and sheltered waters where they consume up to 100 pounds of vegetation daily. The manatee can grow to 12 feet in length and weigh over 500 pounds, its thick, heavy body covered with hairless gray-brown skin. A sluggish, nocturnal bottom feeder, it propels itself with two weak flippers and a beaver-like tail. The female gives birth to one calf every two to five years and uses her flippers to hold the nursing calf to her chest. Both parents care for their young, one holding it while the other dives for food. An endangered species, the manatee has no natural predators but is vulnerable to injury from boat propellers, and is found in the coastal waters of Central America, the West Indies and Florida, where it's protected by law.

*A pair of manatees surfaces in the coastal waters of Florida.*

# PART II

## *THE VOYAGE AND THE PORTS*

## THE CARIBBEAN

CRUISE ROUTES: - - - - - - -

N

Miles
0     300

### CARIBBEAN CRUISE DISTANCES

FROM MIAMI TO:

| | |
|---|---|
| San Juan | 1100 miles |
| St. Thomas | 1180 miles |
| St Maarten | 1280 miles |
| Dominica | 1475 miles |
| Barbados | 1650 miles |
| Curacao | 1320 miles |
| Colon | 1430 miles |

UNITED STATES

Houston •
Galveston •
New Orleans •

GULF of MEXICO

Tropic of Cancer

Florida

Tampa ⊙

Port Canaveral ⊙

Fort Lauderdale ⊙
Miami ⊙
Key West

MEXICO

Yucatan

Progreso •
Cancun •
Playa del Carmen •
COZUMEL
Costa Maya (Majahual) •

Havana ⊙

CUBA

CAYMAN IS.

The Bahamas

Freeport •

Nassau •

Greater Antilles

Turks & Caicos
G. Turk I.

DOMINICAN REPUBLIC

Santo Domingo ⊙

HAITI

JAMAICA

Ocho Rios •
Kingston ⊙

BELIZE

Belize City •

Puerto Cortes •
ROATAN IS.
Bay Islands

GUATEMALA

HONDURAS

NICARAGUA

Managua ★

CARIBBEAN SEA

CARIBBEAN

EASTERN

Tropic of Cancer

ATLANTIC OCEAN

Lesser Antilles

ANGUILLA
ST. MAARTEN
ST. KITTS
ANTIGUA
MONTSERRAT
GUADELOUPE
DOMINICA
MARTINIQUE
ST. LUCIA
ST. VINCENT
BARBADOS
GRENADA
TOBAGO
TRINIDAD

San Juan ⊙ ST. THOMAS
PUERTO RICO
VIRGIN ISLANDS
ST. CROIX

SOUTHERN CARIBBEAN

ISLA DE MARGARITA

ARUBA
CURACAO
BONAIRE
Willemstad •

La Guaira
Caracas ⊙

VENEZUELA

Cartagena •

San Blas Is.

Colon ⊙
Panama City ⊙
Panama Canal

PANAMA

San Jose ⊙
Limon •
COSTA RICA
Puntarenas •

COLOMBIA

PACIFIC OCEAN

WESTERN

CARIBBEAN

# THE CARIBBEAN

The azure, island-dotted Caribbean Sea is the most popular cruising area in the world. The beauty of its beaches is legendary and, with almost no tidal range, its turquoise waters remain warm year round – ideal conditions for swimming, snorkeling and other water sports.

Yet there's more to the Caribbean than white sand and swaying palm trees. The West Indies were once important European-controlled colonies used for the cultivation of sugarcane, and each island nation has its own history and local flavor – an exotic mix of African, European, Indian and Asian cultures called Creole.

For travellers yearning to escape the grey grip of winter, there is no mystery to the appeal the Caribbean holds. The senses are reawakened here, where the air is soft and warm, carrying the fragrance of flowers and sweet spices.

Cruise ships often pull into port as dawn is breaking, treating their passengers to the magic of a seaborne arrival as the golden sun rises above a rippled sea and the verdant shores of a volcanic island draw ever nearer. The departure is equally special, the ship easing away from shore and heading out to sea as the setting sun casts its Caribbean colors across the sky.

The islands regularly visited on a Panama Canal cruise are covered in this section, as are the Florida ports of Miami and Fort Lauderdale.

*(Right) A beach stop in the Caribbean. (Below) A Caribbean-bound cruise ship glides past Miami Beach.*

# FLORIDA

lorida is America's gateway to the Caribbean. Warmed by subtropical waters, cooled by trade winds, this southern state of swaying palms and coral cays counts its visitors in the millions. Every conceivable 'fun in the sun' attraction is here – palm-shaded swimming pools, championship golf courses, tennis camps, shopping malls, sporting events and theme parks galore. Yet it is water more than anything that defines Florida. The sea is readily accessible from any point in the state and some of the best beaches lie on barrier cays lining much of the splendid coastline. And the water doesn't stop at the seashore. Rivers and canals meander past cypress stands and waterfront homes, linking many of the lakes and lagoons that make Florida an angler's paradise. Bird life abounds in wetlands that are protected as wildlife refuges and the state's seemingly endless shoreline of beaches and resorts is dotted with parks, preserves and public recreation areas.

*(Above) Port Everglades viewed from John U. Lloyd Park.*
*(Below) South Pointe Park and Miami Beach.*

## A Brief History of Florida

The first European to arrive on Florida's shores was Spanish explorer Ponce de Leon. Seeking the fabled Fountain of Youth, he landed near the future site of St. Augustine in 1513 during the Easter season (*Pascua Florida*) and mistook the long peninsula for an island, which he claimed for Spain. Commissioned by the Spanish king to colonize the 'isle of Florida,' Ponce de Leon returned in 1521, landing his two vessels near Charlotte Harbor.

The Native Americans living in the area had built their dwellings on high rectangular mounds surrounded by waterways and boat basins. Called Caloosa, they didn't take kindly to the sight of strangers settling on their land, and they attacked the Spanish party, fatally wounding Ponce de Leon with a poisoned arrow and forcing the Spanish to leave.

Spain abandoned any further plans to colonize Florida until the French began encroaching upon the area. St. Augustine was founded in 1565 to protect Spain's shipping route through the Straits of Florida, but Spain's tenuous hold on Florida ended in 1819 when it was ceded to the United States. Official U.S. occupation took place in 1821 with Andrew Jackson appointed military governor. The next year Florida became a territory, with settlers from other states soon establishing cotton and tobacco plantations around the new capital of Tallahassee.

When the New York financier Henry Flagler paid a visit to Florida's east coast in the late 1800s, he envisioned the state as the perfect winter playground and proceeded to build a business empire of railroads, steamships and palatial hotels, while anonymously donating to the construction of schools, churches and hospitals. Another industrial tycoon, Henry Plant, built railroads and hotels on Florida's west coast, laying the groundwork for Florida's enduring allure as America's Sunshine State.

*Key Largo*

# Miami

Named for an American Indian tribe, Miami was a trading post when Henry Flagler, having built grand hotels at St. Augustine and Palm Beach, set his sights on this southern port. He made Miami a railroad terminus in 1896, the year it was incorporated, then proceeded to dredge the harbor to accommodate his fleet of steamships. Set on a low ridge overlooking Biscayne Bay, Miami is now the transportation and business hub of south Florida. It is also the busiest cruise port in the world, receiving four million passengers a year.

## Getting Around

The Port of Miami's cruise port is a two-island complex in Biscayne Bay adjacent to downtown Miami. The port, consisting of numerous passenger terminals, is located eight miles from Miami International Airport (a $24 taxi ride). There is long-term parking with a complimentary shuttle service at each terminal ($20 per day) and no reservations required.

It's a short ($10) taxi ride from the cruise terminals to **Bayside Marketplace** **1**, a bustling waterfront development of shops, restaurants and open-air entertainment. Tour boats depart daily from Bayside on 90-minute narrated tours of the port, affording passengers a view of the Miami skyline, waterfront mansions and other sights.

Gray Line operates two hop-on hop-off bus tours from Bayfront Park's Central Station – the Beach Loop stops at various attractions in Miami Beach and South Beach; the City Loop stops at attractions such as Vizcaya, the Biltmore Hotel, Coral Gables and Little Havana.

Trolley tours also depart regularly from Bayside, as do water taxis, which ply the waters of Biscayne Bay, stopping at various waterfront attractions. The elevated Metromover links downtown Miami's major hotels and shopping areas.

*Miami's busy cruise port.*

## Where to Stay

The selection of hotels in Greater Miami is extensive and includes a plethora of luxury properties. In downtown Miami, the Intercontinental Miami is within walking distance of Bayside. Its stunning lobby features a massive marble sculpture called *Spindle* by Henry Moore. Yesteryear's elegance can be enjoyed at the **Biltmore Hotel**, built in 1926 as the centerpiece of Coral Gables. In a lovely setting of waterways, tennis courts and golf links, this is a classic grand hotel with a vaulted lobby and an opulent swimming pool/bar area.

The **Fountainebleau** is Miami Beach's most famous hotel, which first opened in 1954 and has been featured over the years in numerous movies and television shows, including the James Bond film *Goldfinger*. Other hotels in the vicinity include **Eden Roc Renaissance** and **Sheraton Four Points**.

*Downtown Miami viewed from The Rusty Pelican restaurant.*

In the stylish Art Deco District of South Beach, the selection of boutique hotels along Ocean Drive includes the **Beacon Hotel**, built in 1937 and recently renovated. A few blocks north, at 1116 Ocean Drive, is **The Villa** by Barton G. This luxury boutique hotel is housed in a 1930s gated palazzo formerly owned by slain fashion designer Gianni Versace.

## Shopping & Dining

Bayside Marketplace is a great spot for visiting cruise passengers to soak in the local atmosphere while browsing the waterfront shops or enjoying an authentic Cuban sandwich to the sound of live Latin music.

Other shopping/dining areas include Coconut Grove where interesting shops, open-air bistros and sidewalk cafes line CocoWalk on Grand Avenue.

At Coral Gables the Miracle Mile (the main shopping thoroughfare on Coral Way between Southwest 42nd Avenue and Douglas Road) is lined with some of Miami's best restaurants.

For a taste of Latin America and Miami's famous Cuban coffee, try one of the eateries on **Calle Ocho** **2** in Little Havana.

In South Beach, the family-owned Joe's Stone Crab Restaurant at 11 Washington Avenue (just off South Point Drive) is a legendary seafood restaurant, established in 1913 by Hungarian-born Joseph Weiss. Also in South Beach is the popular Mango's Tropical Cafe, offering lively beachfront dining.

For a sunset view of the Miami skyline, try The Rusty Pelican on Key Biscayne (at 3201 Rickenbacker Causeway).

**Golf** – The Doral Resort near the Miami International Airport, has four 18-hole courses including one of the most challenging courses in the Miami area. The Links at Key Biscayne, a top-ranked municipal course, is built around lagoons and contains four waterside holes with views of the Miami skyline. The city-owned Biltmore Golf Course in Coral Gables opened in 1925 and was recently refurbished.

## Miami Attractions

Greater Miami encompasses the City of Miami, Miami Beach, Coral Gables, Hialeah and many smaller communities. About half of the City of Miami's population is Hispanic, many of Cuban descent, with hundreds of thousands of Cuban refugees moving here from the late 1950s to early 70s, settling in the city's Little Havana section. **Calle Ocho** (Southwest Eighth Street) is the main thoroughfare and scene of an annual Hispanic festival that's held in March and stretches the length of 23 lively blocks of music and dancing.

**Miami Beach 3**, located on a barrier island in Biscayne Bay, was a mangrove swamp until connected to the mainland by a wooden bridge in 1913. Opulent hotels and huge estates were soon built here, while the **South Beach 4** area was sub-divided into smaller lots and developed as a middle-class resort of mod-

*Versace's former palazzo is now The Villa by Barton G.*

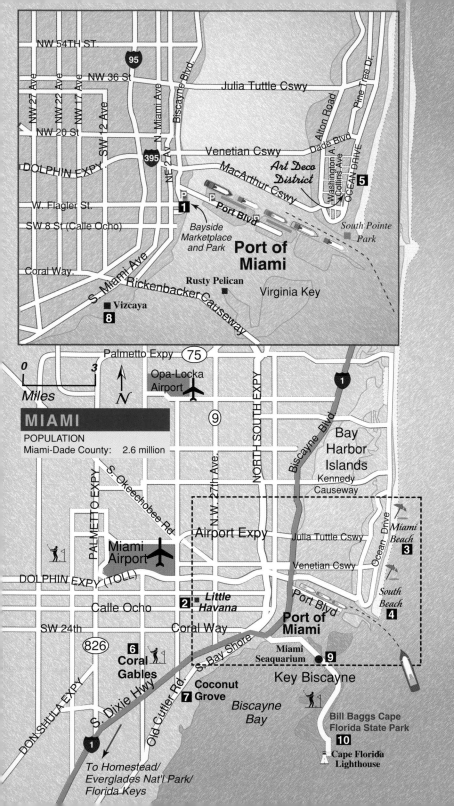

est hotels and apartments. Many of these buildings went up during the Depression, when visitors came to Miami Beach to temporarily escape their worries. The area suffered a decline following World War II. Then, in 1979, South Beach's square-mile area of Art Deco structures, their style of smooth lines and white exteriors sometimes referred to as Tropical Deco, was declared a national historic district.

During South Beach's revitalization in the late 1980s and early 90s, many of the run-down hotels were refurbished and repainted in pastel colors. Today the area is one of the trendiest in America, where a steady stream of pedestrian and car traffic along Ocean Drive includes movie stars and fashion models who frequent the stylish eateries and nightclubs.

The **Art Deco Welcome Center** **5** at 1001 Ocean Drive is a good place to start a tour of South Beach. Local attractions include South Pointe Park, the bohemian outdoor cafes of Espanola Way

*(Top) South Beach's Ocean Drive. (Above) A boardwalk connects Miami Beach with South Beach/Art Deco District.*

(a favored setting for episodes of *Miami Vice*) and the shops, galleries and sidewalk cafes of the Lincoln Road pedestrian mall. A beachside boardwalk runs from 23rd Street to 46th Street, along the Miami Beach waterfront.

**Coral Gables** **6**, situated four miles south of downtown Miami, was founded in 1925 at the height of the Florida land boom. A planned city designed by George Merrick, its Mediterranean architecture includes such highlights as the Venetian Pool – a huge municipal pool set in a coral quarry with caves, waterfalls and arched bridges. Merrick's boyhood home, a gabled plantation house on Coral Way, is open to the public. His dream city of canals, plazas and tree-shaded streets is also home to the University of Miami, where the Lowe Art Museum houses a permanent collection of Renaissance and baroque art, as well as Spanish and American paintings and artwork by North American Indians. The Orange Bowl Classic & Festival has been a major annual event in Miami since 1933 when the University of Miami played the Manhattan University.

**Coconut Grove** **7**, on the waterfront east of Coral Gables, was settled in the late 19th century by New England intellectuals and Bahamian seamen. The conical home of founding father Ralph Munroe, a New York yacht designer, is called the Barnacle

and is open to the public at 3485 Main Highway. Also in Coconut Grove is the **Vizcaya Museum and Gardens** **8** (3251 S. Miami Avenue), a restored Italian Renaissance-style villa completed in 1916 as a winter residence for industrialist John Deering. The 34-room mansion, set in grounds of formal gardens and amid fountains overlooking Biscayne Bay, has been designated a National Historic Landmark. It contains Renaissance and baroque antiques and artwork, and has been visited by such dignitaries as Pope John Paul II and Queen Elizabeth, and President Clinton who hosted the 1994 Summit of the Americas at Vizcaya.

A toll causeway links the mainland with Virginia Key, location of the **Miami Seaquarium** **9**, and with **Key Biscayne**, where attractions include Crandon Park's white-sand beach, 18-hole championship golf course and 26-court tennis center. At the southern tip of Key Biscayne is the **Bill Baggs Cape Florida State Park** **10** with nature trails, picnic areas, open-air restaurants and a concession renting bicycles, kayaks, beach chairs and umbrellas. Overlooking the park's swimming beach is the historic **Cape Florida Lighthouse**.

## South of Miami

**Homestead**, south of Miami, is the gateway to Everglades National Park, Biscayne National Park and the Florida Keys. The center of Florida's fruit and nursery production, one of its major attractions is **Coral Castle**, built from massive blocks of coral by

a Latvian immigrant in the 1920s and '30s.

**Biscayne National Park**, nine miles east of Homestead on SW 328 Street, is an undeveloped underwater park containing miles of coral reefs. Its shallow waters are very clear and warm – a natural habitat for sponges, crabs, manatees and more than 500 different kinds of fish. The park is primarily accessible by boat, with tour boats operating out of park headquarters at Convoy Point.

## The Everglades

This unique wilderness region of shallow, slow-flowing water covers more than 4,000 square miles. Sawgrass and hammocks (island-like masses of vegetation) grow here in the solidly packed black muck, which has formed over millions of years from vegetation decaying in the nearly stagnant water. Lake Okeechobee (along with Big Cypress Swamp) is a chief source of water for the Everglades, sections of which were drained, starting in 1906. When conservation measures were introduced in the 1980s, drained swampland was reflooded and the amount of phosphorus fertilizer used on farmers' fields was reduced so that cleaner water is now running off their land into the Everglades ecosystem.

**Everglades National Park** includes Florida Bay and its many islets and islands, and contains a great variety of flora and fauna, including palms, pines and mangrove forests. The park is a sanctuary for manatees, crocodiles, alligators, sea turtles and nearly 300 kinds of land and wading birds. Mosquitoes proliferate from May to November, and insect repellent is recommended year-round.

Parachute Key Visitor Center is located at the park's southeast entrance and another, the Royal Palm Visitor Center, is just inside the park. A road leads through the southern half of the Everglades to the Flamingo Ranger Station and Visitor Center on Florida Bay. In addition to boardwalks and nature trails in the Flamingo area, tours can be taken of Florida Bay and the backcountry. Charter fishing boats and canoe rentals are available. Airboat tours can be taken within the park, including those operated out of Gator Park.

*(Opposite) Vizcaya Museum.*
*(Below) View from Cape Florida Lighthouse in Key Biscayne.*

# The Keys

A chain of small coral islands extending 110 miles from the southern tip of Florida, the Keys are both exotic and all-American. Their tropical vegetation, steady trade winds and coral reefs are quintessentially Caribbean, while Key West's clapboard houses and white picket fences are reminiscent of a New England coastal town. The Keys' reef-riddled waters supported a thriving salvage industry in the mid-19th century before modern lighthouses and steam vessels brought an end to the steady stream of ships that were snared in the reefs off Key West.

**Key Largo**, the largest of the islands at the 'top' of the Keys, is the location of **John Pennekamp Coral Reef State Park** – America's first underwater park, established in 1960. Over time,

adjoining sanctuaries were established to protect the threatened reefs from boats hitting them with their props and anchors. In 1997, the **Florida Keys National Marine Sanctuary** was established to encompass the entire length of the Keys. Glass-bottom boat cruises depart from the Holiday Inn dock in Key Largo to view the coral reefs.

## Key West

The southernmost point of the continental United States, and only 90 miles from Cuba, Key West is the largest center in the Keys, with about 25,000 residents. It was once a base of operation against pirates, who preyed on Spanish treasure ships as they sailed from Cuba to Spain via the Straits of Florida. When Florida was ceded by Spain to the United States in 1819, Key West became a haven for exiled Cubans, including revolutionary leaders trying to rid their country of Spanish rule. The sinking of the battleship *Maine* in Havana harbor in 1898 led the U.S. to declare war on Spain, and some of the 266 men who died in that incident are buried in the Key West Cemetery.

In 1912 the Keys became linked with the mainland upon completion of Henry Flagler's railroad. The rail line was abandoned after sustaining hurricane damage in 1935, and was replaced a few years later with the 123-mile Overseas Highway that includes 42 bridges. Despite this well-travelled connection to the rest of Florida, the Keys have retained an island ambiance and sense of seclusion.

As a port of call, Key West holds many attractions. The cruise ship dock is located close to the downtown's tree-lined streets of shops, restaurants and colonial homes, a number of which are listed on the National Register of Historic Places. President Harry Truman had a presidential retreat in Key West, and other illustrious names associated with Key West include Haitian-born and French-educated John James Audubon, for whom one of the oldest and best-known U.S. environmental organizations is named, who visited Key West in 1832 to study and sketch the native birds.

Key West has long been an enclave for writers and artists drawn to the tiny island's exotic locale, including Winslow Homer, Robert Frost and Tennessee Williams. Of Key West's famous former residents, the one whose presence is most pervasive is Ernest Hemingway. For years Key West celebrated this Nobel Laureate with an annual Hemingway Days Festival, which included a writers' workshop, short-story contest, Caribbean street fair and a concert on the grounds of his former home. However, in 1997 Hemingway's sons denounced the festivities as tacky and threatened to sue if they weren't given control of the festival and a cut of the proceeds, prompting the festival's cancellation. However, Sloppy Joe's bar still stages its annual Ernest Hemingway look-alike contest.

## Getting Around

The cruise ship docks are near Mallory Square, a bustling waterfront that attracts artists, entertainers and sunset watchers. Most major sights are within walking distance of the cruise pier but

*(Opposite) Key West's colorful past lives on. (Below) Key West's cruise port.*

another option is to board either the Conch Tour Train at Mallory Square, or the Old Town Trolley at one of numerous stops, for a 90-minute narrated tour of Key West. Bicycles and mopeds can also be rented within the town.

**Shopping & Dining** – A shopping arcade is located near the cruise docks between Wall Street and Mallory Square, and jewelry stores are concentrated on Duval Street. An excellent gift shop is located in the Mel Fisher Maritime Museum. Sloppy Joe's (Hemingway's favorite watering hole at the corner of Greene and Duval) sells clothing and souvenirs. Fresh seafood can be enjoyed at the Hyatt's waterfront **Shor Seafood Grill** and at **A&B Lobster House** at the foot of Front Street.

**Beaches & Watersports** – Local scuba diving, snorkeling and sailing excursions are available. Departing just north of Mallory Square are glass-bottom boat rides to the nearby coral reef. The beach at Fort Zachary Taylor is popular for swimming and snorkeling along its artificial reef.

**Golf** – Southernmost course in the continental U.S., Key West Golf & Country Club (Par 70; 6,500 yards) features rolling fairways and dense mangroves.

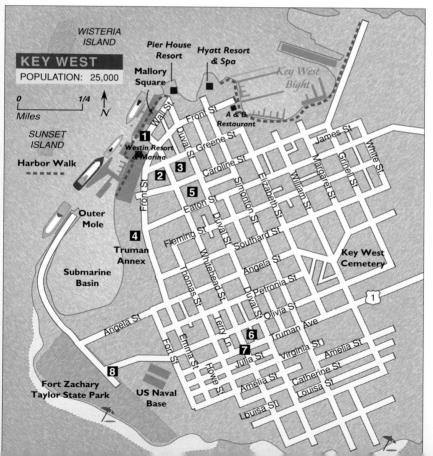

## Local Attractions

**The Key West Aquarium 1**, beside Mallory Square, presents sea life of the Atlantic Ocean and Gulf of Mexico.

**The Mel Fisher Maritime Museum 2**, at 200 Greene Street, features artifacts and treasures retrieved from two Spanish galleons that sank off Key West in 1622. Beginning in the 1970s, Mel Fisher Enterprises, the legendary treasure hunters, recovered hundreds of millions of dollars in booty from these gold-laden ships.

**The Audubon House & Tropical Gardens 3** at 205 Whitehead Street is housed in a restored 19th-century building. The museum commemorates John James Audubon's 1832 visit to Key West and contains a collection of his original engravings.

**Harry S. Truman Little White House 4** contains original furnishings and artifacts, which recreate the Truman era of the 1940s when the mansion was a presidential retreat.

At 322 Duval Street (near Eaton Street) stands Key West's oldest home, built in 1829 for a wrecker and sea captain. It now houses the **Wreckers' Museum 5** with exhibits including marine artifacts and ship models. Other historic homes of note are the Curry Mansion (on Caroline near Duval) and the Donkey Milk House Museum, at 613 Eaton Street, a restored 19th-century mansion listed on the National Register of Historic Places. Named for the back alleyway along which donkeys used to pull milk delivery carts, the award-winning mansion

*Ernest Hemingway's Key West home is now a museum.*

features hand-decorated ceilings, Spanish tile floors and verandas off every room.

**The Ernest Hemingway Home & Museum 6** at 907 Whitehead Street is a Registered National Historic Landmark. The home was built in 1851 in the Spanish colonial style and contains furnishings and other items that Hemingway and his second wife, Pauline, collected in their travels to Spain, Africa and Cuba. Hemingway wrote some of his greatest works while living here in the 1930s and 40s, and his study in the loft of the pool house remains intact with his desk and typewriter on display. The home exudes Hemingway's forceful presence, and dozens of cats, descendants of those owned by the famous author, still wander the lushly landscaped grounds. Sloppy Joe's, Hemingway's favorite watering hole, was moved in 1937 from Greene Street to the corner of Duval and Greene. Its owner, Joe Russell, was Hemingway's boat pilot, fishing companion and a model for the character Freddy in *To Have and Have Not*, which was set in Key West and Cuba.

The **Lighthouse Museum 7** at 938 Whitehead Street features the keeper's clapboard house and the lighthouse itself, built in 1847, with a magnificent view of Key West at the top of its 98 steps.

**Fort Zachary Taylor State Historic Site 8** was part of Florida's coastal defence system. Built from 1845-66, the fort became a base for the Union blockade of Confederate shipping during the Civil War, with captured ships brought to its harbor. Artifacts, models and one of the largest collections of Civil War armaments are on display.

## Fort Lauderdale

Situated on the New River, this retirement and resort city was settled around a fort built by Major William Lauderdale in 1838, during the Seminole War. Fort Lauderdale was incorporated in 1911, and the city grew rapidly during the Florida land boom of the 1920s. Its suburbs continue to expand, and today about 5.5 million people live in the metro area.

Fort Lauderdale's seaport was originally a small lake used by recreational boaters. Locally known as Bay Mabel Harbor, it came to the attention of a developer and businessman named Joseph Young, who moved to the area in the early 1920s, purchased 1,440 acres adjacent to the lake and created the Hollywood Harbor Development Company. On February 28, 1927, expectant spectators gathered to watch an

*Port Everglades is Florida's second busiest cruise port.*

explosion that would remove the lake's rock barrier to the ocean. At the appointed time, President Calvin Coolidge pressed a detonator in the White House, but nothing happened. Nonetheless, the harbor was officially opened that day and the rock barrier was removed a short while later. In 1930, the new seaport was named **Port Everglades** – chosen from submissions to a naming contest.

## Getting Around

Port Everglades is less than two miles from Fort Lauderdale/ Hollywood International Airport ($20 taxi ride) and is 30 to 45 minutes from Miami International Airport via I-95 ($85 taxi ride). Long-term parking is available in self-parking garages near the cruise terminals. For more information, visit www.broward.org/ port.

The cruise port is serviced by several car rental companies that provide shuttle service between the port and their rental lots. A taxi from the cruise port to downtown Fort Lauderdale costs $20 to $25.

Water taxis and tour boats are a pleasant way to explore Fort Lauderdale's scenic waterways. Water Taxi operates from 10 a.m. to midnight, with 11 convenient stops along its route, including the Convention Center (at the north end of the cruise port), Pier 66, 15th Street Fisheries, Riverwalk

*(Above) Fort Lauderdale's Water Taxi. (Below) The Hilton Fort Lauderdale Marina.*

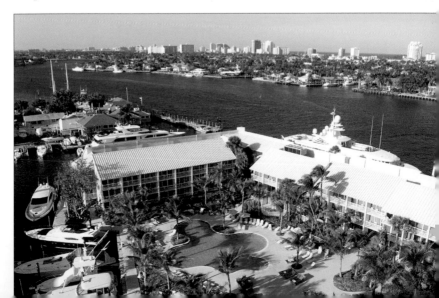

and several beach access points. Tickets are sold on board, cash only; an all-day pass is $13.

**Shopping & Dining** Las Olas Boulevard, the 'Rodeo Drive' of Fort Lauderdale, is lined with boutiques, galleries and several fine restaurants, including the Grill Room at the Riverside Hotel, a heritage property built in 1936.

In Lauderdale-By-The-Sea, the **Sea Watch** serves excellent seafood, as does the legendary **15th Street Fisheries** restaurant at Lauderdale Marina, which is a stop on the Water Taxi route.

**Where to Stay** – Fort Lauderdale has shed its image as a spring break destination for col-

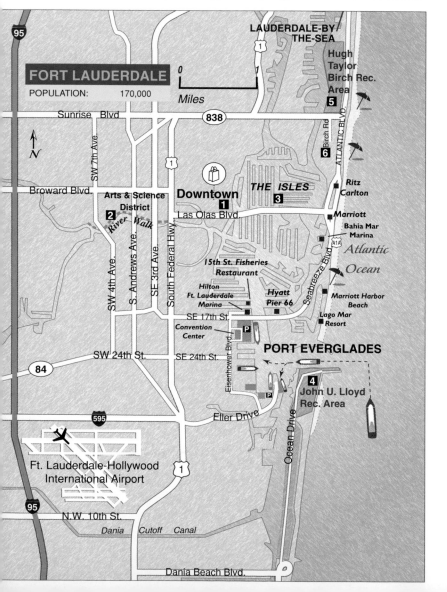

lege students and the opening of several luxury hotels, including a Ritz-Carlton, is bringing upscale sophistication to the city's selection of accommodations. The **Hilton Fort Lauderdale Marina** (formerly the Grande Hotel & Yacht Club) is conveniently located across the street from the Convention Center and Port Everglades. **Hyatt Pier 66** is a hotel resort situated on the other side of the Intracoastal Waterway, offering a waterside setting of lushly landscaped grounds. The beachfront **Lago Mar Resort & Club** and **Marriott Harbor Beach** are four-diamond hotels located in the Harbor Beach neighborhood.

The busy hotel strip opposite Fort Lauderdale Beach features a **Marriott** and **Ritz-Carlton** (formerly St. Regis). For a taste of 'Old Florida', the family-owned **Riverside Hotel** on Las Olas Boulevard is distinctly decorated with tropical murals and finely appointed rooms. North of downtown, in Lauderdale-by-the-Sea, the wide array of comfortable small hotels and motels includes **A Little Inn By The Sea**, with its bright and airy rooms overlooking a beach-side swimming pool.

**Beaches** – Fort Lauderdale's famous stretch of beach is overlooked by hotels, restaurants and a pedestrian promenade. This oceanfront boulevard proceeds north to Lauderdale-by-the-Sea, and beyond to Pompano Beach,

Hillsboro Beach and Deerfield Beach. South of Fort Lauderdale are the beaches of John U. Lloyd State Recreation Area, Dania and Hollywood. There are 23 miles of beach in the Fort Lauderdale area, the shoreline punctuated by fishing piers.

**Golf** – There are over 50 golf courses in the Fort Lauderdale area. The Emerald Hills Golf Club in Hollywood, about two miles south of the airport, is one of many open to the public.

## Local Attractions

**Las Olas Boulevard** 1 is an upscale shopping street of boutiques and restaurants. The Greater Fort Lauderdale Convention & Visitors Bureau is located at 200 E. Las Olas Boulevard

At the western end of Las

*Fort Lauderdale's beachfront promenade.*

*(Above) Port Everglades viewed from John U. Lloyd Recreation Area.*
*(Below) Fort Lauderdale's Riverwalk.*

Olas is **Riverwalk 2**, a lovely promenade on the north bank of the New River. Attractions in the Riverwalk area – also known as the **Arts and Science District** – include Esplanade Park, with outdoor exhibits on astronomy and navigation; the Museum of Art; a complex housing the Museum of Discovery and Science and Blockbuster IMAX Theater; the Broward Center for the Performing Arts; and the Fort Lauderdale Historical Society Museum.

Called the 'Venice of America', Fort Lauderdale is interwoven with more than 270 miles of natural and artificial waterways, and the eastern half of Las Olas runs through an exclusive residential area of canal-lined streets called **The Isles 3**, where both cars and yachts can be seen parked outside the palm-shaded homes. Nearby is the Bahia Mar Marina and the International Swimming Hall of Fame.

The cruise ship port is located opposite **John U. Lloyd Beach State Recreation Area 4**, situated on 251 acres of barrier island separating the Intracoastal Waterway from the Atlantic Ocean. The park is named in memory of a local attorney whose efforts helped bring about its creation. The park is entered at its south end via Dania Beach Boulevard, and its broad flat beach – popular for swimming and sunning – is also one of Broward County's most important sea turtle nesting beaches. A jetty at the north end is excellent for fishing and watching the comings and goings of cruise ships.

Manatees frequent the mangrove-lined tidal waterway that runs down the middle of the John Lloyd park. The Florida manatee is a protected species and in winter months these sluggish sea mammals frequent the Port, where they are attracted to the heated effluent from the Florida Power & Light plant. When calving mothers were found to be utilizing the FPL discharge canal, a section of it became designated a 'Manatee Nursery' and access to it was restricted.

Across the road from Fort Lauderdale Beach is the **Hugh Taylor Birch State Recreation Area 5** with nature trails, picnic facilities and a museum. Directly south, on the other side of Sunrise Boulevard, is **Bonnet House 6** – the 35-acre estate of Frederic and Evelyn Bartlett. Now a wildlife preserve, the tranquil grounds feature a swan pond. The Bartletts' paintings and seashell collection are displayed inside the house.

*The Breakers at Palm Beach*

## North of Fort Lauderdale

The coastal drive north of Fort Lauderdale to Palm Beach follows a scenic highway, bordered by the Atlantic Ocean to the east and the Intracoastal Waterway to the west. **Spanish River Park**, in Boca Raton, provides access to an ocean beach and contains a lagoon, nature trails and picnic sites.

The **Arthur R. Marshall Loxahatchee National Wildlife Refuge**, located west of Boca Raton, is the last northernmost portion of the Everglades and is habitat for the American alligator and over 200 species of birds. Visitor facilities include walking and biking trails, a canoe trail, boat ramps and a fishing platform, as well as a visitor center, butterfly garden and observation towers.

**Palm Beach** is where you'll see some of Florida's most palatial estates along Ocean Boulevard, including President Kennedy's Winter White House at 1095 North Ocean Boulevard, which the family sold in 1995. For a taste of Old Florida, visit **The Breakers** (on County Road) – a luxury grand hotel originally built by tycoon Henry Flagler in the late 1800s. Rebuilt in 1926, the resort's Italian Renaissance architecture includes vaulted ceilings, frescoes and Florentine fountains outside the main entrance. Nearby, on Cocoanut Row, is **Whitehall** – a mansion built by Flagler in 1901 and now a museum containing original furnishings and railroad exhibits.

# Tampa

Located on Tampa Bay, an inlet of the Gulf of Mexico, Tampa is the third largest city in Florida and one of the largest ports in the U.S. Incorporated in 1855, Tampa has long been a shipping and manufacturing hub on the Gulf Coast. First visited by Panfilo de Narvaez in 1528, the Spanish negotiated a peace treaty with the Native Americans, on the present site of the University of Tampa, but they remained hostile and for two centuries Europeans avoided the area.

The first white settlement began in 1823 and Fort Brooke was built the next year. The late 1800s brought a surge in development with the construction of railroads, an expanding fishing industry and the introduction of cigar making in **Ybor City**, the center of Tampa's Hispanic population. During the Spanish-American War, Tampa became a military base with Theodore Roosevelt training his Rough Riders there.

A commercial center, Tampa also has a thriving arts and culture scene, which includes the

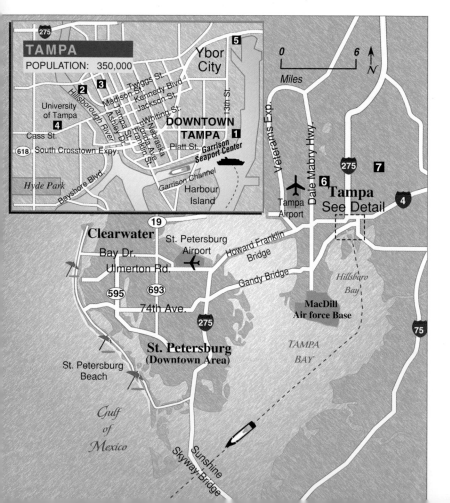

Florida Symphony Orchestra and the Tampa Ballet. It's also a sports-oriented city, and several major league baseball teams have spring training camps in area.

Tampa shares the shores of Tampa Bay with neighboring St. Petersburg and Clearwater. **St. Petersburg** is a popular resort and retirement community, its places of interest including a municipal pier, the **Salvador Dali Museum** and a **Museum of Fine Arts**, all located on the Bay waterfront. Clearwater's white sand beaches have supported a thriving tourist industry dating back to 1896, when railroad baron Henry Plant built a luxury resort called The Belleview on a bluff overlooking the water. The Bay Area's beaches are concentrated on the barrier islands of Clearwater and St. Petersburg, a popular one being Indian Rocks Beach on Sand Key.

## Getting Around

Tampa International Airport is located 12 miles from downtown and the Garrison Seaport Center where the cruise ships dock. Long-term parking and valet service are available at the port. Terminal #2, home to Carnival Cruise Line, is directly across the street from the port's parking facilities, and the Florida Aquarium and Channelside Bay Plaza are on either side of the terminal. Terminal #3, home to Norwegian Cruise Line and Royal Caribbean International, is across the street from the parking garage and within walking distance of the Aquarium and Channelside, as is Terminal #6, which is used by Holland America Line.

The Tampa-Ybor Trolley offers daily service around downtown Tampa, Ybor City and Garrison Seaport Center. A Visitor Information Center is located downtown at the corner of Ashley and Madison streets.

## Shopping & Dining

A selection of shops and eateries is located beside the cruise port at Channelside Bay Plaza. **Hyde Park Village** in the historic Hyde Park area of Tampa contains more than 60 shops, as well as restaurants and movie theaters.

**Ybor Square** is another historic marketplace, consisting of three large brick buildings converted into shops and restaurants, including the popular Columbia Restaurant, which opened in 1905 and serves Spanish-Cuban cuisine accompanied by nightly flamenco dance performances.

Gift shops are located in the Tampa Museum of Art in Tampa and the Salvador Dali Museum in downtown St. Petersburg.

**Where to Stay** – Numerous hotels are located within a mile of the cruise port, including Marriott Waterside, Westin Harbour Island, Sheraton Riverwalk and the Hilton. The Vinoy Renaissance Resort, named to the National Register of Historic Places, is situated south of downtown on the shores of Tampa Bay on a 14-acre site. The original Vinoy Park hotel was built in 1925 and luminaries such as Babe Ruth and Jimmy Stewart stayed at this elegant hotel, which was rebuilt in the 1990s. Facilities include an 18-hole championship golf course.

**Golf –** There are over 90 courses in the Tampa Bay area, many of which are open to the public. Babe Zaharias Golf Course, Rogers Park Golf Course and USF Golf Course are all located north of downtown; the Rocky Point Golf Course is just west of the Tampa International Airport.

## Local Attractions

The **Florida Aquarium** 1 is located right beside the passenger terminals at Garrison Seaport Center. It features sea creatures in near-natural habitats, as well as a fascinating exhibit in which visitors follow the path of a water drop from its underground source to the open sea, viewing aquatic animals and plants native to Florida along the way.

The **Tampa Bay Performing Arts Center** and **Tampa Museum of Art** 2 are located downtown overlooking the Hillsborough River. East on Franklin Street is the Spanish-Mediterranean-style **Tampa Theatre** 3, a restored 1926 movie palace.

Across the Hillsborough River, on the University of Tampa campus, is the **Henry B. Plant Museum** 4, housed in a wing of an opulent building originally built as the Tampa Bay Hotel by Henry Plant in 1891. It's a striking example of Moorish-Revival architecture and is a city landmark with its domed spires.

Northeast of the downtown core is historic **Ybor City** 5. Settled by Cubans, Spaniards and other Europeans, this designated national landmark district features Mediterranean-style buildings housing art galleries, cafes and antique stores. Popular attractions here include the Tampa Rico Cigar Company (a retail store with cigar-rolling demonstrations) and tours of the Ybor City Brewing Company, located in a 100-year-old cigar factory.

Animals in their natural habitats can be seen at **Lowry Park** 6 Zoological Garden, which also operates a manatee research and rehabilitation center. The **Busch Gardens** 7 theme park is famous for its large African zoo, tropical garden and rides, such as the

*Tampa's Florida Aquarium*

inverted roller coaster. Another area attraction is the Florida Botanical Gardens, containing 250 acres of themed gardens.

## Gulf Coast

A drive south of Tampa takes in historic Bradenton and nearby **Anna Maria Island**, with its public pier and numerous white sand beaches. Next is **Sarasota**, a cultural center of Florida, its bay protected by a string of keys connected by bridges. One of Sarasota's noted attractions is the **Ringling Museum of Art**, located on the circus baron's winter estate built in the Italian Renaissance style with fountains, courtyards and gardens. The art museum's huge galleries are lined with priceless paintings, including one of America's largest Baroque art collections.

**Venice**, to the south of Sarasota, is another upscale community of palm-lined streets and waterfront restaurants. Near Naples, off Route 846, is the **Corkscrew Swamp Sanctuary**, maintained by the National Audubon Society,

where a boardwalk winds through marshland which is habitat for great egrets, blue herons and alligators.

**Fort Myers**, about 50 miles south of Venice, was once a resort getaway for the wealthy. The winter estates of Thomas Edison and Henry Ford are now museums featuring daily guided tours of these restored homes, including Edison's laboratory. Ford bought his place in 1916 because it was next door to the winter home of his friend Edison.

Nearby **Sanibel Island**, a barrier island joined by a causeway to Fort Myers, is famous for the hundreds of species of sea shells that wash ashore. Ardent collectors assume the 'Sanibel stoop' while scouring the sandy beaches. Each summer hundreds of loggerhead turtles drag their heavy bodies onto shore to dig a nest and lay eggs, their welfare overseen by a group called Turtle Time, based in Fort Myers, which monitors the beach to ensure the hatchlings are undisturbed.

*The pier at Anna Maria Island.*

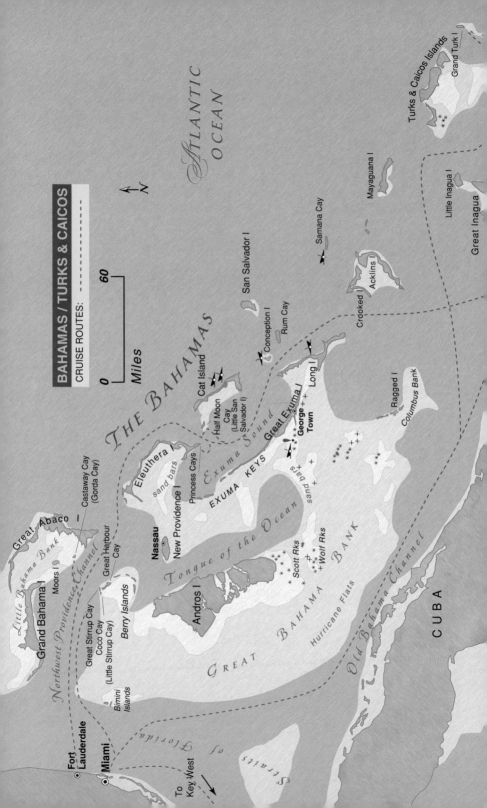

# BAHAMAS
## & GRAND TURK

Once a haven for pirates, the Bahamas now attract seclusion-seeking celebrities, such as Johnny Depp, Nicholas Cage and Eddie Murphy, who own private, beach-lined cays. Numbering in the hundreds, the islands and islets of the Bahamas form a chain that starts 50 miles off the coast of Florida and extends for 600 miles in a southeasterly direction toward Haiti. These small, limestone islands lie low on the horizon and are surrounded by clear turquoise seas filled with coral gardens and sunken wrecks. A diver's delight, they were treacherous waterways in the days of piracy when buc-

*Beautiful beaches fringe the many islands of the Bahamas.*

caneers, intent on pillage, would lure passing ships into these shallow reef-strewn waters.

These far-flung islands were originally inhabited by a seafaring tribe of Arawaks called Lucayans who lived here in fishing villages. Their solitude was shattered in 1492 by the arrival of an unexpected visitor, for the Bahamian island of Guanahani is where Christopher Columbus first stepped ashore after crossing the Atlantic. Relieved to have reached what he assumed were the islands of Asia, Columbus called the island San Salvador and claimed it for Spain.

The Spanish, seeking gold, were not interested in colonizing these *cayos* (cays) situated in what Columbus called a *baja mar* (shallow sea). They did, howev-

er, enslave the Lucayans to work in the gold mines on Hispaniola, and the first inhabitants of the Bahamas were soon exterminated.

The islands remained deserted until the mid-17th century when a group of English Puritans arrived from Bermuda. They settled at Preacher's Cave on Eleuthera and tried to scratch out an existence from the thin soil, but conditions were harsh. The Bahamas rise from a vast submarine plateau, their brackish lakes connected with the ocean by underground passages, and rainfall was the settlers' only source of fresh water.

Some of the English settlers moved to the Turks and Caicos and began extracting salt, which supplied the cod-fishing fleet of New England. Others moved to New Providence Island where they established Charles Towne, renamed Nassau in 1695. The town became a haven for pirates and for runaway slaves flee-

*A private cabana overlooks the beach at Half Moon Cay.*

ing the American colonies, who would stow away on Bahama-bound merchant ships. When the American Revolutionary War broke out in 1776, hundreds of loyalists also fled to the Bahamas.

Over time, the islands' inhabitants developed a unique culture of Goombay music, Junkanoo dance and straw crafts, but the influence of British colonialism remained strong, with English nobility maintaining beautiful homes and gardens on New Providence Island. Wealthy Americans began vacationing in the Bahamas in the late 1800s, but it wasn't until after World War II that tourism flourished.

In 1972 a newly elected Bahamian government negotiated independence from Britain and the following year this British crown colony became the Commonwealth of the Bahamas. The Turks and Caicos, which had been separately administered by Great Britain since 1848, remained a crown colony.

## Private Islands

Numerous islands in the Bahamas are privately owned, some by wealthy individuals seeking solitude, others by cruise lines seeking a private-island experience for their guests. These private islands are very popular with cruisers and offer them a chance to spend a relaxing day at the beach. A barbecue buffet lunch and beach towels are usually provided, as are beach chairs, but there is a charge to rent watersports equipment or a private beach cabana.

The cruise companies strive to retain the pristine beauty of these tropical islands while providing guest amenities, such as open-air beach bars and crafts markets (bring cash to purchase locally made souvenirs). Passengers are tendered ashore at most private islands (one exception is Disney Cruise Line's Castaway Cay, which has a ship pier).

*(Top) Entrance to the Welcome Center at Half Moon Cay. (Above and below) Watersports equipment is available at private island calls.*

The following is a brief list of the islands owned by the major cruise companies. Visit the cruise lines' websites to learn more about these private islands and the Caribbean and/or Panama Canal itineraries that include them as a port of call.

## Castaway Cay

Disney Cruise Line's private port of call in the Bahamas, this island was originally called Gorda Cay and is where Tom Hanks first encountered Daryl Hannah on the beach in the 1980s movie *Splash.* Since being acquired by Disney Cruise Line, the island's amenities include open-air BBQ dining locations and tram transportation around the island. Swimming, kayaking and water sports can be enjoyed at the age-appropriate beach areas and shore excursions include stingray interactions, glass-bottom boat tours, parasailing and fishing. Free childcare is available and adults can partake of open-air massages, yoga classes and a bar at the secluded, adults-only beach.

*Castaway Cay*

## Coco Cay

Called Little Stirrup Cay when acquired by Royal Caribbean Cruises Ltd., this island is 140 acres in size. Its shoreline is indented with crescent beaches and guest amenities include beach hammocks and island-style seaside barbecues. There is a fee to enter the aqua park, and shore excursions include parasailing, kayaking, snorkeling and guided nature walks.

## Great Stirrup Cay

Norwegian Cruise Line pioneered the concept of a private-island experience when it bought Great Stirrup Cay from Belcher Oil in 1977. The island had served various roles over the centuries, including U.S. Air Force satellite tracking station and WWII base for American troops. A British naval captain named Allan Bertram lived and died on the island in the early 1800s (his grave overlooks Bertram Cove) and the island's lighthouse was built in 1863, despite protests by the locals who earned their livelihood from shipwreck salvaging.

Today this private island (250 acres in size) welcomes NCL passengers who are tendered ashore. Facilities include a bandstand, several beach bars and a BBQ lunch buffet. Beach chairs are available (first come, first serve) and guests can rent clamshell sun shades, mats and floats. Activities include snorkeling, parasailing and beach volleyball. Kayak tours and catamaran tours are also available. Other island amenities are a 40-foot high water slide and a Bahamian arts and crafts bazaar.

## Half Moon Cay

Originally called Little San Salvador, this island was purchased in 1997 by Holland America Line. Designated a Wild Bird Reserve by the Bahamian National Trust, the island is an important nesting ground for terns, shearwaters and herons. Only two percent of the island has been developed, with the rest preserved as a bird sanctuary.

HAL passengers are tendered ashore to enjoy Half Moon Cay's beautiful crescent-shaped beach – two miles of white, powdery sand. An aqua park for kids features a pirate ship, water slide and water cannon. The island also has interpretive nature trails and a 1K running course. A luncheon barbecue is served in the covered dining pavilion.

Private cabanas with optional butler service can be reserved in advance and shore excursions include feeding stingrays in a natural lagoon, horseback riding, personal

watercraft tours and eco tours by glass-bottom boat. Snorkeling, windsurfing, parasailing, kayaking and sailing are all available, as are beachside massages. The island also has open-air beach bars, a Bahamian chapel for weddings and vow renewals, and a straw market run by locals from the neighboring island of Eleuthera.

## Princess Cays

Not technically a private island, Princess Cays is a private 40-acre resort located on the southern tip of Eleuthera. Princess passengers can enjoy the resort's half-mile beach of white sand and take in the views from the observation tower. All of Princess Cays' facilities are linked by walkways, and a barbecue lunch is served. Various amenities can be pre-booked, such as snorkel equipment, sea boards, kayaks, paddle wheelers, beach clamshells and bungalows. Shore excursions to the rest of the island are also offered.

*The view from a private cabana on Half Moon Cay.*

# Grand Turk

The **Turks and Caicos Islands**, lying southeast of the Bahamas, consist of more than 30 cays and islands (six of which are inhabited). Tourism began on the Turks & Caicos in the 1960s when several millionaires (including Teddy Roosevelt III) leased land from the British government and built a small airstrip for their private planes and a deep-water anchorage for their yachts

Grand Turk is the capital and home to a cruise port developed by Carnival Corporation that opened in 2006 at the island's south end. The island, six miles long and a mile wide, was chosen for its deepwater port, colonial charm and natural attractions of sugary beaches and fabulous snorkeling and diving.

The cruise terminal provides direct access to a private beach and a supersized swimming pool, with changing rooms and watersports equipment for rent. Admission to the FlowRider surfing pool can be booked ahead of time as a shore excursion.

## What's In A Name?

Some say the Turks & Caicos were named for the indigenous Turk's Head cactus and for *caya hico*, which means 'string of islands' in Lucayan. Others say the name Turk meant 'pirate' during the days of the Ottoman Empire. Mail sent to the islands is sometimes misdirected to Turkey but eventually arrives at its destination, even when mistakenly addressed to the Turks & Tacos!

Facilities at the terminal include an outpost of Jimmy Buffet's Margaritaville restaurant, as well as duty-free shopping, an internet cafe, and car, jeep and bicycle rentals. The local buses provide a continuous loop service around the island, and you can jump off and on at several stops.

**Cockburn Town** has been the seat of government since 1766 and its colonial architecture includes the **Turks & Caicos National Museum** with displays of artifacts recovered from the Molasses Reef Wreck (1513) – one of the oldest known shipwrecks in the New World. Some locals claim that Christopher Columbus made his first landfall on Grand Turk (a stone monument attests to this), but most historians believe that Ponce de Leon was the first European to visit these islands in 1512.

One historic landing that is not open to debate is that of John Glenn, the first American astronaut to orbit the earth, whose space capsule splashed down in local waters on February 20, 1962. This event can be relived at the cruise port's Splashdown Grand Turk – its interactive exhibits and spacecraft replicas developed with the assistance of NASA's Kennedy Space Center.

From the early 1950s until 1984, a U.S. Air Force tracking station operated on the island's west coast, and the remains of a U.S. Navy base are located at the island's northeast point, where a lighthouse stands.

**Conch World** is a new attraction built on a hill overlooking the ocean on the island's east coast.

*Grand Turk's cruise terminal*

This conch farm facility is dedicated to the conservation and preservation of the Queen Conch and features museum-quality exhibits, a cafe and gift shop. Tours from the cruise port include time to swim or snorkel off a secluded beach.

## Shore Excursions

*Grand Turk*

Shore excursions include a trolley train ride to Governor's Beach for a beach break with snorkeling. Scuba diving (both beginner and certified) is offered, as are stingray encounters, blue water fishing, aqua boats, power snorkel, snuba, semi-submersible glass-bottom boat rides and sea trek helmet diving (walking on the sea floor). Guided bike tours, horseback riding, horse-and-buggy rides, and 4X4 safaris are also featured. as is a visit to Conch World.

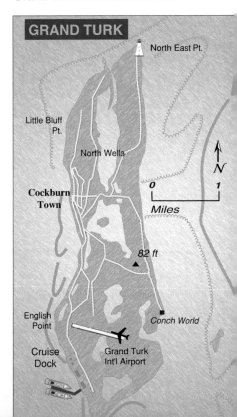

**JAMAICA**

AREA 4,244 sq mi
POPULATION 2.7 million
CAPITAL Kingston
LANGUAGE English, patois
CURRENCY Jamaican dollar
GOVERNMENT Parl amentary democracy

Port Antonio

▲ 7402 ft

BLUE MOUNTAINS

Oracabessa Bay

**Kingston**

Port Royal

**Ocho Rios**

Spanish Town

Portmore

Dunn's River Falls

Runaway Bay

Discovery Bay

3235 ft

Falmouth

Martha Brae R.

Cockpit Country

**Appleton Rum Distillery**

Black River

May Pen

Mandeville

Portland Bight

**Montego Bay**

Great River

Lucea

Negril

Savanna-la Mar

Bluefields Bay

Long Bay

Great Pedro Bay

Caribbean Sea

N

20

0

Miles

©OCEAN CRUISE GUIDES LTD.

# JAMAICA

Jamaica, third largest island of the West Indies after Cuba and Hispaniola, is one of the most beautiful in the Caribbean. A lush and mountainous island, Jamaica has long attracted a diversity of peoples to its shores, from famous buccaneers to accomplished artists. The country's official motto is "Out of many, one people" – acknowledging the range of races and nationalities that have colonized this island nation. Its history is turbulent and social problems still exist, but a 'No problem mon' attitude sums up the buoyant spirit of Jamaicans.

Arawaks, an agricultural people, were the first to inhabit the island about a thousand years ago. The Spanish began colonizing Jamaica in 1509 under licence from Christopher Columbus's son, and the Arawaks soon died out under Spanish occupation. Captured by the British in 1655 and formally ceded to England in 1670, the island was a haven for buccaneers before becoming a major sugar producer in the 18th century.

The island is a limestone plateau more than 3,000 feet above sea level, its mountainous backbone rising at its eastern end to the Blue Mountains. Fertile slopes and broad river valleys lead down to narrow coastal plains and support large plantations of sugarcane, bananas and other crops, including the famous Blue Mountain Coffee.

Rainfall, abundant in the mountainous regions, diminishes westward across a rugged plateau of streams and subterranean rivers. The heart of this plateau, called the Cockpits, is used for livestock grazing. During Jamaica's colonial days, escaped or freed slaves – called maroons – fled to Cockpit country where they lived in villages and organized frequent uprisings against the European landowners.

Half of Jamaica's population is still rural, with much of the work force employed in agriculture. However, the continuing trend is one of migration to the cities. Of the country's 2.6 million residents, about 600,000 live in the capital of Kingston. Situated on a deep, landlocked harbor, Kingston was established in 1692 after an earthquake destroyed Port Royal at the tip of the peninsula that forms the harbor. This British outpost and pirate haven suddenly sank 33 feet into the sea, taking 2,000 inhabitants with it. When a subsequent tsunami swept ashore, a British naval frigate was carried across the sunken townsite and deposited inland.

Plans are now underway to recreate 17th-century Port Royal, which wasn't properly excavated until 1965, although some

*Jamaica's scenic north coast.*

of its treasure was salvaged at once. The most famous name associated with Port Royal is Sir Henry Morgan, a Welsh privateer whose daring exploits included the sacking of Portobelo in 1668 and the capture of Panama in 1671. He was eventually arrested on charges of piracy and sent to England where, with war against Spain threatening once more, he was knighted and returned to Jamaica as deputy-governor.

The entire north coast, from Negril at its western end to Port Antonio at its eastern end, is dotted with beach-lined bays and palm-shaded resorts, including some of the most exclusive in the Caribbean. It also contains Jamaica's two main cruise ports – Ocho Rios and Montego Bay.

Many a famous person has spent time living or vacationing in Jamaica, beginning with Christopher Columbus who first stepped ashore in 1494 at Rio Bueno. On his fourth voyage to the West Indies in 1503,

Columbus beached his damaged ships on the island's north shore and spent a year on Jamaican soil awaiting rescue. In more recent times, the swashbuckling movie star Errol Flynn pulled into Port Antonio in his private yacht to escape a storm and ended up building a home there on Navy Island.

For a relatively small country, Jamaica has had a far-reaching impact on the rest of the world with its music, dance and art. Jamaicans are international in outlook and many of its citizens have migrated to other countries, most notably Britain. Over 90% of Jamaicans are of West African descent with Asians and Europeans adding to the cultural tapestry of this dynamic island nation. Yet, the country's rich social fabric has at times appeared to be unraveling, with political tribalism resulting in election violence.

The People's National Party (PNP) was founded in 1938 by Norman Manley. His cousin, Sir Alexander Bustamante, founded the Jamaica Labour Party (JLP).

These two parties, their roots in rival trade unions, have dominated Jamaican politics since 1944 when universal adult suffrage was introduced. Jamaica gained its independence from Britain in 1962 but remains a member of the British Commonwealth. The country's economy is one of the more prosperous in the West Indies, despite a recession that persisted throughout the 1970s and 80s. After embracing socialism in the 1970s, Jamaica now has a free market economy based on tourism, agricultural products and the export of bauxite, from which alumina is extracted.

Hurricane Gilbert caused widespread devastation when it swept the length of the island in 1988 and the country's tourism industry was crippled. The island has since regained its prominence as a popular Caribbean destination but many tourists stay at all-inclusive resorts. The government is trying to counter this insular attitude with a Meet the People program in which the tourist board will arrange for a visitor to spend time with a Jamaican host who shares a common interest.

Cruise passengers who might be apprehensive about venturing ashore can simply book a shore excursion. Those who prefer to strike out on their own will find the Jamaican people, despite their reputation for aggressively selling their wares (including narcotics), are an outgoing and friendly people who will respond to a polite but firm 'No thank you' with a 'No problem mon' wave of the hand. Most Jamaicans have a good sense of humor and this is usually the best way to fend off persistent advances.

## Reggae & Rastafarianism

Rastafarianism is a religious-cultural movement that began in Jamaica in the 1930s when Haile Selassie (also named Ras Tafari) became Emperor of Ethiopia, as predicted by Jamaican hero Marcus Garvey. Selassie was hailed as the movement's messiah, Ethiopia was the promised land, and Garvey was considered a major prophet and early leader in creating black awareness and unity.

Reggae, which originated in the 1960s among the poor blacks of Kingston, is the protest music of the Rastafarian faith. Its sound is characterized by an off-beat rhythm that draws on American soul and traditional African and Jamaican folk music. Reggae's most famous performer is the late Bob Marley, a Jamaican singer, songwriter and guitarist to whom a museum is dedicated in Kingston.

*Bob Marley, the 'King of Reggae Music', died at age 36.*

Born in 1945 and deserted by his white Jamaican father, Marley was raised by his mother in Nine Miles village on Jamaica's north coast. As a youth, he and his mother moved to the poor shanty area of Kingston where he worked in the welding trade while seeking success as a musician. Fame finally came to Marley in the 1970s when his new group began playing reggae and their songs soared in the charts. When Marley died of cancer at the age of 36, he had achieved international stardom and received his country's highest public honor, the Order of Merit. The worldwide popularity of reggae is attributed in large part to Marley, whose songs supported his belief in non-violence and the Rastafarian religion.

Rastas, who object to shaving and cutting hair, wear their hair in long braids called dreadlocks – a symbolic connection with the Ethiopian lion. They are vegetarians who prefer natural foods and many of them smoke ganga, locally grown marijuana. Not everyone wearing dreadlocks is a Rasta and most 'real' Rastas are congenial, generally preferring the country to urban areas.

## Ocho Rios

The original Spanish name for Ocho Rios was Las Chorreras – The Waterfalls – an appropriate name for a port situated at the base of lush mountains where rivers and streams spill into the sea. A former fishing village, Ocho Rios has been developed as a tourist destination with high-rise hotels and condominiums lining the beaches to the east of Ocho Rios Bay. The local population numbers about 11,000 and residents speak an English-based patois. Ocho Rios Bay contains two piers – the Reynolds Pier and the new cruise ship pier which is joined by a jetty to shore where telephones, tourist information and a handful of shops are located.

## Getting Around

The cruise lines offer organized excursions to the major attractions, or you can hire a taxi. A visitor information booth is located in the terminal building and the taxi fares to various destinations are posted nearby. A dispatcher is also stationed there and, upon telling him where you want to go, he will hail you a driver whose car will carry the red Public Passenger Vehicle (PPV) license plates. If you want to visit a number of destinations, negotiate the fare with your driver before getting in. The fare is per taxi, so travelling in groups of four is the most economical. Some sample taxi tour rates for one to four persons: Dunn's River Falls – $20; Prospect Plantation – $30.

**Shopping** – Jamaica offers good buys in duty-free goods and great bargains in locally produced clothing, wood carvings, coffee and rum. Beautiful, hand-carved walking sticks can be bought for $15 and tee shirts screened with unique Jamaican designs sell for as little as $5. More expensive are the beautiful batik cottons and silks. The exchange rate is approximately 70 Jamaican dollars for 1 US dollar, but there's no need to exchange money because American currency and credit cards are widely accepted.

Within walking distance of the cruise ship pier are the **Taj Mahal Centre** 1 and **Soni's Plaza** 2, or you can take a shopping shuttle which costs $2 per person. In between are the **Old Market Craft Shoppes** 3 and **Craft Park** 4, where local artisans sell their wares. Excellent arts and crafts can also be bought at the Dunn's River Falls marketplace, and paintings by acclaimed Jamaican artists are on display at the **Harmony Hall Gallery** 9, five miles east of the cruise port.

**Best Beaches** – Beautiful white sand beaches line the shoreline east of Ocho Rios Bay. Most of these are backed by hotels and have controlled access to protect tourists from pedlars. The admission fee is usually $1.00 per person. Closest to the pier is Turtle Beach, and an excellent beach lies on the other side of The Point at Mallards Bay.

*(Above) A hotel resort at Turtle Beach. (Below) The waterfront at Ocho Rios.*

**Dive & Snorkel Sites** – excursions are available out of Ocho Rios to nearby shallow coral gardens, some of which have been damaged in recent years by hurricanes. Serious divers recommend going deeper to see an abundance of coral and sponge life. Wall diving is popular at Runaway Bay.

**Sandal's Golf & Country Club**, overlooking Mallards Bay, is considered one of the most scenic in Jamaica, situated 700 feet up into the mountains. This 18-hole par-71 course was designed by P.K. Sanders and totals 6,500 yards.

## Local Attractions

A botanical garden and bird sanctuary, **Shaw Park Gardens'** 5

*Turtle Beach is a short walk from the cruise pier.*

hillside location provides panoramic views in a tropical setting. The Coyaba River flows through **Coyaba Garden** 6 where riverside paths and boardwalks lead past waterfalls and pools filled with koi carp and turtles. The museum contains pre-Columbian artifacts and the gallery displays creative works by Jamaicans.

## Area Highlights

**Fern Gully** 7, a former riverbed that went dry following an earthquake, is a three-mile stretch of road that winds into the Blue Mountains and leads, eventually, to Kingston on the other side of the island. The many species of fern that grow in this gully form a lush canopy for vehicles passing beneath it.

One of Jamaica's most popular attractions, **Dunn's River Falls** 8 consist of clear mountain water flowing seaward across a tiered limestone bed. Visitors are charged $5 US to enter the park area, which includes a guided climb up this stunning set of falls. Guides lead visitors, in single file, along a known route. Operators of the park are fairly insistent you remain part of a guided climb to prevent personal injury. For an additional $5, a guide will hold your camera and other belongings as you scramble up the falls. A pair of running shoes or aqua socks (which can be rented) are recommended for the climb over slippery stones and rushing, knee-deep water. Dunn's Falls are about 1.5 miles by road from Ocho Rios and can also be reached by boat, a popular excur-

## Shore Excursions

### *Ocho Rios & Montego Bay*

Ocho Rios and Montego Bay are located about 50 miles apart on Jamaica's north coast, and several area attractions are covered by ship-organized excursions from either port, namely Dunn's River Falls, Dolphin Cove and river rafting on the **Martha Brae**, which lies between Montego Bay and Ocho Rios. On bamboo rafts carrying two people, the raft man uses a pole to guide the raft gently downstream past bamboo groves and chirping birds. The drive from Ocho Rios to Martha Brae takes 1.5 hours along the winding coastal highway, and the river ride is just over an hour in length. An organized shore excursion lasts about five hours, often with a stop at Columbus Park, near Discovery Bay, where Columbus first landed at Jamaica. Other nota-

ble places along this stretch of coastline include Nine Miles village, the birthplace and gravesite of Bob Marley, and the 18th-century Georgian town of Falmouth near the mouth of the Martha Brae, about 20 miles east of Montego Bay.

Excursions specific to **Ocho Rios** include visits to Prospect Plantation and Coyaba Gardens. Other organized excursions include ocean and river kayaking, and biking expeditions.

**Montego Bay** excursions include tours of Appleton Rum Estate or of a local great house (see box on page 183). Beach time can be enjoyed at nearby Negril's Margaritaville, which features a 100-foot waterslide, or at Doctor's Cave Beach, the latter included with snorkeling excursions at Montego Bay Marine Park.

Both ports feature party boat excursions, horseback riding, river tubing and a rainforest canopy adventure.

sion being one of the party cruises that depart the cruise pier for a relaxing yacht ride to the mouth of Dunn's River and back, with time allowed for climbing the falls. Mountain biking excursions are also popular and involve an

uphill drive followed by a downhill bike ride from Murphy Hill to Dunn's River Falls. **Dolphin Cove**, located beside Dunn's River Falls, is a new attraction where visitors can feed, pet and swim with dolphins.

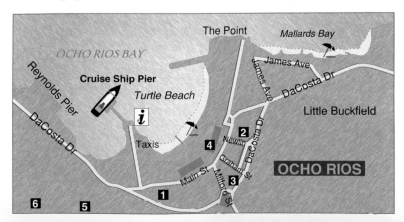

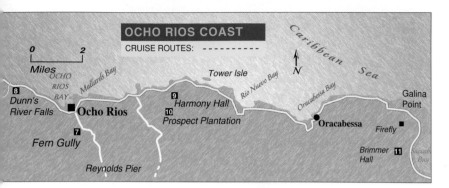

Anyone interested in Jamaican folk art will enjoy a visit to **Harmony Hall** 9, a restored Victorian great house. Set on a small plantation estate four miles east of Ocho Rios, it contains an art gallery, craft and book shops, boutique and restaurant.

**Prospect Plantation** 10 is a working plantation estate where guides take visitors on tractor-drawn jitneys past various flora and agricultural crops including bananas, sugarcane and coffee, as well as the White River

Gorge and Sir Harold's Viewpoint, where Cuba, about 100 miles due north, can be seen on a clear day. Horseback tours are also available on each of three varied trails that traverse the 900 acres of grounds, which also contain a miniature golf course and a gift shop selling local crafts and souvenirs.

About 10 miles east of Prospect Plantation, **Brimmer Hall Plantation** 11 is another working plantation providing tours by tractor-drawn jitney. The beautiful grounds contain an 18th-century great house open for viewing, as well as a swimming pool, bar and shops.

**Firefly**, Noel Coward's "earthly paradise" set atop a plateau with a dramatic view of the surf pounding into Saccabus Bay, was the famous playwright's home for the last 25 years of his life and the place where he wrote some of his most celebrated works. Screen stars and British royalty would come to visit, but when Coward died in 1973 he asked that no fuss be made, and the site of his grave was where he often sat with friends sipping a pre-dinner

*River rafting on the Martha Brae.*

*The tiered falls at Dunn's River.*

cocktail while looking out to sea. Coward's home and contents were bequeathed to Jamaica in 1975 and restored as a museum run on behalf of the National Heritage Trust by Island Outpost, which is owned by Chris Blackwell, the multi-millionaire founder of Island Records. However, Firefly failed to attract enough visitors and in early 2000 plans were made to auction many of Coward's belongings and rent the property out for private receptions.

At **Oracabessa** ('Golden Head' in Spanish), the road winds past Goldeneye, an estate overlooking a private cove. This was the former winter retreat of the late Ian Fleming, who wrote his James Bond novels at this idyllic location. Noel Coward referred to Fleming's rather plain U-shaped house as the, "Goldeneye, nose and throat clinic," while describing the cove's crescent beach of dazzling white sand as "unbelievable." Chris Blackwell's Island Outpost now owns the property and has converted it into a boutique-style luxury resort.

# Montego Bay

Jamaica's second-largest city, Montego Bay is one of the Caribbean's most popular resorts, beautifully situated on a beach-lined bay surrounded by green hills. A commercial center and shipping port, it's a growing city of over 70,000 residents, many of whom live in shanty towns on the outskirts. On the lower slopes of the Miranda Hills are luxury hotels set in manicured grounds.

## Getting Around

The cruise ships dock at Freeport, about three miles from downtown. An information booth and telephones are situated on the dock. Nearby is the Montego Freeport duty-free shopping area. The taxi fare into town is about $12 for up to four people, and only JUTA (Jamaica Union of Travellers Association) taxis and mini-vans should be rented.

**Best Beaches – Montego Bay Marine Park** encompasses all of Montego Bay, its office located at Pier 1. Beautiful beaches and good snorkel sites lie within the park's boundaries. **Doctor's Cave**

**Beach**, located just north of the town center, is Montego Bay's most celebrated beach. Named after Dr. Alexander McCatty who donated the beach to a local bathing club, the beach was originally accessible through a small cave, destroyed by a hurricane in 1932. Today it's Montego Bay's most popular beach, with an entry charge that includes change facilities. Other good stretches of sand are found at **Walter Fletcher Beach**, south of Doctor's Cave, and at **Cornwall Beach**, which lies directly north of Doctor's Cave . Coral sea gardens can be viewed by glass-bottom boat in the clear, sheltered waters of Doctor's Cave, which offers good snorkeling for beginners. Unity Hall at the eastern end of Montego Bay Marine Park, is another premier snorkel site with plenty of coral and juvenile fish

*Famous beaches lure cruise visitors to Montego Bay such as Doctor's Cave beach below.*

inside the reef that lies in front of Sahara De La Mer Hotel.

**Golf** – A championship golf course (7,130 yards, par 72) is located at the **Half Moon Golf Course**, near the sea on the eastern outskirts of Montego Bay. The White Witch course (6,820 yards, par 71) is part of the Ritz-Carlton Rose Hall Resort.

**Local Sights & Shopping** – The city's business district includes a few historic landmarks, most of them situated on or near **Sam Sharpe Square 1**– named for a Jamaican hero who was hanged in 1831 for leading a slave revolt. On the southwest side of the square stands the Court House, an early-19th century colonial building. The Cage, a small building of the same period on the square's northeast corner, was used for detaining runaway slaves. Nearby, on Church Street, are a number of restored Georgian buildings including St. James's Parish Church which was rebuilt

## Shore Excursions

### *Montego Bay*

Shore excursions from Montego Bay include visits to Dunn's River Falls, Dolphin Cove and river rafting on the Martha Brae (see page 179), as well as other attractions, such as Greenwood Great House and Rose Hall Great House. **Greenwood Great House**, located 16 miles east of Montego Bay, was built by relatives of poet Elizabeth Barrett Browning, and the stately mansion is furnished with antiques and contains a rare-book library. A tour of Greenwood gives visitors an inside look at the privileged lives once enjoyed by plantation owners.

**Rose Hall**, a British mansion built in 1770, lies about 10 miles east of Montego Bay and is Jamaica's most famous great house thanks to a legendary mistress by the name of Annie Palmer. She lived here around 1820 and is said to have murdered three husbands and numerous slave lovers whom she controlled through witchcraft. According to one version of the legend, she was finally murdered by a lover who felt he was destined to be next on Annie's hit list.

after suffering major damage in a 1957 earthquake. South of Church Street, near the water, is the colorful **Crafts Market 2**. A few blocks to the north, along the waterfront, stand the remains of Fort Montego which was built by the British in 1752. From here Gloucester Avenue, the main shopping thoroughfare, wends north past the hotel strip.

Area Attractions – **Rockland Bird Sanctuary 3**, nine miles south of Montego Bay, is popular with visitors, as is the **Appleton Estate Express 4**, a train that departs daily from Montego Bay and heads into Cockpit Country, location of the famous Appleton Rum Distillery and the Ipswich Caves with their limestone stalagmites and stalactites.

East of Montego Bay are Rose Hall, Greenwood Great House and the Martha Brae River (see box above).

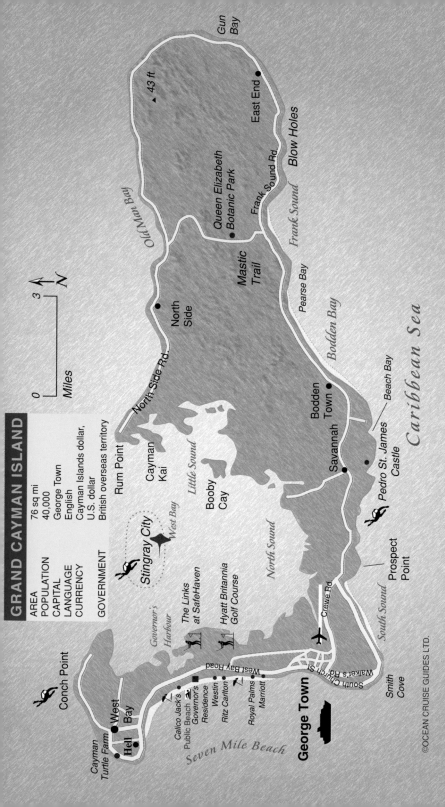

# GRAND CAYMAN ISLAND

| | |
|---|---|
| AREA | 76 sq mi |
| POPULATION | 40,000 |
| CAPITAL | George Town |
| LANGUAGE | English |
| CURRENCY | Cayman Islands dollar, |
| | U.S. dollar |
| GOVERNMENT | British overseas territory |

N

0    3
Miles

Conch Point

Cayman
Turtle Farm

Hell

West
Bay

West Bay

Calico Jack's
Public Beach
Governor's
Residence
Westin
Ritz Carlton
Royal Palms
Marriott

Seven Mile Beach

West Bay Road

Governor's Harbour

The Links
at SafeHaven

Hyatt Britannia
Golf Course

Stingray City

Rum Point

Cayman
Kai

Little Sound

Booby
Cay

North Sound

Old Man Bay

North
Side

North Side Rd

43 ft

Queen Elizabeth
Botanic Park

Mastic
Trail

Gun
Bay

East End

Blow Holes

Frank Sound Rd

Frank Sound

Pearse Bay

Bodden Bay

Bodden
Town

Savannah

Pedro St. James
Castle

Beach Bay

Caribbean Sea

Prospect
Point

South Sound

Smith
Cove

George Town

South Church St

Walker's Rd

Crewe Rd

©OCEAN CRUISE GUIDES LTD.

# GRAND CAYMAN

**G**rand Cayman is one of the best-rated dive locations in the world, its varied underwater terrain ranging from shallow coral reefs to submarine canyons. But a person needn't even get wet to enjoy some of the island's remarkable aquatic sights, for a variety of vessels and observatories allow visitors to see the reefs, wrecks and marine life for which the Cayman Islands are famous.

Grand Cayman is the largest of a three-island group which includes Little Cayman and Cayman Brac – a Gaelic word for cliff. The name Cayman is derived from a Carib word for crocodile, although the Caymans were first called Las Tortugas by Columbus when he observed, in 1503, the hundreds of turtles living on these uninhabited islands. The Spanish paid these flat coral outcrops little attention but English, Dutch and French ships pulled in regularly to take on fresh water and salted turtle meat

Today, the green sea turtle is a protected species and the Cayman Turtle Farm, initially established to supply the demand for turtle products without depleting wild populations, is

now a major research and release facility. Preservation zones have been established in Grand Cayman to provide year-round protection of conch and lobster breeding grounds. Line fishing from shore or beyond the drop-off are the only forms of harvesting allowed. Permanent moorings have been installed to protect the reefs, which were becoming damaged by the anchors of dive boats.

These progressive conservation measures have extended onto land with the establishment of animal sanctuaries and a botanical park. Bird watching is popular, with more than a hundred species of birds observed here.

The Cayman Islands, a British Crown Colony since 1670, were

*Stingray City is a unique attraction in Grand Cayman.*

settled by a motley collection of British army deserters, shipwrecked sailors, retired pirates and African slaves who gained freedom when ships carrying them foundered on local reefs.

Today, about 45,000 people live on the three islands, the majority on Grand Cayman. With few natural resources on these mangrove-covered islands, the

Cayman men traditionally made their living from the sea – turtle fishing, ship building and serving in the merchant marine.

Grand Cayman remained an isolated backwater until 1954, when an airfield was built. But it wasn't until the island's troublesome mosquitoes were brought under control in the 1970s that tourists began arriving in droves. Cayman's political stability and attractive tax laws also make it an ideal environment for offshore banking interests.

Grand Cayman was devastated by Hurricane Ivan in September 2004. With winds gusting to 200 miles per hour, Ivan was the worst storm to hit the island in 86 years. There was no direct loss of life but property damage was extensive.

## Getting Around

The cruise ships anchor off George Town and tender their passengers ashore to one of three harborfront docks. Royal Watler Terminal is the largest and offers the most facilities, including a visitor information booth, telephones and shops. The town's shops and major sights are a short walk from all three tender docks.

A taxi stand is located at Royal Watler where you can catch a shuttle to Seven Mile Beach for a fee of $4 or $5 per person, depending on which drop-off spot you request. The further north you go, the quieter the beach tends to be. To return to George Town from Seven Mile Beach, simply walk out to the road and hail a taxi van by raising your hand. It takes about 15 minutes

## Shore Excursions

*Grand Cayman*

Shore excursions include driving tours to various attractions, such as the Botanic Park, Butterfly Farm, Pedro St. James, Hell and Turtle Farm. Stingray City is featured in various boat excursions, and some cruise lines offer excursions to Dolphin Discovery. Marine life can be viewed on an Atlantis submarine, Seaworld semi-submarine, snorkeling tours and dive expeditions. Beach breaks, kayaking safaris and horseback riding are also offered, as are bicycle tours. Visit your cruise line's website for detail on excursions offered.

to walk from the tendering docks to the south end of Seven Mile Beach, and another 15 minutes to reach the Marriott Resort on foot.

Ship-organized excursions (see box) cover the island's major attractions. Passengers interested in touring the island independently have several options, which include renting a car, jeep, scooter or bicycle. Car rentals start at about $55 per day for a compact model. The major rental agencies are located in Grand Cayman, including Cico Avis which offers a courtesy pickup service at the Blue Iguana souvenir shop on the waterfront (to reserve online, visit www.aviscayman.co). Cayman Auto Rentals (which also rents scooters and bicycles) is located three blocks from the main tendering dock (see map) and offers a drop-off service at the end of a rental (caymanautorentals.com) The terrain is fairly flat on Grand Cayman, and driving is on the left, with most cars equipped with a right-hand drive.

*(Right) Shopping on Harbour Drive in George Town. (Below) Tendering back to the ship.*

Mini-buses bearing blue licence plates are another way to get around. The bus depot is located beside the library on Edward Street (see map) and buses depart every 15 minutes for West Bay. The fare is CI$2.00.

Several of Grand Cayman's major attractions can be visited independently but be sure to factor in your taxi fare if there is no courtesy shuttle. Cayman Turtle Farm at Boatswain's Beach can be booked on-line ($45 per adult;

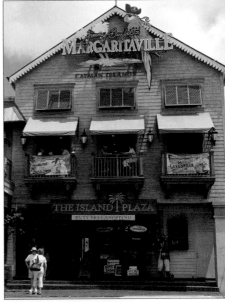

$25 per child; includes admission to the marine park's snorkeling lagoon, swimming pool with viewing panel and nature trail) and there's a 20% discount on advance bookings (boatswainsbeach.ky). Stingray City Trips offers tours to this famous sand bar, barrier reef and coral gardens at a cost of $45 per person ($27.50 for children ages 4 to 11). This price includes snorkeling equipment and a courtesy shuttle that picks up in George Town (stingraycitytrips.com). Dolphin Discovery also takes online reservations; the cost is $99 to $159 per adult, depending on which dolphin interaction you book, and visitors are advised to check in 30 minutes ahead of time.

**Shopping** – A free port, Grand Cayman carries an assortment of duty-free goods. George Town is where the majority of shops are located (many of which are closed on Sundays) and is very clean and orderly with no pedlars. Local items to look for include numismatic jewelry, crafted from old coins retrieved from sunken vessels and featured in exquisite gold-and-diamond settings.

Unique to the Cayman Islands are sculptures and jewelry made of an earth-toned, hard dolomite stone called caymanite that was discovered at East End. Another island specialty is Tortuga Rum Cake, baked according to a century-old family recipe and coated with an aromatic syrup made with specially blended, five-year-old Tortuga Gold rum stored in oak barrels.

The Cayman Island dollar equals about $1.25 US, but American currency is accepted throughout the islands. American and Canadian visitors should be aware it is against customs regulations to import turtle products into their countries.

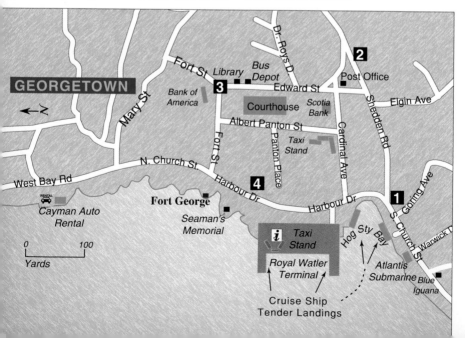

**Local Sights** – Overlooking the pier area is the **1** **Cayman Islands National Museum**, housed in the former courthouse and containing displays on the islands' natural and cultural history, including artifacts of pirate lore. Cardinal, one of the main shopping streets, leads to the post office and the adjacent **Elizabethan Square** **2**. A few blocks north on Edward is the Public Library. Across the street is a small park containing a massive fig tree. At the intersection of Edward and Fort Streets is **Clock Tower** **3**, a monument to Britain's King George V. Fort Street leads down to the waterfront where the remains of Fort George can be seen, built in the 17th century to protect the island from pirate attacks. Nearby, on Harbour Drive, is the restored 19th-century **Elmslie Memorial Church** **4**.

**Best Beaches** – The natural choice for cruise passengers is **Seven Mile Beach**, one of the finest in the Caribbean, which starts just north of George Town and stretches for about five miles along the island's western shore. Lined with hotels, this beautiful white-sand beach is free of pedlars and is ideal for swimming, snorkeling and other water sports. Sailboards and other equipment can be rented at a sports center beside the public beach, which is usually uncrowded. Government House, the Governor's official residence, is near the public beach area.

*(Above) Cayman Islands National Museum. (Below) Seven Mile Beach.*

**Dive & Snorkel Sites** – Grand Cayman is the top of a submerged mountain and its offshore coral reefs form the famous 'Cayman Wall'. An estimated 60 miles of drop-offs encircle Grand Cayman where the underwater visibility extends to depths of 150 feet. There are more than a hundred dive sites surrounding the island, and they include numerous shipwrecks as well as coral gardens, grottos, caves and canyons which are habitat for rays, turtles, tropical fish and huge, colorful sponges. Whether snorkeling, shore diving or deep diving, Cayman Island offers crystal clear water, an abundance of marine life and a variety of underwater terrain.

This fascinating marine world can also be viewed from vessels that operate out of George Town, including a glass-bottom boat and the Seaworld semi-submarine operated by Atlantis. There are reefs and wrecks to explore right in Hog Sty Bay, such as Cheeseburger Reef and the wreck of the *Cali*. Other easily accessible dive sites include Eden Rock and Devil's Grotto, just south of George Town, as well as those along Seven Mile Beach. Dive boats take certified divers to the island's incredible drop-offs, such as the West Wall, which lies about nine miles offshore. Atlantis Submarine operates out of George Town and offers non-divers the opportunity to view the famous Cayman Wall. Several dive and snorkel shops are located within walking distance of the tender pier, and the cruise lines also offer snorkel and dive excursions.

**Golf** – There are two golf courses on Grand Cayman, both a few miles north of George Town along West Bay Road. Closest to town is the Hyatt Britannia Golf Course, designed by Jack Nicklaus and offering three courses in one: a nine-hole championship course, an 18-hole course and one played with a special Cayman ball. The Links at SafeHaven is an 18-hole championship course and is reminiscent of those in Scotland.

## Island Attractions

**Stingray City**, located in the protected waters of North Sound, has been described in National Geographic as "one of the most rewarding experiences in the undersea world." Visitors are taken by boat to this shallow sandbar where for decades fishermen used to

*(Left) Cheeseburger Reef*

clean fish, their discarded entrails attracting stingrays who would arrive at the sound of a ship's motor. In 1987 some divers began frequenting this spot, bringing squid for the normally shy stingrays who gradually got used to the divers' presence. Now 30 to 50 stingrays show up daily to be hand fed, stroked and held by humans. Visitors can watch from an observatory or snorkel with the stingrays.

**Cayman Turtle Farm** was originally established in 1968 to raise and market turtle products, but now concentrates on research and breeding. Green sea turtles and hawksbill turtles are bred, hatched, raised and tagged before being released into local waters. The touch tanks allow visitors to hold the baby turtles. The turtle farm was moved further inland following hurricane damage in 2001, is now part of Boatswain's Beach park where attractions include a rock swimming pool with waterfall, snorkeling lagoon, predator tank, nature trail and aviary with exotic birds (www.boatswainsbeach.ky).

**Dolphin Discovery** is located at the Turtle Farm's old location, and is where visitors can interact with dolphins.

Some visitors like to stop at nearby **Hell** so they can send a postcard, the real attraction is the weathered outcrop of iron shore which, although said to look like the charred remains of a hell fire, is actually made of black limestone about 1.5 million years old.

East of George Town the attractions include **Pedro St. James Castle**, an 18th-century great house beautifully situated on landscaped grounds atop a bluff. **Bodden Town**, with its legendary Pirate Cave, is where pirates are said to have hidden their loot in a series of tunnels. Nearby is the Meagre Bay Bird Sanctuary and further east is the **Botanic Park**, officially opened by Queen Elizabeth in 1994. The park's 60 acres of grounds include a floral garden and an interpretive trail that winds through woodlands, wetlands, swamps and thickets. Adjacent to the park is the **Mastic Trail**, a restored 200-year-old footpath that winds for two miles through primary woodlands and mangrove swamps. The island's eastern shores contain **The Blow Holes**, saltwater geysers spouting from the coral rock as waves crash onto shore. East End is the oldest town on the island, founded in the late 17th century.

*Viewing young sea turtles at the Cayman Turtle Farm.*

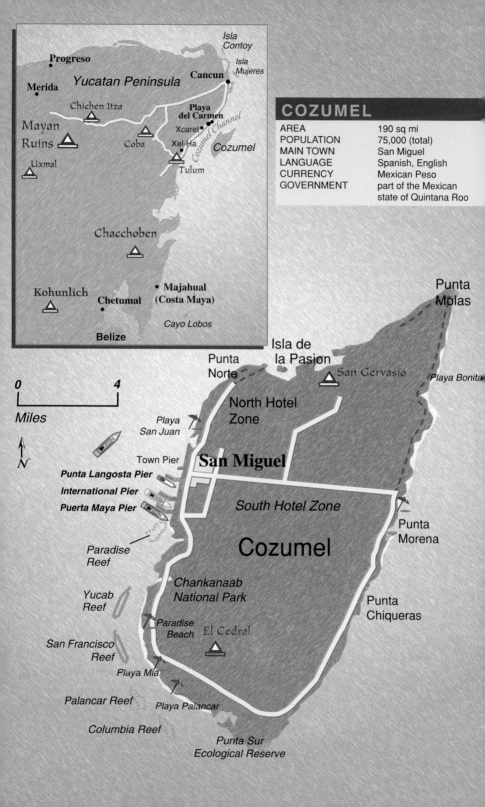

## COZUMEL

| | |
|---|---|
| AREA | 190 sq mi |
| POPULATION | 75,000 (total) |
| MAIN TOWN | San Miguel |
| LANGUAGE | Spanish, English |
| CURRENCY | Mexican Peso |
| GOVERNMENT | part of the Mexican state of Quintana Roo |

**Inset map — Yucatan Peninsula:**

Isla Contoy

Isla Mujeres

Progreso

**Cancun**

Yucatan Peninsula

**Merida**

Chichen Itza

**Playa del Carmen**

Mayan Ruins

Coba

Xcaret

Cozumel Channel

Xel-Ha

Cozumel

Uxmal

Tulum

Chacchoben

Kohunlich

**Chetumal**

**Majahual (Costa Maya)**

Cayo Lobos

**Belize**

**Main map — Cozumel:**

Punta Molas

Punta Norte

Isla de la Pasion

San Gervasio

Playa Bonita

North Hotel Zone

Playa San Juan

**San Miguel**

Town Pier

**Punta Langosta Pier**

**International Pier**

South Hotel Zone

**Puerta Maya Pier**

Punta Morena

Paradise Reef

**Cozumel**

Yucab Reef

Chankanaab National Park

Punta Chiqueras

San Francisco Reef

Paradise Beach

El Cedral

Playa Mia

Palancar Reef

Playa Palancar

Columbia Reef

Punta Sur Ecological Reserve

0   4
Miles

N

# COZUMEL & COSTA MAYA

The coral-fringed island of Cozumel was a sleepy hideaway when Jacques Cousteau paid it a visit in the early 1960s and introduced the world to one of the Caribbean's top dive sites. The documentary Cousteau filmed here captured the brilliance of Cozumel's extensive coral reefs, which thrive in crystal-clear waters teeming with tropical fish and other marine life. The clarity of the water is unsurpassed anywhere in the Caribbean, and the underwater caves and spectacular sponges are considered some of the best in the world. The island is also popular for its beautiful beaches and fascinating Mayan ruins.

The ancient **Maya**, from which Cozumel's inhabitants descend, named the island 'Land of Swallows' and dedicated it to Ixchel, the moon goddess of fertility. Remnants of temples and religious artifacts have been found throughout the island which lies 12 miles off the **Yucatan Peninsula**. The Yucatan, low and flat like Cozumel, is a limestone tableland. No rivers run through this area and the light rainfall is absorbed by the porous limestone where it collects in underground rivers and wells (cenotes), and in surface pools called *aguadas*.

Scattered throughout the low hills are thousands of pre-Columbian archaeological sites, for the Yucatan was once the seat of the great Mayan civilization that flourished for three millennium, beginning in about 1500 B.C.

**El Mundo Maya** (The Maya World) extended from the Yucatan peninsula into parts of El Salvador and Honduras. An advanced society with an understanding of astronomy and engineering, the Maya built their pyramidal structures oriented to the spring and fall equinoxes. Kilns were used to reduce the region's limestone into lime, which was mixed with white earth and water to create the mortar used in constructing the walls, corbelled arches and roof combs of massive stone temples – often decorated with elaborate carvings and ceramic paintings.

Mayan civilization reached its height during the Classic period (300 to 900 AD), followed by a rapid decline during which the population plummeted. In the Yucatan, the arrival of the Toltec from Central Mexico brought another advanced civilization of master builders.

The Spanish arrived in the early 1500s and imposed a new religious and political organization on the Mayan population. But assimilation was far from complete, especially among the rural peasants. In the mid-1800s, the

Maya tried to drive all Europeans off the Yucatan peninsula but were unsuccessful.

Following the Mexican Revolution of 1910-17, a land redistribution program guaranteed the rural Maya would no longer have their village lands expropriated.

## Cozumel

Cozumel is a flat island, its highest point only 35 feet above sea level, and is covered with scrub jungle. The majority of islanders live in the town of San Miguel, located on the island's sheltered west coast overlooking Cozumel Channel. While no longer the quiet seaside town that greeted visitors back in the 1950s, San Miguel has retained much of its early charm. Safe and compact, the port is laid out in a grid pattern with streets running parallel and perpendicular to the waterfront. The locals, of Mayan descent, are generally shorter than the average Mexican and most speak Spanish as well as some English. The Mexican peso is the official currency but American currency is widely accepted.

### Getting Around

The three cruise ship piers are located south of San Miguel. The closest, **Punta Langosta**, is a short walk from the town center. The **International Pier** and **Puerta Maya Pier** are a 10-minute taxi ride from town (about 45 minutes on foot). Ships that anchor off San Miguel transport their passengers by tender to the town pier, opposite the central

plaza. Taxis are plentiful at the cruise dock; the fare (for 4 passengers) from Puerta Maya pier to San Miguel is $11; to Playa Mia is $16. Renting a car (about $50 a day) is another option; the highways are paved and parking is free at most beachside lots. A passenger ferry runs between San Miguel and Playa del Carmen on the mainland (a 45-minute trip), where cruise passengers disembark on organized shore excursions to the Yucatan's Mayan sites and other attractions.

### Shopping

Cozumel offers excellent shopping, and there are outdoor malls located at Puerta Maya and Punta Langosta. The local flea market is located off 5th Avenue between Calles 2 and 4, while the town's upscale boutiques and restaurants are located on the waterfront's Avenue Rafael E. Melgar. Mexican handicrafts are among the finest in the world and include ceramics, glassware and whimsical hand-painted wooden animals. Quality leather goods include wallets, belts and sandals, while hand-woven products range from baskets, rugs and hammocks to embroidered blouses and colorful woolen shawls called *serapes*. Gold and silver filigree (intricate ornamental work) is another Mexican specialty, creating exquisite earrings, necklaces and bracelets. Mayan craftsmanship includes elaborate weavings, decorative stitching and ceremonial masks. Mexican-made products are duty-exempt and good buys are available in products made of silver, onyx and leather. Small discounts are often given for cash purchases and most stores accept U.S. dollars. Passengers visiting the mainland will also have an opportunity to buy local Mayan crafts at outdoor markets.

## Beaches

Sheltered beaches lie south of San Miguel, starting with **Chankanaab Bay** ($12 entry fee) where a full-service beach offers water sports and a restaurant.

Next is **Paradise Beach** (one of three beach clubs lying along a lovely three-mile stretch of sand formerly known as San Francisco Beach) with free beach chairs and umbrellas, and a bar/restaurant; kayaks and other watersports equipment can be rented.

South of Paradise Beach is **Playa Mia** (formerly Playa Del Sol) which is the island's party beach. Its pier is used by a local tour boat offering day cruises. An entry fee of $16 provides access to the beach, swimming pool, sun loungers, change rooms and other facilities.

Further south is **Mr. Sancho's Beach,** where facilities at this smaller, quieter beach include a bar-restaurant, beach palapas, watersports rentals and a small open-air shopping arcade. Horseback riding and ATV jungle tours are also available.

One of the island's southernmost beaches, **Playa Palancar**, is quieter than those closer to the cruise terminals. Divers and snorkelers come here to explore the famous Palancar Reef (see next section), and facilities include a bar, restaurant, beach chairs and umbrellas.

Good beaches north of San Miguel include **Playa San Juan**, just north of the Melia Mayan Hotel, offering shade and calm water. Several hotels offer day passes for cruise ship passengers, starting at $45 per person, which provide access to the resort's private beach and guest facilities.

The east coast beaches are pounded with surf and less crowded than the sheltered west side. **Punta Morena** is an excellent beach with palapas, a beach bar and restaurant, and souvenir stand.

**Dive & Snorkel Sites** – A strong current flows through Cozumel Channel, so drift div-

*Popular Paradise Beach is*
*quietest in the morning.*

# COZUMEL
## & the YUCATAN

*(Above and right) San Miguel's charming museum features a replica Mayan home. (Below) Tulum was an ancient trading center of the Maya-Toltec.*

*(Top) Chichen Itza is an important Maya-Toltec site on the Yucatan peninsula. (Middle, right) San Miguel's main shopping street is lined with lively restaurants.*
*(Belowt) A Mayan family sells crafts outside the walls of Tulum.*
*(Bottom) The view from Puerta Maya, looking toward the adjacent International Pier.*

ing is how the offshore reefs are explored. The continual current carries food to the reefs, which is why the sponge growth is so spectacular. Many of these sponges and soft corals were torn when Hurricane Wilma pounded local waters, but the hard corals and sea life are doing fine. Some of the shallower reefs suffered damage, but reefs at 35 feet and deeper were unscathed and the local dive community spent three months clearing away bags of debris deposited on the sea floor by Hurricane Wilma. One of Cozumel's most famous dive sites is three-mile **Palancar Reef** at the southern tip of the island, with seven different dive sites ranging from 35 to over 80 feet. Other good dive sites include: Columbia Reef; Punta Sur with caverns and steep drop-offs; Santa Rosa Reef with its huge coral mounds; San Francisco Reef's valleys and vertical wall; and Yucab Reef, an extensive and shallow dive site encompassing a wide variety of coral formations and fish species.

Cozumel's reefs were protected by presidential decree in 1980, so construction of a new cruise pier near Paradise Reef in the late 1990s was greeted with protests from several environmental groups, as well as local residents and dive operators. Paradise Wall begins at a depth of 50 feet and contains an abundance of marine life including giant sponges.

The best **snorkel sites** are the shallow reefs at Paradise Beach (a.k.a. Playa San Francisco) and the reefs of Chankanaab Bay.

**Cozumel Golf & Country Club** features a championship 18-hole golf course.

## Local Attractions

**Main Square 1**, located opposite San Miguel's town pier, is pleasant for strolling with its shaded areas, large gazebo, clock tower and a monument to motherhood.

**Museum de le Isla de Cozumel 2**, located on the waterfront between Calle 4 Norte and Calle 6 Norte, is a welcome retreat from the busy street and bustling boutiques. For a small admission charge, you can enjoy exhibits ranging from Cozumel's natural habitat to its Mayan and

SAN MIGUEL

## Shore Excursions

*Cozumel*

The following is a sampling of shore excursions offered by the cruise ships calling at Cozumel. Most ships also offer tours to the Yucatan peninsula, to visit various Mayan sites and parks, but these will vary from ship to ship. For more detail, log onto each cruise line's website or, if you have booked your cruise, refer to the shore excursion booklet provided.
• Adventure Park, Zip Line & Snorkel Combo
• Jungle Adventure by ATV or Bike

• Certified Two Tank Dive
• Clear Kayak & Snorkel Adventure
• Cozumel Golf & Country Club
• Deep Sea Fishing
• Sail, Snorkel & Beach Party
• Isla Pasion – beach, kayak or jeep adventure
• Playa Mia Beach Break
• Dolphin Encounter / Swim
• Sunset Catamaran Cruise
• Night Dive
YUCATAN EXCURSIONS -
• Mayan ruins of Tulum
• Mayan ruins of Coba
• Cenote Cavern Dive
• Cenote Snorkeling, Zip Line & Biking
• Xcaret Eco-Archaeological Park

colonial history. A highlight is the replica Mayan house, set in a courtyard, with a garden outside and authentic tools and furnishings inside. A Mayan host demonstrates the various stone tools, identifies foodstuffs on display and generally brings to life the workings of a typical village home. An open-air restaurant on the museum's second floor provides a lovely view out to sea.

**Cozumel Archaeological Park** ❸ contains full-size replicas of Mayan and Toltec stone carvings set in a jungle setting. A guided walking tour is included in the admission fee.

**Chankanaab Park** ($12 admission) is part of Isla Cozumel's Reefs National Marine Park and contains a natural underwater preserve connected to the sea by underground channels (*chankanaab* means 'small lake' or 'little sea' in Mayan). This beautiful lagoon is filled with bright corals and surrounded by a botanical garden, where visitors can stand and watch the colorful

fish. The lagoon itself is off-limits to snorkeling and swimming to protect the marine life from harmful suntan lotions, but there is good snorkeling among the reefs of Chankanaab Bay. Other attractions include Dolphin Discovery (visitors can swim with dolphins), a sea lion show, and a reproduction of a Mayan village. Atlantis Submarine operates daily tours of Chankanaab Bay's underwater coral heads and tropical fish, with passengers transported to the dive site by ferry from various pick-up points, including the cruise piers.

**Punta Sur Light House** is an ecological park and nature reserve featuring mangrove forests and white sand beaches where sea turtles come ashore between June and August to lay their eggs. Crocodiles can be viewed from a look-out tower, while the old lighthouse and navigation museum are rich in nautical history.

Although there are numerous archaeological sites on Cozumel, none reach the scale and architectural significance of those found on the Yucatan peninsula. The most important island site is the Mayan temple of Ixchel located at San Gervasio, about 10 miles from San Miguel.

## Yucatan Peninsula

**Progreso** – The lure of Mayan ruins and dazzling white beaches has prompted the construction of several cruise ship ports on the Yucatan Peninsula. Progreso, a tiny fishing village on the north coast, is now home to a cruise pier providing access to Merida (22 miles) and the Mayan sites of Uxmal (49 miles) and Chichen Itza (72 miles). Other shore excursions feature nearby caves and cenotes, dune buggy sightseeing or a visit to a flamingo reserve where these birds nest and feed among the mangroves. Spanish colonialism is revisited at the area's haciendas and the town of Izamal. Maya-themed excursions include a visit to the ruins at Dzibilchaltun, or to the Mayan community of Dzemul with its thatched roof palapa houses. Golf can be enjoyed at La Ceiba Golf & Country Club's 18-hole championship course (par 72, 6,528 yards) which was designed by Jack Nicklaus.

**Merida** – Once called the White City for its clean streets of gleaming white buildings where rooftop windmills are used to pump water from underground wells and streams, this Spanish colonial town was founded in 1542 by Francisco de Montejo, who conquered the Yucatan peninsula after his father withdrew due to fierce resistance. Built on the site of a ruined Mayan city, Merida became the cultural center of the Yucatan peninsula, its Cathedral of San Ildelfonso completed in 1599. Today, as the Yucatan state capital with a population exceeding 1/2 million, Merida's colonial heritage endures in its public buildings and the elegant old mansions of Paseo Montejo.

**Uxmal** – Situated in the Puuc hills (and pronounced *oosh-mal*), this important center of education flourished between 600 and 900 and is considered one of the finest examples of the Maya's Late Classic architecture. The site's impressive structures include the unique Pyramid of the Magician; the Governor's Palace, its facade decorated with some 20,0000 carved stone elements; and the Nunnery Quadrangle, the equivalent of a modern university.

**Chichen Itza** – This well-restored and popular Mayan site was founded around two large cenotes (deep, natural wells) in circa 514 by the Itza – the last strong, independent Mayan tribe. A political and religious center, the site was occupied at various times until 1194 when it was abandoned for the last time. The buildings span two periods of Mayan civilization. The Classic style is reflected in massive structures and heavy, decorative sculpture; the Post-Classic period, with a strong Toltec influence, produced plainer buildings, columns and sculpture based on the Mexican feathered serpent motif. The site's highlights include the Castillo temple, a ball court and, unusual among Mayan buildings, a round tower called the Caracol (snail shell) which was built in the Post-Classic period, probably as an astronomical observatory. Offerings, including human sacrifices, were thrown into Chichen Itza's sacred well which was a mecca for pilgrimages by other Mayan tribes of Central America and Mexico.

**Cancun** – Originally a Mayan settlement, its name meaning 'vessel at the end of the rainbow', Cancun consisted of a few hundred inhabitants before an international holiday resort was built on its offshore island in the early 1970s. Long and narrow, the island is lined with powdery white beaches and connected to the mainland by a bridge at each end. Its hotel zone contains first-class hotels and recreation facilities that draw over two million visitors annually, mostly from the U.S. The L-shaped island forms a lagoon where water sports can be enjoyed, and the outer beaches are sheltered by coral reefs. Isla Mujeres is a short ferry or water taxi ride from Cancun, and this tiny island (5 miles long and 1 mile wide) of secluded beaches and lagoons contains the National Marine Park El Garrafon at its southern tip – a snorkeling and diving paradise.

**Coba** – Dozens of stone roads and causeways once led to Coba – a commercial hub of the Maya, which flourished from 400 to 1100. The largest settlement found to date, much of this site is still overgrown but those structures that have been excavated include the 80-foot-high Iglesia temple-pyramid, the Crossword pyramid, and the Nohochmul pyramid, which is the tallest on the Yucatan peninsula with 120 steps climbing to the top of its 138-foot-high face.

**Calica** is a cruise terminal located about five miles south of Playa del Carmen. Two natural parks are in the vicinity, the nearest being **Xcaret** ('little inlet'), which is an eco-archeological park built around the ruins of a Mayan ceremonial center. Visitors can don life vests and ride the gentle currents along an underground river, through caves illuminated by shafts of sunlight. The grounds include a botanical gardens, butterfly pavilion, turtle farm, swimming lagoons and restaurants.

Further south (about 15 miles) along the coast is **Xel-Ha**, touted as the world's largest natural aquarium. The park's limestone shoreline has been sculpted by the sea and freshwater springs, forming turquoise lagoons filled with tropical fish that can viewed from wooden platforms above the rocky shore. Snorkelers can swim in the lagoons and along the Xel-

*One of several temples at Coba.*

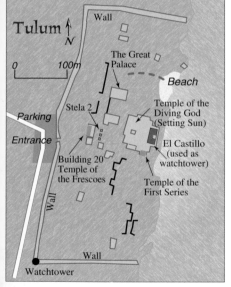

*Visitors explore the site of*
*Tulum, shown on map at left.*

of a bluff overlooking the sea. Its stone buildings are surrounded on three sides by a stone wall that dates from 1200 AD and is 16 feet thick in places. Tulum, 'City of the New Dawn', was the only Mayan city still occupied when the Spanish arrived in the early 1500s. The beach-lined cove at the base of this site is ideal for swimming and snorkeling.

# Costa Maya

This cruise port near Majahual was custom built for cruise ships and features a shopping arcade, a small beach, saltwater swimming pool and an amphitheater where Mexican folkloric shows are staged. The port was badly damaged by Hurricane Dean in 2007. Extensively repaired, the port reopened in fall 2008. Majahual is a pleasant fishing village with a lovely beach backed by restau-

Ha river. A footpath also leads to the river and into the jungle where two cenotes and the Cave of Miracles, a massive underground cavern, can be viewed.

**Tulum** – The only known walled city of the Maya, this ancient trading center is a stunning sight perched on the edge

rant-bars. It can be reached by shuttle bus or taxi from Puerto Costa Maya; the shuttle bus is $3 per person, the shuttle van is $2, and a private taxi is $2 per person. Fares are for each way.

Excursions from Costa Maya highlight the area's beautiful beaches, lagoons and coral reefs, which can be explored in clear-bottom kayaks and on guided scuba dives and snorkel expeditions. **Banco Chinchorro**, a huge coral reef the size of Cozumel Island, lies offshore and provides diving and snorkeling

*(Above) The swimming beach at Majahual. (Below) Puerto Costa Maya's modern cruise terminal.*

opportunities. Land-based tours include dune buggy rides, 4X4 safaris, horseback riding and bicycling. The area's notable Mayan ruins include **Chacchoben** (City of Red Corn), which dates to the 4th century, and **Kohunlich**, discovered in 1912, its Temple of Masks featuring a staircase lined with stucco masks adorned with features of the Sun God.

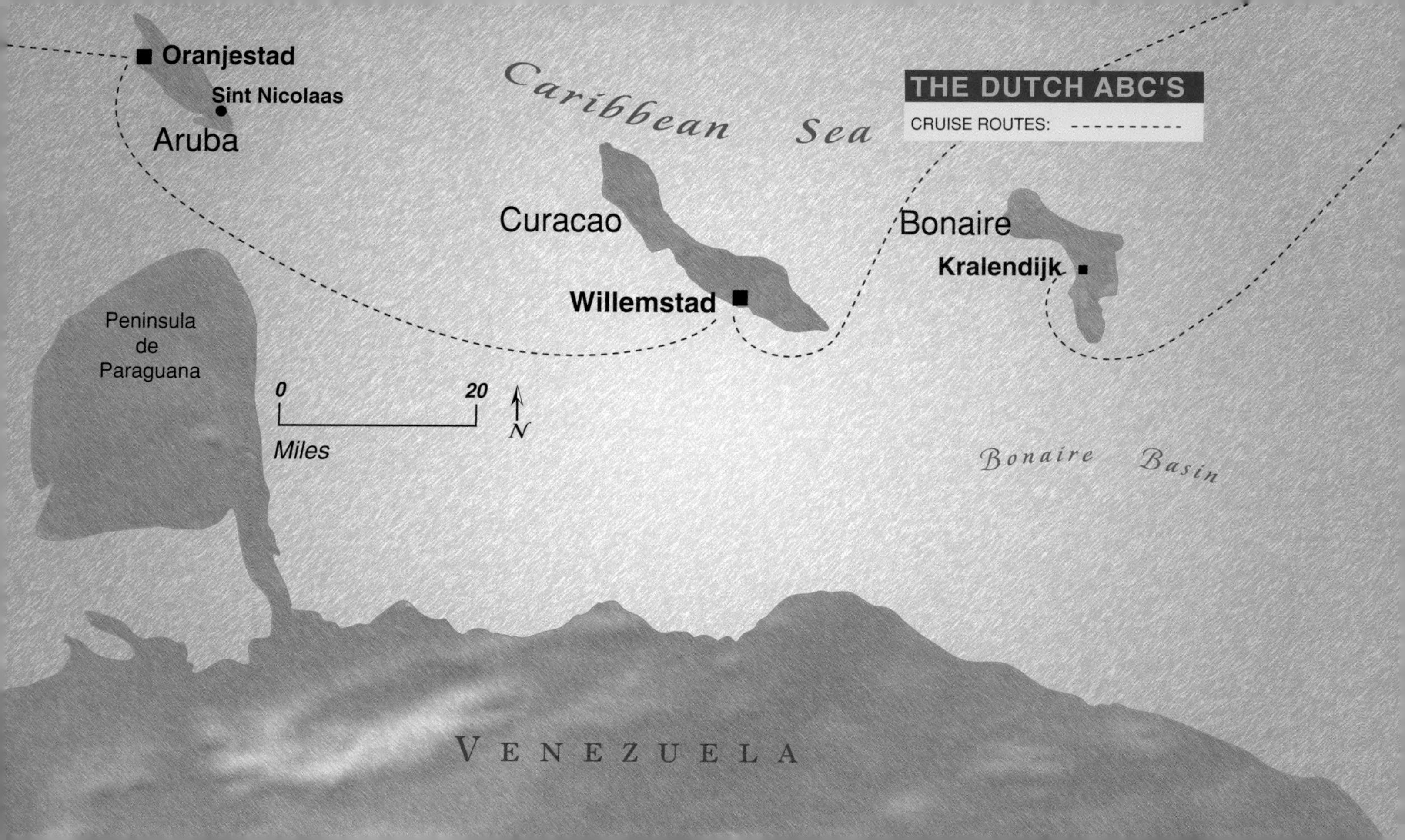

THE DUTCH ABC'S

CRUISE ROUTES: - - - - - - -

*Caribbean Sea*

*Bonaire Basin*

Bonaire

**Kralendijk** ■

Curacao

■ **Willemstad**

N

20

0

*Miles*

Oranjestad ■
**Sint Nicolaas**

Aruba

Peninsula
de
Paraguana

VENEZUELA

# ARUBA, CURACAO & BONAIRE

The Dutch-founded islands of Aruba, Bonaire and Curacao (the ABCs) lie off the coast of Venezuela, outside the hurricane belt. They receive little rain in summer, their vegetation consisting of drought-resistant cacti and divi-divi trees bent by the steady trade winds. Their stark landscapes of wave-eroded rock formations and blinding white beaches are in contrast to the picturesque ports where brightly colored, Dutch gabled buildings line the waterfront.

The islands were inhabited at the time by Arawak Indians who lived in villages and caves. Their food came mostly from the rich bounty of the sea, while other foodstuffs were obtained from mainland tribes in exchange for salt – one of the few natural resources found on these barren islands.

Treasure-seeking Spaniards discovered the ABCs when, in 1499, a Spanish sea captain en route to South America left some of his scurvy-afflicted sailors on one of the islands to die. When he returned less than a year later, he found them all alive and well. Hence the name Curacao – based on the Portuguese word for 'the cure.'

Yet, despite its promising name, Curacao didn't impress the Spanish for it was a dry, prickly place with no apparent

*Dutch gabled buildings line Willemstad's waterfront.*

gold deposits. Even the Valencia orange trees brought from Spain produced a bitter, almost inedible fruit when planted here.

It took the resourceful Dutch to see the potential of Curacao and make it an integral part of their trading empire. The Dutch West India Company seized the island in 1634, transferring the few Spanish settlers and Arawak Indians to the mainland, and made it a base for raiding nearby settlements. Its sheltered harbor was fortified on either side at the entrance and, under the governorship of Peter Stuyvesant, Willemstad became an important trading port and an enormous slave depot.

*Aruba's California Lighthouse stands at the northern tip of this semi-arid island.*

As for those bitter-tasting oranges brought from Spain, it was discovered that their sun-dried peels contained an etheric oil which became the basis for Curacao's famous liqueur. The ABCs remained for the most part Dutch, briefly occupied by British troops in the early 1800s.

Slavery was ended in 1863 and the islands had to develop new resources. Trade with Venezuela became the mainstay of Curacao's economy. On Aruba, alluvial deposits of gold were mined and the aloe plant became an important crop, its gel used in numerous pharmaceuticals. The pods of the divi-divi tree were also exported for use in leather tanning.

Following World War I, oil was discovered at Lake Maracaibo in Venezuela. The oil companies, seeking a stable place to locate their refineries and storage facilities, chose the nearby Dutch islands which made the ABC's a target for submarine attack in World War II.

Dutch – the official language – is taught in schools, and residents are often fluent in English and Spanish, as well as their native tongue of Papiamentu, which is a Creole mixture of Spanish, Portuguese, Dutch, English and Arawak Indian dialects.

Aruba separated from the Netherlands Antilles in 1986. Other member countries, such as Curacao and St. Maarten, also sought greater autonomy and, in 2010, the Netherlands Antilles was dissolved. All three islands are now part of the Kingdom of the Netherlands.

# Aruba

Once a cacti-studded cattle ranch, Aruba is today a holiday paradise with miles of sugary white beaches and crystal-clear turquoise waters. The island's southwest coast has beach resorts, shopping malls and casinos; its rugged northeast coast is where wave action has carved coral cliffs into dramatic sea arches. In between lies a hilly desert of caves, cacti and scrub.

Wells tap into the island's water table but a huge saltwater distillation plant at Spanish Lagoon, once a hideout for pirates, is the island's main source of fresh water.

## Getting Around

The cruise ships dock in the heart of **Oranjestad**, within easy walking distance of the shops and local attractions. Taxis are available at the cruise terminal and bear 'TX' on their licence plates. They are unmetered and rates are fixed, based on a carload of up to five passengers, but be sure to establish a fare before departing. People returning from the beach in wet bathing suits are usually refused, so be sure to dry off and take a cover-up. US currency is accepted, but no bills larger than $20. The minimum rate to any destination is $6, and the hired rate per hour is $45. Some sample fares (in US$) from the cruise terminal: Eagle Beach ($10); Noord ($11); Tierra del Sol ($20); Casibari ($16); Palm Island ($22); Arikok ($23); Baby Beach ($38).

The bus is another way to get to the beaches north of the cruise port. The bus station is a short walk from the pier and all buses to Malmok will stop at other beaches along the way. The fare is US$1.15 one-way and US$2 return (www.visitaruba.com/getting-around/bus-schedule/).

*Dutch colonial buildings line a shopping street in Oranjestad.*

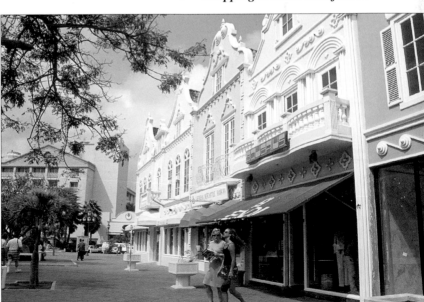

***A ship docks at the Oranjestad cruise terminal.***

Most major American car rental companies operate on Aruba, in addition to several local companies. The cost to rent a car for the day is about $60. A valid driver's license is all that's required to rent a car. The island is 20 miles long by six miles wide, the main roads are paved, and driving is on the right.

The official currency is the Aruban Florin (Afl) but US dollars are readily accepted island wide, and major credit cards are accepted at most establishments. The bank rate of exchange is fixed at 1.80 Afl. to $1 US.

**Beaches** – A string of lovely beaches lies along the coast northwest of the cruise terminal, starting with Druif Beach (about two miles from the cruise ship pier), which is adja-

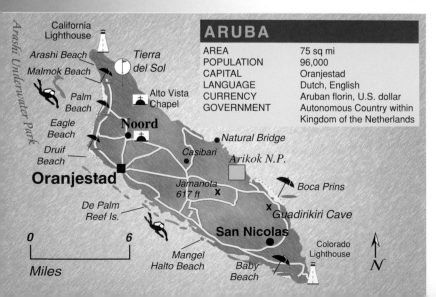

Arashi Underwater Park

California Lighthouse
Arashi Beach
Malmok Beach
Tierra del Sol
Palm Beach
Alto Vista Chapel
Eagle Beach
Noord
Druif Beach
Natural Bridge
Casibari
Arikok N.P.
**Oranjestad**
Jamanota 617 ft
Boca Prins
De Palm Reef Is.
Guadirikiri Cave
**San Nicolas**
Colorado Lighthouse
Mangel Halto Beach
Baby Beach

0      6
*Miles*

N

| ARUBA | |
|---|---|
| AREA | 75 sq mi |
| POPULATION | 96,000 |
| CAPITAL | Oranjestad |
| LANGUAGE | Dutch, English |
| CURRENCY | Aruban florin, U.S. dollar |
| GOVERNMENT | Autonomous Country within Kingdom of the Netherlands |

cent to Manchebo Beach (where hotel facilities are available), which is adjacent to Eagle Beach (where watersports equipment is available). About four miles from the terminal is Palm Beach, considered one of the best beaches in the Caribbean and extremely popular for its swimming, sailing and hotel facilities. Hadikurari is popular with windsurfers (rental equipment is available). Arashi Beach, near the island's northern tip, is a wide expanse of sand dotted with beach huts and within sight of the California Light House. At the island's southeastern tip are Rodgers Beach and Baby Beach, the latter being ideal for young children with its calm, shallow waters and shaded areas. Picnickers enjoy the romantic setting of Boca Prins, backed by sand dunes and pounded by the nearby surf, which makes swimming dangerous.

**Dive and Snorkel Sites** – The shallow waters and abundance of fish off Malmok Beach (8 miles from the terminal) make it an ideal spot for snorkelers but there are no facilities nearby. Arashi Reef and the *Antilla*, a German freighter destroyed during World War II, are popular dive sites, and can also be viewed by semi-submers-

*(Above) Diving at Aruba*
*(Below) Arashi Beach*

ible and submarine, both available through ship-organized shore excursions. Seaworld Explorer transports passengers by bus to the north end of the island where their semi-submersible is boarded, while Atlantis transports passengers to and from their sub site by ferry from Seaport Village Marina. Another good snorkeling beach is Manguel Halto beach, with its nearby barrier reef. De Palm Island (reached by a four-minute ferry crossing) also offers excellent snorkeling; the full-day admission charge ($99 for adults; $75 for children) covers all beach facilities, an open bar and an all-you-can-eat buffet as well as snorkel equipment, instructions and guided tours.

*(Above) Souvenir stand and (top) Seaport Marketplace in Oranjestad. (Opposite) A cruise ship departs Aruba.*

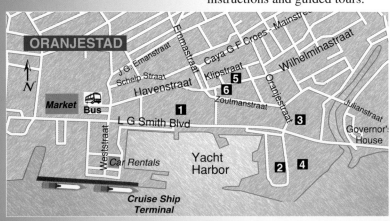

**Golf** – An 18-hole course designed by Robert Trent Jones Jr is situated at Tierra del Sol near the island's northwestern tip. This par-71 course with water on two sides, has stunning sea views and is dotted with giant cacti.

**Shopping** – Shopping malls are located at the harborfront, in  town and stretching northwest along the coast. **Seaport Village Mall** ❶, a five-minute walk from the cruise terminal, is Aruba's largest shopping and entertainment complex with dozens of stores, boutiques and a casino. The nearby **Seaport Marketplace** ❷ is also popular with its shaded central walkway and sidewalk cafes. Oranjestad's main shopping street is Caya G.F. Betico Croes, with chic boutiques and shops.

International items to look for include designer fashions, jewelry and watches. There are also good buys in Peruvian hand-knit sweaters, Venezuelan shoes and handbags, Colombian emeralds, and locally made aloe vera products. Clay pottery and local crafts are sold at outdoor stands along the waterfront and at the flea market beside the bus station.

## Local Sights

**Fort Zoutman** ❸ is the oldest building in Oranjestad, erected in 1796 and named for a Dutch Rear Admiral. Added to the fort in 1868 was King Willem III Tower which served as a lighthouse and now houses a heritage museum.

**Queen Wilhelmina Park** ❹, adjacent to the Seaport Marketplace, contains a marble statue of the former Dutch queen. Wilhelminastraat contains interesting colonial architecture including the **Protestant Church** ❺, built in 1846. The **Archaeological Museum** ❻ on Zoutmanstraat contains artifacts and pottery of the island's first Indian inhabitants.

**Island Attractions** – **Santa Anna Church** in **Noord** was built in the 1770s, and its hand-carved oak altar won the exhibition award in Rome in 1870. The **Chapel of Alto Vista**, built by a Spanish missionary, is a place of pilgrimage situated on the north coast overlooking the sea. **Casibari**'s interesting rock formations can be climbed via some steps for a view of the island. Aruba's most famous landmark was, before it collapsed in 2005, the **Natural Bridge**, made of coral and carved by the sea on the island's windward coast. Still standing is the smaller Baby Natural Bridge.

## Shore Excursions

*Aruba*

Shore excursions include countryside drives and feature such island attractions as the Butterfly Farm (near Palm Beach) and the Ostrich Farm. Also offered are ATV adventures, 4WD safaris, mountain biking and horseback riding, as well as guided hikes in Arikok National Park and historic walking tours of Oranjestad. Submarine rides, semi-submersible cruises and glass-bottom boat rides are available, as are kayaking, snorkeling, helmet diving and scuba diving. Beach breaks include Palm Beach and De Palm Island. Golf is available at Tierra Del Sol.

*A ship docks near the entrance to Curacao's St. Anna Bay.*

**Arikok National Park** contains natural and man-made paths, a restored *cunucu* (countryside house), a traditional stone well and the Natural Pool, near Boca Keto, which is surrounded by rocks and filled with sea water. Several caves are situated along the north coast, including **Guadirikiri Cave**, its caverns containing stalactites and ancient drawings.

# Curacao

Few Caribbean ports of call can surpass the arrival awaiting passengers whose ship docks in **Willemstad**'s St. Anna Bay. The Queen Emma Pontoon Bridge swings open to allow ships entry into this narrow inlet overlooked by the restored waterfront warehouses of colonial Willemstad. Added to UNESCO's World Heritage List in 1997, Willemstad's Dutch gabled buildings were first painted a variety of colors in 1817 when the governor complained that the sun's glare off the stark white buildings was giving him headaches.

Initially founded as Santa Anna by the Spanish, the port's name was changed to Willemstad when Holland took possession of the island in 1634. Settlement grew on both sides of the channel with the eastern side called Punda and the western side Otrabanda (other side). Ferry boats had long transported residents across the channel when, in 1888, a pontoon foot bridge was built – fixed at one end so it could open whenever a vessel had to pass.

A toll charge was based on each person's ability to pay – those wearing shoes were charged 2¢ and those walking barefooted were free. It's said that the poor would borrow shoes to prove their ability to pay, while the rich would take off their shoes to save 2¢. Today there is no charge for either the bridge or the passenger ferries which run continuously throughout the day.

*The trolley train is an easy way to tour the streets of Willemstad.*

## Getting Around

The cruise ships dock either at Mega Pier near the entrance to St. Anna Bay or at Mathey Wharf on the Otrabanda side of the bay.

### CURACAO

| | |
|---|---|
| AREA | 171 sq mi |
| POPULATION | 153,000 |
| CAPITAL | Willemstad |
| LANGUAGE | Dutch, English |
| CURRENCY | N. A. guilder, U.S. dollar |
| GOVERNMENT | Part of Kingdom of the Netherlands |

West Point
Christoffel National Park
**14**
Lagun    1220 ft
Soto    Barber
Daniel
Hato
**15**
Blue Bay    Hilton    Rio Canario
Piscadera Bay    **12**    Santa Rosa
**Willemstad**    **13**
Nieuwpoort    East Point
Seaquarium Beach
*Underwater Marine Park*

N

0    Miles    10

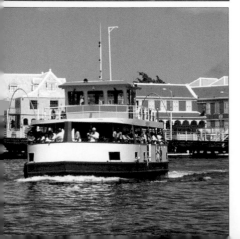

*(Above) Willemstad's Penha Building is a town landmark. (Left) A pontoon bridge and passenger ferry (bottom left) connect the two sides of Willemstad.*

Passengers can make their way to the Punda side on foot over the pontoon bridge, via the free passenger ferry which docks at Mathey Wharf, or by taxi (about US$8) over the Queen Julianna Bridge.

Taxis are unmetered and quoted fares are for up to four passengers. The fare should be agreed upon before departing. Sample fares: Willemstad to Hilton resort $15; to Seaquarium $20; to Blue Bay $30.

The official currency is the Netherlands Antilles guilder (also called the florin) but U.S. dollars are widely accepted.

A trolley train departs Fort Amsterdam daily at 10:00 a.m. on a one-hour city tour ($20 adults, $15 children).

**Beaches** – Curacao's southern coast is indented with beach-lined bays and coves. Private beaches charge a small entrance fee, as do some of the hotel beaches. A popular beach northwest of Willemstad, near the village of Sint Michiel, is Blue Bay (Blauwbaai) – considered one of Curacao's best with its shaded areas, lounge chairs, change facilities, bar and restaurant, and water sports center ($3 admission is charged). Closer to Willemstad is the Hilton Curacao resort. Fine beaches east of Willemstad include Seaquarium Beach, situated right next door to the seaquarium and featuring beautiful white sand, palm trees, change facilities and several bars.

**Dive & Snorkel Sites** Excellent snorkeling and diving are available all around the island with visibility of 60 to 80 feet, and sometimes up to 150 feet. The Curacao Underwater Park, ideal for both diving and snorkeling, protects 12 miles of unspoiled coral reef along which is an underwater nature trail and spectacular dive sites which include coral beds, sheer walls and shipwrecks. A dive center is located at the Hilton resort on Piscadera Bay (a $15 taxi ride from Willemstad), as is Seaworld Explorer, its semi-submarine departing from the Hilton pier. Klein Curacao, lying off East Point, is an uninhabited islet with beautiful beaches and good snorkeling and diving.

**Golf** – A nine-hole course with sand greens is open mornings at the Curacao Golf & Squash Club just north of the Willemstad Harbor.

**Shopping** – Duty-free bargains in Willemstad include brand-name jewelry, watches, European fashions, perfumes, crystal, china, electronics and cameras. Fine stores are located in Punda on Handelskade, Heerenstraat and Breedestraat, with additional shops and boutiques located in the restored **Waterfort Arches**. Local art and crafts are sold at several outdoor markets including one along the Otrobanda waterfront near the pontoon

*The beach and pier at the Hilton Curacao resort.*

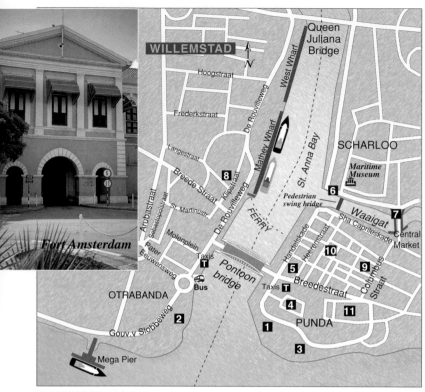

## Shore Excursions

*Curacao*

Organized ship excursions include a trolley train tour of Willemstad; an island tour with stops at the Curacao liqueur distillery and Curacao Seaquarium; a semi-submarine ride along coral reefs; and beach and snorkel excursions. Check your cruise line's website for details.

bridge and another at Wilhelmina Park in Punda. Central Market, located in a large circular building east of the **Floating Market**, sells art and crafts as well as fresh fruit and vegetables, and local Criollo cuisine.

## Local Attractions

Located at the harbor entrance within the battlements of **Waterfort 1** (built in 1634), and within hailing distance of ships entering the harbor, is the Van der Valk Plaza Hotel – one of only two hotels in the world that is covered by marine collision insurance. Still attached to the sea wall are iron rings once used to secure a chain that was stretched across the channel to prevent enemy ships from entering the harbor. During World War II, a steel net was stretched across the channel between **Waterfort** and **Riffort 2** – built on the other side in 1838. Stretching east of Waterfort along the sea front are more old battlements, including the **Waterfort Arches 3**, housing shops and restaurants.

**Fort Amsterdam 4** with its mustard-colored walls, was the center of the fortified town from 1648 to 1861. Today it's the seat of the Netherlands Antilles government. Its inner courtyard, entered through an arched walkway, is formed by the **Governor's Palace** (facing the water), the **Fort Church Museum** (opposite) and government offices on each side. In case of siege, the church was built with a cellar for provisions and an adjacent water cistern. A cannon ball fired in 1804 by English troops, led by Captain Bligh of Bounty fame, remains embedded in its front wall.

The much-photographed **Penha Building 5**, golden yellow with white trim, stands at the corner near the east end of the pontoon bridge. One of Curacao's oldest examples of Dutch colonial architecture, the building was formerly a social club with a gallery overlooking the harbor. Other waterfront buildings along this block resemble the canal houses of Amsterdam, one of which houses **Gallery '86** – a showcase for the works of well-known artists of the Caribbean and Netherlands.

At the other end of the block is the **Floating Market 6** where Venezuelan boats loaded with fruit, vegetables and fish sell their wares. Nearby is the Maritime Museum, and at the east end of the market is the **Queen Wilhelmina Bridge 7**, which spans the Waaigat and leads to the former residential district of **Scharloo**, where wealthy merchants built opulent homes, their architectural styles ranging from 1700s colonial to Victorian.

Across the water from Scharloo. near the ferry dock, is **Kura Hulanda Museum 8**. Built on the town's slave auction site, this museum chronicles the slave trade.

In 1651, a dozen Jewish families from Amsterdam arrived in Willemstad, growing to a community of 2,000 by the early 1700s. The **Mikve Emanuel Synagogue 9**, built in 1732 and similar in style to the old Portuguese one in Amsterdam, is today the oldest active synagogue in the Western Hemisphere. The Jewish Cultural Museum is entered off the synagogue's courtyard.

Other museums in Punda include the **Postal Museum 10**, housed in a 1693 building atthe corner of Keukenstraat and Kuiperstraat.

The town's central park, **Wilhelminaplein 11**, contains a statue of Queen Wilhelmina, as well as shaded benches and a playground. Opposite the park's east side is the former Jewish Reformed Synagogue Temple Emmanuel (the Temple Building) and City Gate, which marks the boundary of Willemstad when it was a fortified settlement.

**Island Attractions**

Outside of Willemstad the attractions include beautiful beaches, secluded coves, village churches and restored land houses, which are former country estates situated on hilltops so the owner could watch over his slaves. Popular attractions include the **Curacao Liqueur Distillery** **12**, located in the former colonial mansion of Chobolobo on the east side of Willemstad's harbor.

The **Curacao Seaquarium** **13** is where visitors can view 400 species of sea life native to local waters, including various sharks and stingrays. It is also the location of the Curacao Dolphin Academy, where visitors can interact with dolphins at various levels, including swimming, snorkeling and open-water diving (prices start at $89 per person). Beside the aquarium is a full-facility beach of white sand.

At the north end of Curacao is **Christoffel National Park** **14**, a 4,500-acre nature reserve containing the island's highest point of Mount Christoffel (1,239 feet), Indian caves and trails.

The prehistoric caves at **Hato** **15** were recently opened to the public, their limestone terraces containing fossilized coral that formed before tectonic uplifting brought the submerged island to the sea's surface.

## Bonaire

Boomerang-shaped Bonaire is one of the best islands in the Caribbean for diving and snorkeling. The island's shoreline is a protected marine park, where coral reefs are home to more than a thousand different species of aquatic creatures, including sea horses and turtles. There are 86 charted dive sites on the island, many of these located on the sheltered western side of the island, clustered north of Kralendijk and around the offshore islet of Klein Bonaire. Reefs and wrecks, beach dives and drop-offs – the variety of dive sites and the clarity of the water is spectacular. Conditions are also ideal for snorkelers, with little current and plenty of shallow water snorkeling sites.

The island capital of **Kralendijk**, meaning 'coral dike', is a quiet place where about 3,000 of the island's 15,000 residents live. Shops carrying duty-free and local items are found at the Harborside Shopping Mall and along the main street which

*Bonaire's famous and protected underwater sites include three vertical wall dives.*

runs parallel with the water-front. Historic sights include Fort Oranje, two churches and a museum. Wild donkeys and goats roam free on this unspoiled island where the centuries-old industry of salt mining has been joined by oil bunkering and tourism.

Bonaire's land-based attrac-tions are as fascinating as its underwater world, for the island is home to one of the largest **flamingo colonies** in the Western Hemisphere. More than 15,000 flamingos nest in the island's

*Pink Beach is ideal for swimming, snorkeling and scuba diving.*

salt pans and, in addition to two flamingo sanctuaries, a 13,500-acre game preserve (Washington-Slagbaai National Park) has been established at Bonaire's north end. Here iguanas and green-tailed liz-ards can be viewed in addition to flamingos and other birds such as yellow-winged parrots, often seen perched on the giant cacti that grow as high as 30 feet.

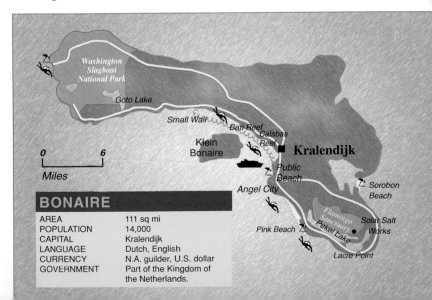

BONAIRE

| | |
|---|---|
| AREA | 111 sq mi |
| POPULATION | 14,000 |
| CAPITAL | Kralendijk |
| LANGUAGE | Dutch, English |
| CURRENCY | N.A. guilder, U.S. dollar |
| GOVERNMENT | Part of the Kingdom of the Netherlands. |

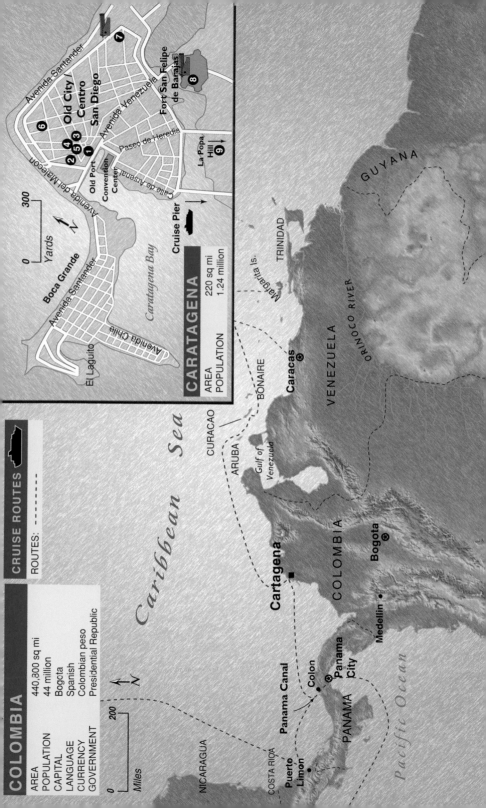

# COLOMBIA

| | |
|---|---|
| AREA | 440,300 sq mi |
| POPULATION | 44 million |
| CAPITAL | Bogota |
| LANGUAGE | Spanish |
| CURRENCY | Colombian peso |
| GOVERNMENT | Presidential Republic |

## CRUISE ROUTES

ROUTES: - - - - - - - -

Caribbean Sea

NICARAGUA

COSTA RICA

Puerto Limón

Panama Canal

Colon

PANAMA

Panama City

Cartagena

COLOMBIA

Medellin

Bogota

Pacific Ocean

Miles
0    200

N

ARUBA

CURACAO

BONAIRE

Gulf of Venezuela

VENEZUELA

Caracas

Margarita Is.

TRINIDAD

ORINOCO RIVER

GUYANA

## CARATAGENA

| | |
|---|---|
| AREA | 220 sq mi |
| POPULATION | 1.24 million |

Boca Grande

Avenida Santander

El Laguito

Avenida Chile

Cartagena Bay

Cruise Pier

Yards
0    300

N

Avenida del Malecon

Old Port

Convention Center

Calle de Arsenal

Paseo de Heredia

Avenida Venezuela

Avenida Santander

Old City / Centro

San Diego

Fort San Felipe de Barajas

La Popa Hill

2 4 5 3 1 6 7 8 9

# CARTAGENA

Cartagena de Indies was, for two centuries, one of Spain's most prized New World ports. Founded in 1533, Cartagena (pronounced *kar-ta-hay-na*) is today a United Nations World Heritage Site. Preserved within its Old City walls are historic churches, Iberian palaces and narrow cobblestone streets.

Back in the days of the Spanish Main, a fleet would call at Cartagena each August to load gold and silver arriving from Portobelo. When the Spanish ships pulled into port loaded with goods from the home country – wines, cheeses, books, clothing and porcelain – Cartagena took on a circus-like atmosphere. The townspeople would crowd the

*(Right) Spanish fortifications guarded the harbor entrance. (Below) Fort San Felipe de Barajas.*

docks where bankers, merchants, agents, pedlars and prostitutes all sought a piece of the action. A few months later, their ship holds loaded with treasure, the fleet would sail for Spain.

A series of forts and massive stone walls, which now divide the Old City from the newer part, were built over time to defend the port against marauding pirates and enemy fleets. Cartagena's history is a bloody one of sieges and sackings, starting with its fall to the English privateer Sir Francis Drake in 1586.

*(Above) The Old City's colonial architecture includes the forbidding entrance to the Palace of the Inquisition. (Below) Cartagena's cruise port viewed from atop La Popa Hill.*

Drake's successful attack prompted the enraged Spanish king, Philip II, to hire an Italian engineer named Antoneli whose task for the next 20 years was to make sure it didn't happen again. A series of forts was built to defend Cartagena from sea approaches and the city remained impregnable for more than a century, until the famous French buccaneer Jean Du Casse arrived in 1697 with 700 men and direct orders from France's King Louis XIV to go ahead and attack. After a fierce battle, the Spanish surrendered to the joint force of French pirates and soldiers, the latter collecting the loot of gold and silver, then refusing to share it with the pirates who turned back to the city and sacked it again.

An unsuccessful British siege in 1741 was led by Edward Vernon, who was able to storm the harbor but whose troops (including a regiment led by George Washington's half brother) succumbed to dysentery, malaria and yellow fever before a final assault could be staged.

Cartagena was the first city in Colombia to officially defy Spain's rule, declaring its independence in 1811. It became

known as the Republic of Cartagena, a base from which Simon Bolivar launched his military campaign to liberate Venezuela. The walled city built by Spanish colonists was, ironically, besieged and captured by Spanish forces in 1815, but the rebel forces regained Cartagena in 1821 and the former treasure city of the Spanish Main was incorporated into Colombia. Its importance waned until the 20th century, when oil refining brought new wealth to the city. In addition to oil, other commodities shipped out of Cartagena's busy port include coffee, bananas, platinum and gold.

Today Cartagena, with a population exceeding one million, is considered an island of peace in a country plagued by poverty and drug violence. The colonial architecture of the city's walled quarter is a big draw for cruise visitors, as are the outlying mangrove forests and island beaches.

*(Below) Cartagena's old port,*
*now overlooked by the*
*Convention Center, is where*
*Spanish galleons once docked.*

## Shore Excursions
### Cartagena

Shore excursions offered by the cruise lines usually include a selection of motorcoach tours (4 to 5 hrs) that cover the Old City's main attractions such as Fort of San Felipe de Barajas, Inquisition Palace, Church of San Pedro Claver and La Popa Monastery, with shopping stops at The Dungeons and Pierino Gallo Mall. An historic walking tour of the Old City is also offered. Should you decide to explore the Old City independently, taxis are plentiful and gather at the port gates (see Getting Around).

Boating tours include a speedboat ride to the colonial Fort of San Jose de Bocachica (built to guard the port entrance), or to the Rosario Islands for a visit to the aquarium at Isla de San Martin with beach time spent snorkeling or sunbathing (6 hrs). Tropical flora and fauna can be viewed while canoeing through a mangrove system (4 hrs), and panoramic tours of the bay can be taken aboard a replica Spanish galleon (2 hrs).

*(Above) Gourmet coffee can be purchased at Pierino Gallo Shopping Center.*
*(Below) A local woman in traditional dress poses for a photo.*

## Getting Around

The entrance to Cartagena harbor is nine miles long and worth viewing as your ship approaches or leaves this historic port. Cruise ships enter Cartagena Bay south of Isla de Tierra Bomba and dock at the cruise ship pier in residential Manga.

Ship-organized city tours are conducted on buses that load at the dock. A free shuttle can be taken from your ship to the terminal building located inside the port entrance. Here you will find an indoor/outdoor cafe, and shops selling local handicrafts. An ATM is located here, but US currency is widely accepted. Near the cruise terminal is a pleasant little park inhabited by monkeys and tropical birds. Taxis line up outside the port gates and can be hired at set rates. The fare from the port entrance to the Old City is about US$20 for one to four passengers.

Take reasonable precautions before heading ashore, i.e. secure your wallet in an inside zipped pocket and refrain from wearing any expensive jewelry.

## Shopping

Cartagena is not a duty-free port but local products worth shopping for include leather goods, ceramics, silver jewelry, semi-precious stones and, of course, emeralds. The world's finest emeralds are mined in Colombia, the world's leading producer of emeralds. Those sold in Cartagena are unique in that centuries-old goldsmithing techniques are used to create handcrafted items of jewelry.

Emeralds, like diamonds, are sold by weight, but the cut of the stone is less important than its color. The darker the emerald, the higher its value, yet a person should buy the color they personally prefer. All emeralds are flawed, so be suspicious of someone offering you a dark green stone with no visible flaws at a low price, for it might be a fake. Also, a green oil is sometimes rubbed on an emerald to hide its flaws and deepen its color – until the oil wears off – so be sure to buy from a reputable dealer.

**Pierino Gallo Shopping Center** at El Laguito is the place to shop for quality merchandise. A number of reputable jewelers are located here, including Adriana's Jewelry, Mister Emerald and Greenfire. The center's other shops carry fine leather goods, pre-Columbian art (including beadwork and ceramic pieces), gourmet coffee products, pottery, hand-painted plates and appliqued t-shirts.

In the Old City, local handicrafts can be bought from street vendors or at **Las Bovedas**, where boutiques are housed in medieval vaults.

*(Above) Shopping at the souvenir stalls in Las Bovedas where some shops sell high-quality handcrafted tableware (below).*

## Local Attractions

The preserved colonial architecture of the walled Old City can be enjoyed on a leisurely stroll of its narrow streets and shaded plazas. Pedlars and street entertainers will be encountered but are not aggressive. The **Clock Tower 1** marks the main entrance to the walled city and opens onto Plaza de los Coches where a visitor information center is located.

From this square, Casa de la Aduana leads past beautiful arcaded buildings to San Pedro Square, which is overlooked by **Church of San Pedro Claver 2**, named for a Jesuit monk who was canonized 200 years after his death in the mid-1600s for his life's work defending African slaves.

From here it's a short walk to **Plaza Bolivar**, which is the center of the Old City. This shaded park contains an equestrian statue of Simon Bolivar and is where you will find Cartagena's main **Cathedral 3**, the **Palace of the Inquisition 4** with its museums, and the **Gold Museum 5** with an excellent collection of pre-Columbian gold work. Cartagena's historic cathedral was built in 1575 and partially destroyed by Francis Drake in 1586, after which it was fortified to serve as a defensive post.

Close by is the **Church of Santo Domingo 6** – the oldest in the city – which overlooks a lovely square filled with outdoor cafes.

*(Above) The Bell Tower marks the main entrance to the walled Old City. (Below) Spanish colonial architecture lines the streets of Cartagena's Old City.*

Other highlights of a city tour include the fortifications at **Las Bovedas (The Dungeons)** **7**. These arcades, built between two fortresses, were designed as storage vaults and were later used as prison cells during the civil wars of the 19th century. Today they house shops visited by tourists.

Across a bridge from the Old City stands **San Felipe de Barajas** **8**, a massive fort dating back to 1536 and extensively expanded in 1657. The fort is a superb example of Spanish military construction and provides an excellent view of the city, as does the 17th-century monastery at **La Popa Hill** **9**. A winding road leads up the hillside to the monastery, devoted to Saint Monica, and each February 2nd (Saint Monica's Day) the faithful of Cartagena ascend this road on an annual pilgrimage.

Cartagena's beach and hotel strip, the Boca Grande, is directly south of the city's historic core. The upscale **Pierino Gallo Shopping Center** is at the far end of the strip, in between the Hotel Las Velas and the **Hotel Cartagena Hilton**.

*(Above right) 16th-century Church of San Pedro Claver. (Right) A street leading to Cartagena's famous cathedral – Iglesia Santa Catalina.*

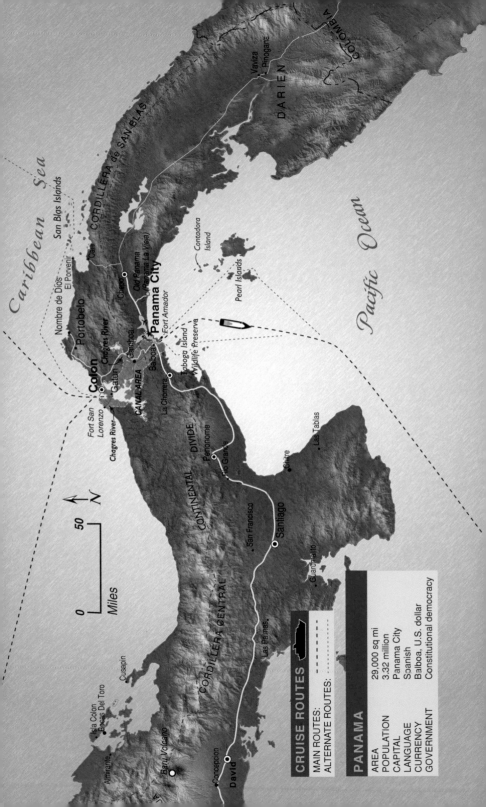

Caribbean Sea

COLOMBIA

Pacific Ocean

San Blas Islands

CORDILLERA de SAN BLAS

VAVIZA

Pinogana

DARIEN

Nombre de Dios
El Porvenir

Cani

Portobelo

Chagres River

Colón

Fort San
Lorenzo

Chagres River

Gatún

CANAL AREA

Chilibre

Old Panama (Panama La Vieja)

Panama City

Fort Amador

Balboa

Contadora
Island

Pearl Islands

Taboga Island
Wildlife Preserve

La Chorrera

CONTINENTAL DIVIDE

Penonomé

Rio Grande

Las Tablas

Chitré

San Francisco

Santiago

CORDILLERA CENTRAL

Guararlito

Las Palmas

Cusapin

Almirante

Isla Colón
Bocas Del Toro

Baru Volcano

Concepción

David

N

50

0

Miles

**CRUISE ROUTES**
MAIN ROUTES: — — —
ALTERNATE ROUTES: ·········

**PANAMA**
AREA          29,000 sq mi
POPULATION    3.32 million
CAPITAL       Panama City
LANGUAGE      Spanish
CURRENCY      Balboa, U.S. dollar
GOVERNMENT    Constitutional democracy

# PANAMA – THE CANAL & THE PORTS

The Panama Canal, carved through dense jungle across the Isthmus of Panama, has created more controversy and intrigue than any other waterway on earth. It took a revolution, endless landslides and the deaths of thousands of workers to construct this man-made wonder linking the Atlantic Ocean with the Pacific. Once of huge importance to the United States for its strategic and economic value, the canal's usefulness faded following World War II when Harry Truman was the first American president to propose "ditching the Big Ditch."

Today the Panama Canal is thriving. Not only is it undergoing expansion with construction of additional locks large enough to accommodate massive cargo ships and mega-cruise liners, the canal has beome a major tourist destination – especially among cruise passengers who line the ship's rail to watch firsthand the incredible sight of their ship being raised 85 feet above sea level in the canal's colossal locks.

The Panama Canal is one of the world's greatest human endeavors. As an engineering achievement it is unparalleled and, situated in a unique and strategic location between the world's two largest oceans, the Panama Canal has exerted a profound influence on world trade patterns since opening in 1914.

*A ship, lifted 85 feet above sea level at Gatun Locks, prepares to move into Gatun Lake.*

A canal transit is a voyage along one of the modern wonders of the world and the beauty of this perpetual-motion machine is its simplicity – using gravity and the region's abundant rainfall. Some might view a transit of this famous waterway as eight hours of slow steaming through a tropical jungle. And, in a way, that is what the builders of the canal wanted – a safe and efficient passage from sea to sea, without incident or delay.

An intriguing aspect of the Panama Canal is its configuration. The isthmus, which connects Central and South America, is actually S-shaped. As a result, a cruise ship travels in a southeasterly direction when going from the Atlantic side to the Pacific side. Upon exiting the canal at Balboa, a ship is actually 23 nautical miles further east than when it started at Limon Bay. The sun, when viewed from the canal, rises over the Pacific and sets over the Atlantic.

Since the locks first opened on August 15, 1914, more than 850,000 vessels have transited the 50-mile-long canal. Currently about 14,000 vessels transit the canal each year, almost 40 a day, and of these nearly 50 percent are Panamax-sized vessels – the largest the waterway can accommodate (the maximum size allowed is 965 feet in length and 106 feet in width). A cruise ship's transit toll (based on passenger capacity) is prepaid through the cruise line's agent. One of the highest tolls ever paid was by the *Norwegian Pearl* in April 2010 when the amount charged was $375,600. The lowest toll ever charged was 36 cents, paid by Richard Halliburton when he swam through the canal in 1928.

The United States, which built the canal after taking over a failed French attempt in 1904, relinquished administrative control of the Canal Zone to Panama in

## Embera Natives

The majority of Panama's Embera Indians live in the sparsely inhabited jungles of Darien province, but a substantial number also live on the shores of Gatun Lake. Their houses, built with cone-shaped roofs made of palm leaves, are erected on stilts about 10 feet above the ground to escape pesky night critters. The Embera build superb dugout canoes with very shallow drafts, called piraguas, and the Panama Canal Authority has purchased a number of these watercraft to access the upper reaches of the Canal's watershed. The U.S. Air Force has also recruited Embera natives to teach jungle survival to its pilots and astronauts at Fort Sherman near Colon.

## PANAMA AT A GLANCE

The Republic of Panama has a population exceeding 3 million. Its capital and largest city is Panama City. The official language is Spanish, although English is widely understood in the urban centers.

Panama's monetary unit is the Balboa (fixed at parity with the US dollar) and American paper money is used throughout Panama. Coins are identical in shape and value to US coins.

The best duty-free shopping for cruisers is at Flamenco Shopping Plaza at the end of the Amador Causeway on the Pacific side of the canal. Local handicrafts can be purchased throughout the Canal Area at shopping malls and outdoor markets. Look for baskets woven by Embera Indians and colorful *molas* (reversed applique patterns) stitched by Kuna Indian women and sewn onto beach bags, shirts and other textiles. As for the Panama hat, this brimmed straw hat is actually made in Ecuador but was once shipped in large quantities through Panama to markets worldwide.

The climate of Panama is pleasantly tropical, with year-round temperatures ranging from 73 to 83 degrees F in coastal areas. The heat, however, can be stifling at mid-day when your ship is passing through Culebra Cut, with temperatures often in the 90s. Panama's average rainfall is 65 inches on the Pacific side and 120 inches on the Atlantic side, most of this falling during the wet season (from May to December) when you can expect showers. During the dry season, the trade winds blow steadily from the southeast.

Panamanian cuisine includes tamales wrapped in plantain leaves, *dorado en salsa de coco* (fish in coconut sauce) and a fried bread called *ojaldas*. Cinnamon tea is popular, as is *cafe con leche* – a frothy cup of coffee made with locally grown beans. Local beers – Soberana, Balboa and Atlas – are light and thirst-quenching.

1999 while retaining the right to defend it in the interest of national security. Since then the canal has been run as a profitable enterprise instead of a public utility, with the citizens of Panama benefiting economically under the terms the treaty their government signed with the United States.

Panama has made changes to the former Canal Zone, now called the **Canal Area**, where investment in tourism has soared and new cruise-ship facilities at Colon and Fort Amador have transformed Panama into an attractive port of call.

The canal is still the big draw, but the country is also one of the world's richest in terms of biodiversity. Panama's rainforests support such an abundance of flora and fauna, the Smithsonian has been conducting tropical research here since 1946. Panama, always a short cut, is now a destination.

## Colon

Built on a swampy island near the canal's Atlantic entrance, Colon is named for Christopher Columbus. Rebuilt in the French colonial style following a fire in 1885, the city was often scourged

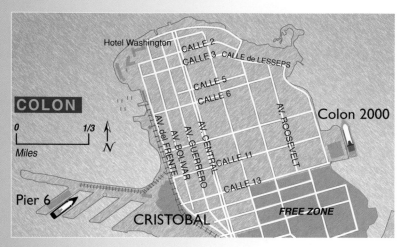

by yellow fever, a situation that prevailed until sanitary work (enclosing sewers and paving streets) was completed by the Americans. Upon completion of the canal, thousands of international workers returned home and Colon – which had been a prosperous and cosmopolitan city – was plunged into a protracted economic decline as its affluent residents moved to Panama City and elsewhere. In an attempt to revive investment, the southeast part of the city in 1948 was turned into a Free Zone. Here traders

*Colon 2000 pier*

from around the world buy and sell at wholesale and avoid paying taxes. This has made Colon one of the world's busiest free ports. With a population of 200,000, Colon is Panama's second largest city, but much of the population lives in slums.

Cruise ships dock at one of two facilities in Colon. **Cristobal Cruise Terminal (Pier 6)** is located in a suburb on the west side of Colon. The port facilities here include a shopping complex and access to local tours. The **Colon 2000 pier** (on the east side of Colon) is located just outside

## Shore Excursions

*Panama*

*(Top) Kayaking on Gatun Lake*

*(Bottom) Fort San Lorenzo*

Whether you ship docks in Colon (Atlantic side) or Fort Amador (Pacific side), numerous companies offer tours throughout the Canal Area. If your ship is making a full transit of the canal with no port stop at either end, you may be able to book a shore excursion involving tenders that take you ashore at one end of the canal and return you to the ship when it emerges from the other end. If your ship is doing a partial transit, you will disembark by tender in Gatun Lake (if you are booked on a shore excursion) and reboard your ship in Colon.

Shore excursions offered from both Colon and Fort Amador include a ride on the railroad that straddles the Isthmus of Panama. Other excursions feature visits to the observation areas at Gatun Locks (Atlantic side) and Miraflores Locks (Pacific side) where the workings of the locks can be viewed up close. This is often combined with other local attractions, such as a tour of Portobelo or of San Lorenzo (which was the fort captured by Henry Morgan in 1671).

Nature tours include the Gamboa Rain Forest Aerial Tram for viewing some of the most renowned rainforest canopy in Central America, and boat tours and kayaking expeditions on island-dotted Gatun Lake. Guided rainforest walks and tours of an Embera native village are also offered.

the Free Zone. This cruise terminal features a duty free mall, crafts boutiques, an internet cafe, lounge areas and restaurants. (An overhead walkway connects the terminal with the shopping complex.) Taxis can be hired at the terminal's central desk and prices are fixed. (The tourism taxis enter the port parking area once the cruise tours have left.) A taxi ride into Colon is about US$3. Places worth visiting include the cathedral on Calle 5, and the restored Washington Hotel where you can enjoy lunch on the terrace while watching ships enter Limon Bay to commence a canal transit.

## Fort Amador

This new cruise port lies at the Pacific entrance to the canal. It is situated at the end of the Amador Causeway, which connects a string of small islands with the mainland and Panama City. (See page 232 for information on the Amador Causeway's attractions and page 231 for information on Panama City.) Taxi drivers looking for a fare will honk; wave to flag one down, and settle on a price at the start of the ride.

# Building the Canal
## The French Attempt

For over a decade, starting in 1880, France was caught up in a heroic attempt to build the Panama Canal. In the face of death and despair, young French engineers stayed on the job and did not flee. Conditions were appalling, even unimaginable to those back home. Poisonous snakes, deadly insects and a suffocating heat combined with tropical humidity and torrential rainfall, made conditions hellish. Floods prevailed during the wet season, and the French engineer Bunau-Varilla reported inspecting the rail line by canoe after one

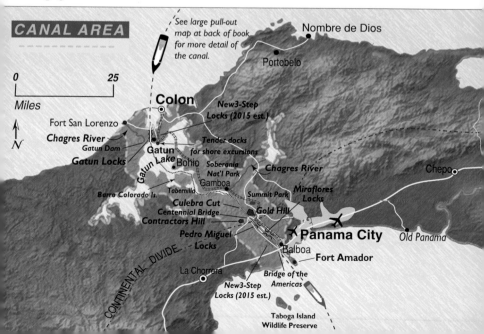

storm and floating past tree tops that were "black with millions of tarantulas."

Death stalked the workers in the form of tropical diseases – cholera, dysentery, malaria and the dreaded yellow fever. The loss of life (especially among laborers from the Caribbean) was staggering. In just 10 years, some 20,000 workers died.

The French attempt at building a canal, led by Ferdinand de Lesseps, was long on enthusiasm but short on the technology needed for such a massive project. The steam shovels used were only a fraction of the size of the later American Bucyrus. At the rate the French were digging, it's been estimated they would have taken 50 years to dig a sea-level canal. The excavated earth and rock (called spoil) was hauled by undersized cars on light-gauge rail to dumping areas too close to the canal, contributing to the slides, and much of the unloading was done by hand.

Perhaps the biggest obstacle was the mindset of de Lesseps, who insisted on building a sea-level canal. Had a lock system been adopted at the beginning, as was suggested by French engineer Godin de Lépinay at a canal congress in 1879, French prospects would have improved. But even then, the canal would have been quickly obsolete because of the small lock size (a width of only 59 feet) the French engineers were contemplating.

When the United States government bought out the French concession to build the Canal for $40 million, it got a partly dug canal from which about 30 million cubic yards of spoil had been removed – barely one tenth of the finished canal's total excavation of 264 million cubic yards. The French had dug a canal 25 feet deep and 70 feet from Colon to Bohio, a distance of 11 miles. They had also lowered the Culebra Cut saddle by over 160 feet and had excavated a small channel from Miraflores to the Pacific. American engineers arriving at Panama marvelled at how much had been accomplished by the French.

In many ways the United States was destined to build this greatest of the world's canals. This immense undertaking meshed with the confident mood and military interests of America, not to mention the expanding economy and ability of the United States to underwrite such a large venture. And, as is often the case, the right man – President Theodore Roosevelt – came along at the right time to make it all happen.

*Unstable soil triggered numerous landslides for the canal workers.*

*(Above) The Panama Canal Railway's station in Colon. (Left) A hostess directs passengers to their railcar. (Below) The passing view of dense jungle from a railcar's observation deck.*

*(Top) The railroad runs parallel
with the canal along Culebra Cut.
(Above) The canal's vessel traffic
can be seen from the railcars.
(Right) A standard car on the
Panama Canal Railway.*

## America Chooses a High-Level Lock Canal

At first the United States wasn't sure what kind of canal should be built. The French had focused their efforts almost entirely on a sea-level canal – similar to their success with the Suez Canal. Digging a long ditch or strait to connect the two oceans would eliminate the need for locks lifting ships up to an intermediate lake. However, as American engineers pondered the task, it became obvious that the effort required to dig a sea-level canal was just too enormous. Chief Engineer George Goethals at one point commented that there wasn't enough money in the world to build a sea-level canal at Panama. There was simply too much earth to excavate. Early estimates predicted it would take double the time and money to built a sea-level canal and, it was emphasized, there was no

*Slides plagued construction near Culebra Cut.*

guarantee a safe navigable canal would be the end result. Even if the ongoing landslides were manageable, the final canal would be a narrow, tortuous channel. And, it was pointed out, at least one lock would be necessary to deal with the difference in water levels due to the Pacific Ocean's large tides.

The greatest challenge, however, was the Chagres River. This was "the lion in the path" of any canal according to one Panama governor. Chief engineer John Stevens stated during Senate hearings that, "The one great problem in the construction of any canal down there is the control of the Chagres River. That overshadows everything else." During the wet season, frequent heavy rains often resulted in spectacular flooding, with the river rising as much as 40 feet in a single day. Such conditions would obliterate canal banks, making navigation difficult, and the strong river currents would make the passage extremely dangerous for ships transiting the tight twisting channel.

A sea-level canal was favored in the American public's mind – on a map it looked easy to cut a trench canal through the narrow isthmus. But to field engineers wading through the sawgrass and the humid heat, it was an impossible and impracticable dream. The vote in favor of a lock canal was very close in the Senate (36 to 31), but this momentous decision proved to be the right one.

## False start leads to success

Although the scale of the project was huge and many of the needed technologies were in their infancy, the mood was upbeat among both American engineers and the general public. However, as American workers arrived in Panama under the leadership of John Wallace (who brought his wife and two metal caskets to Panama), the first steps were tentative. The sheer scale of the project bore down on the engineers who were unsure how to begin or where to start. Within a year morale was low. Panic set in when an epidemic of yellow fever broke out in 1905 and terrified workers filled the ships leaving for the U.S.

At the dismissal of John Wallace, President Theodore Roosevelt found an ideal replacement in John Stevens, who inspired workers and turned the situation around. Stevens was on the scene just a few days, reviewing the canal's progress, when he abruptly ordered all work to stop and began sending thousands of employees home. Stevens, the railwayman who discov-

ered the Marias Pass over the Continental Divide in the Rocky Mountains, saw the challenges he was facing – proper planning and engineering of the project, eradicating disease, and building a smooth organization to execute the plans.

On this last point, Stevens reorganized everything. His first goal was making the canal a "fit" place to live. He built thousands of new houses, mess halls, apartments, offices and warehouses. He brought in shipments of fresh food and sold it to workers in stores or mess halls at cost. Eggs, fresh fruit, even ice cream were available to workers. The health of the workers became a priority and he gave the Sanitation Department carte blanche in ridding the Canal Zone of tropical diseases. Stevens' direct manner

*John Stevens excavated Culebra Cut with an ingenious system that kept rail cars and steam shovels in constant motion.*

and sense of purpose calmed the men and, with morale improved, the planning of the canal's construction moved ahead.

Engineering challenges included the biggest excavation ever attempted by man – one that would ultimately equal three Suez Canals. The project required construction of the largest earth dam ever built; designing the most massive canal locks ever built; constructing the largest gates ever swung; and solving watershed problems of enormous proportions.

By early 1906, with the organization in place and diseases in check, Stevens began calling men from the United States back to the canal. Excavation resumed and, with the United States Senate approving a lock canal in June 1906, the dirt finally began to fly. The planned canal would lift ships 85 feet in three locks (or steps) to a summit-level lake and then lower the ships again to sea level in three more locks.

Plans included building an earth dam to create the world's largest man-made lake extending, halfway across the Isthmus. Gatun Lake's creation was considered a serious challenge, yet construction of the dam went like clockwork, and the bigger engineering challenge proved to be breaching the Continental Divide at Culebra Cut.

As slides continued, excavation at the cut nearly doubled to 100,000,000 cubic yards – an unprecedented excavation, comparable to drilling a 12-foot-square hole through the center of the earth. Nothing like this had been attempted in the engineering history of the world.

The saddle (low point) at Culebra Cut (just north of Gold Hill) was initially 335 feet above sea level. The French had whittled this down to 200 feet, but there was still an estimated 60 million cubic yards of tedious digging to be done throughout the length of the nine-mile-long cut

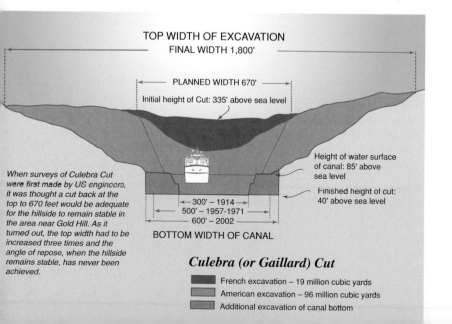

TOP WIDTH OF EXCAVATION
FINAL WIDTH 1,800'

PLANNED WIDTH 670'

Initial height of Cut: 335' above sea level

When surveys of Culebra Cut were first made by US engineers, it was thought a cut back at the top to 670 feet would be adequate for the hillside to remain stable in the area near Gold Hill. As it turned out, the top width had to be increased three times and the angle of repose, when the hillside remains stable, has never been achieved.

Height of water surface of canal: 85' above sea level

Finished height of cut: 40' above sea level

300' – 1914
500' – 1957-1971
600' – 2002

BOTTOM WIDTH OF CANAL

### Culebra (or Gaillard) Cut

French excavation – 19 million cubic yards
American excavation – 96 million cubic yards
Additional excavation of canal bottom

to lower the canal bed to 40 feet above sea level. Engineers first designed this gorge at the saddle to be 200 feet wide at the bottom and about 670 feet wide at the top. However, to attain the necessary angle of repose for the adjacent hill-sides, the bottom had to be widened to 300 feet and the top to more than 1800 feet.

Stevens saw the key to success at the Cut as one of efficiently removing spoil – making sure there was a continuous, smoothly running conveyor of dirt flowing from the cut to safe dump sites. With decades of experience in rail construction in Canada and the U.S., Stevens developed an efficient working "plant" of spoil removal. Flatbed cars were specially designed for ease of loading and unloading. These were brought uphill to the steam shovels where they were loaded and departed downhill.

*(Above) Culebra Cut on a Sunday. Noise levels in the cut were said to be deafening on work days. (Below) SS Ancon marked the official opening of the Canal in 1914.*

## PILOTS AND THE CANAL

Every ship and boat transiting the Panama Canal requires a pilot, and large ships will often have two on board throughout their lock transits. Pilots normally board the ship near the ocean entrances – at the breakwater near Colon on the Atlantic side and at the end of the channel near Naos Island on the Pacific side. The ship's captain and the pilots work together, but it's the pilot who gives the helmsman all navigational orders. While in the locks, the pilot is in constant contact by radio to the locomotive operators and, working in tandem with the ship's captain, tries to ensure the ship does not "touch" the side walls of the locks. (You can usually see the pilot and captain on the bridge wings at this point.) Even the slightest jar of the ship's hull against the concrete walls will scrape off chunks of paint, adding an extra cost to the already expensive Panama transit.

*Pilots use laptop computers which show the exact position of the ship during the canal transit.*

With the help of a laptop computer, electronic charts and the Global Positioning System (which works by satellite), a pilot can tell exactly where the ship is throughout its transit of the canal. The Maritime Traffic Control Center in Balboa sends information about all ships in the canal to the pilot's computer, allowing him to view a "live" map showing the position of all transiting vessels. The pilot can easily find out the time and meeting point with other vessels. Pilots can also monitor the ship's speed, and distances to the canal banks, to other vessels, and to the locks.

On any given day during peak excavation, up to 200 trains a day were running in and out of the Cut. Engineers, track switchers and traffic managers all ensured the system ran smoothly so there was no delay for the empty trains arriving at the steam shovels. Several dump sites became building sites, such as the earth dam at Gatun and the breakwaters on both sides of the canal.

Once the problem of spoil removal was solved, Stevens realized other engineering challenges still lay ahead, namely the design and building of the massive locks, and the complex machinery required for their operation. Even more daunting, perhaps, to a man who had little experience with hydraulic engineering, was the construction of the world's largest earth dam at Gatun to maintain the Gatun Lake level at 85 feet above sea level and to tame the wild Chagres River.

It was at this point, in late 1906, when real progress was apparent and shortly after the successful visit to the canal by President Theodore Roosevelt, that Stevens resigned. The reasons for his resignation remain a mystery but it seems most probable that the work load had become too much. President Roosevelt placed Army engineer Colonel George Goethals in charge, whose great attention to detail saw the Canal to completion. But Goethals always credited Stevens with laying the foundation for building the canal.

Stevens was right about one very important aspect of the canal and that was the need to turn the Chagres River from terrible adversary to useful ally. Whereas the French envisaged digging channels to divert the Chagres away from the canal, or even over the Continental Divide into the Pacific, the Americans understood all this water could be used instead to create a huge man-made lake upon which ships could travel most of the way across the Isthmus. The Chagres became the key to the success of the project or, in Stevens' words, the "servant, instead of the master of the situation." Without Panama's abundant rainfall, without its massive watershed of over 1300 square miles, without its annual supply of new

*Water from Gatun Lake floods into the lock chambers through 100 holes to reduce turbulence when lifting ships.*

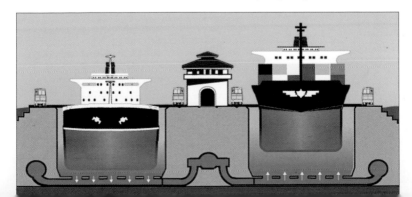

water flowing down the Chagres and its 20 odd tributaries, through some of the wettest real estate in the world, the Panama Canal may have remained a dream even to this day.

On August 3, 1914, the Cristobal was the first oceangoing ship to complete a transit of the canal. By a bizarre twist of fate, World War I broke out the same day and the official opening of the canal two weeks later, transited by the SS Ancon, was something of an anticlimax, the news buried on the back pages behind reports of the war in Europe.

When George Goethals replaced John Stevens as Chief Engineer in 1907, he partitioned the canal work into three divisions – Atlantic, Central and Pacific. The Central Division was charged with clearing a path through the Continental Divide, while the Atlantic and Pacific Divisions were assigned the job of building the massive concrete locks and steel gates needed at each end of the canal. Goethals placed an army engineer, Major William Sibert, in charge of the Atlantic Division and a civilian engineer, Sydney Williamson, in charge of the Pacific Division. As Goethals anticipated, an intense competition developed between the two to see which could be most efficient and competent in the completion of their tasks. In the end, the match proved to be a draw, as the results at both ends of the canal were excellent.

# Cruising the Canal:
## Gatun Locks

Although the Gatun Locks is a unique triple set of locks and is the largest and longest set of locks in the world, it has many aspects in common with the canal's other locks, such as the miter gates and operating mechanisms. Each lock

*Side wall of Gatun Locks compared to a six-storey building. Publications at the time emphasized the scale of the locks.*

is 110 feet wide, 1,000 feet in length and can hold a ship up to a maximum of 106 feet in width and 965 feet in length. Each also has the ability to section itself into a smaller lock depending on the size of the ship. The locks were built in pairs to accommodate passing traffic. One variation between the Atlantic and Pacific locks is the height of their gates. The Pacific side locks were built to accommodate a tidal range of 20 feet. Ships that existed in 1909, when the locks were designed, had plenty of room, but today's large cruise ships clear the lock walls with inches to spare.

The locks, whether on the Pacific or Atlantic side, use water from Gatun Lake; no pumps are needed – the whole system is gravity-fed with lake water entering huge 18-foot-high culverts running the length of the center and side walls of each lock. The water leads into a system of cross-culverts under the lock floors to rapidly fill the lock. Each cross-culvert has five openings for a total of 100 holes in each chamber floor for water to enter or drain, depending on which valves are opened or closed. This large number of openings distributes the water evenly over the lock floor to control turbulence while the lock is being filled.

All movement of water is handled by the operators in the red-roofed control building in the center of each of the locks. Here a control board with a waist-high working representation of the locks shows the operator what is taking place. Everything that happens in the locks happens

*(Above) An archival shot of a canal worker inspecting Gatun Locks. (Below) View of a lock during maintenance.*

on the control board at precisely the same time. The switches to work the lock gates are located beside the representation of that device on the control board. To lift a huge ocean-going ship in a lock chamber, the operator has only to turn a small chrome handle. Another ingenious part of the system are elaborate racks of interlocking bars below the control board to make the switches mechanically interlock. Each handle must be turned in proper sequence or it will not turn. This eliminates doing anything out of order or forgetting a step, ensuring safe operation.

Whether you enter the Panama Canal from the Atlantic or Pacific side, your ship is raised by water which has already lifted two other ships through the two locks ahead of you. To save water from Gatun Lake, it is reused by draining into each successive lock, lifting a ship each time. At Gatun, each lock, is a 28-foot rise and it takes

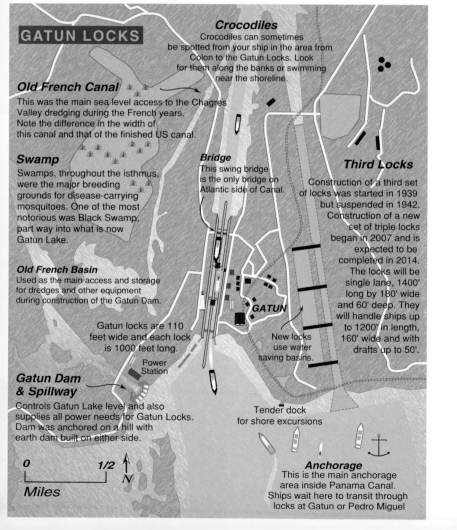

**GATUN LOCKS**

**Crocodiles**
Crocodiles can sometimes be spotted from your ship in the area from Colon to the Gatun Locks. Look for them along the banks or swimming near the shoreline.

**Old French Canal**
This was the main sea level access to the Chagres Valley dredging during the French years. Note the difference in the width of this canal and that of the finished US canal.

**Swamp**
Swamps, throughout the isthmus, were the major breeding grounds for disease-carrying mosquitoes. One of the most notorious was Black Swamp, part way into what is now Gatun Lake.

**Bridge**
This swing bridge is the only bridge on Atlantic side of Canal.

**Third Locks**
Construction of a third set of locks was started in 1939 but suspended in 1942. Construction of a new set of triple locks began in 2007 and is expected to be completed in 2014. The locks will be single lane, 1400' long by 180' wide and 60' deep. They will handle ships up to 1200' in length, 160' wide and with drafts up to 50'.

**Old French Basin**
Used as the main access and storage for dredges and other equipment during construction of the Gatun Dam.

Gatun locks are 110 feet wide and each lock is 1000 feet long.

**GATUN**

New locks use water saving basins.

Power Station

**Gatun Dam & Spillway**
Controls Gatun Lake level and also supplies all power needs for Gatun Locks. Dam was anchored on a hill with earth dam built on either side.

Tender dock for shore excursions

0　　1/2　↑
|_____|　N

**Miles**

**Anchorage**
This is the main anchorage area inside Panama Canal. Ships wait here to transit through locks at Gatun or Pedro Miguel

about 10 minutes to bring a ship up to the next lock in the system. For large cruise ships, 52 million gallons of water are used to transit the canal – equal to a one-day supply for a city of 100,000.

One of the great innovations of the locks was the use of electricity in operating motors, valves, lock gates and the unique electric towing locomotives (known as mules) which help keep ships in position. Designed by Edward Schildhauer, the locomotives work on tracks built atop the lock walls. Operating at a speed of about two miles per hour with a towing pull of 70,000 pounds, these locomotives were specially designed to travel the 45-degree incline between the lock chambers. The original cost for each one was $13,000. Today, new mules cost $2 million each.

During construction of the Gatun Locks, concerns were raised about the foundation on which the massive triple-lock structure would rest. Built with two million cubic yards of concrete, each 1000-foot-long lock is a huge structure which, if stood on end, would compare with the tallest buildings of the modern world. Even lying flat as they do, the walls of the locks are taller than a six-storey building. Each lock floor is between 12 and 20 feet thick and the total length of the Gatun triple locks, including the center guide walls, is over a mile. If any uneven settling had taken place, the locks might have cracked but hasn't happened.

Numerous borings were taken in the area and it was found the underlying shale-like material was superb as a base for the locks.

## WEIGHING IN ON CONCRETE

Until the late 1800s, concrete had been little used in building, and then mostly for floors and basements. There was still a great deal to be learned in the science of concrete production, which requires specific, controlled measurements of water with cement and sand. The concrete work in Panama was an unprecedented challenge that would stand unequalled in total volume until construction of the Boulder Dam in the 1930s. So much cement was used, Goethals estimated saving $50,000 just by shaking out each bag. In spite of the newness of the science, the results were extraordinary. After nearly a hundred years of service, the concrete of the Canal's locks and dams remains in excellent condition, a fact regarded by modern engineers as one of the most astounding aspects of the entire Canal.

*Huge cantilevered cranes were used at the Pacific Division to pour concrete.*

*(Above) Arrow confirms lane to pilot. (Middle) Mules help guide a ship forward. (Bottom) Water flowing from Gatun Lake lifts the ships.*

Chief Engineer Stevens said early in the construction that "if nature had intended triple locks there she could not have arranged matters better." It was crucial for the integrity of the entire canal that the bedrock extending from Gatun Locks to the hills west of Gatun Dam be absolutely stable and impervious to water and this, fortunately, turned out to be the case.

It took four years to build the locks once the first concrete was poured at Gatun on August 24, 1909. These were four intense years of planning, preparing the site, building steel-and-wood forms to mold the thousands of tons of concrete, and organizing a complex overhead system of pouring the concrete into the molds. The sand came from Nombre de Dios and the gravel came from Portobelo, where a large crushing plant was built and where Sir Francis Drake, who died of dysentery in 1595, still lies offshore in a lead casket.

A small automatic railway brought the appropriate amounts of gravel, sand and cement to a location near the Gatun spillway where the concrete was mixed. When the concrete was ready to be

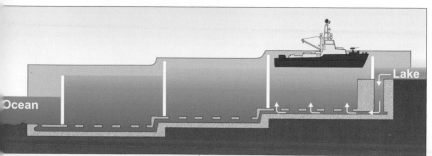

poured, large buckets carrying six tons of concrete were whisked upwards by an overhead cableway. Suspended 85 feet above the ground and travelling at a speed of 20 miles an hour, the buckets were raced to the locks and lowered to the men below who would evenly spread the concrete. The whole system – the gigantic cableway towers and large steel forms – was on tracks and as the work progressed, the entire structure was moved forward.

Three locks are used at each end of the canal (rather than one or two) to provide a wide margin of safety. A single lock holding back a 130-foot-high head of water (depth of channel plus 85-foot height of Gatun Lake) would be dangerous. If the gates ever gave way, through a fault in the structure or by a ship collision, the results would be catastrophic for the ship, those on board, and the entire canal. The risks of gate failure are greatly reduced by having three locks and each with the added precaution of double gates.

The gates, the canal's most dra-

*(Above) Two Holland America ships proceed into Gatun Lake from Gatun Locks. (Below) Passengers watch as their ship, with lines connected to a mule, is raised in the Gatun Locks.*

*Coral Princess emerges from the Gatun Locks. The old French basin is in background.*

## The Third Set of Locks

The canal has been, to some extent, a victim of its own success. Because it offers such an efficient short-cut between the Pacific and Atlantic oceans, an increasing demand for its use has prompted the government to add another lane for larger ships. This project is expected to be completed in 2015.

The new lock chambers will be larger than the existing locks at 1400' long by 180' wide by 60' deep (as compared to 1000' by 110' by 50') which would accommodate the largest cruise ships currently sailing. Also, the new locks will use rolling gates instead of miter gates, allowing for a quicker turnover for the use of the lock, and will use tugboats instead of locomotives.

The new locks will be beside the Gatun Locks on the Atlantic side and the Miraflores Locks on the Pacific side. The locks at the Pacific side will be in a single set of three steps, eliminating the need for a single-step lock at the existing Pedro Miguel locks.

matic moving parts, swing like double doors, closing in a shallow V with the pressure of the rising water helping to seal the gates. The gates weigh several hundred tons each but are nearly weightless in water due to the lower half being a hollow watertight compartment. Not only does this greatly reduce the strain on the gate hinges but requires only a small 40 horsepower electric motor to open and close each gate leaf. The leaves are 65 feet wide by seven feet thick. However, they vary in height from 47 to 82 feet, depending on their position. The lower gates of Miraflores Locks are the highest due to the extreme variation of Pacific Ocean tides.

Upon approaching the Gatun Locks from the Caribbean, a ship is directed to one of the two canal lanes by a large green arrow at the front of the center wall facing the bow of the ship. This arrow is a visual confirmation of orders the pilot has received. Rowboats approach the ships to receive lines and send aboard heavy steel towing cables from the electric locomotives (mules) which are then attached to the ship.

The ship eases into the first lock and by this point will be secured to six to eight mules. It is slowly pulled forward by the mules, and the pilot and captain work in tandem to position the ship in the lock during its upward lift. When the water in the first lock equalizes the level of the next lock, the gates slowly swing open and the ship is pulled into the next lock. After being 'locked' three times, a cruise ship has been lifted 85 feet to Gatun Lake, which marks the start of a beautiful cruise past the tropical rainforest surrounding the lake.

## Gatun Dam

The Gatun Dam, extending westward from Gatun Locks across the Chagres Valley, is connected to hills a mile and half away. A small solid hill right in the middle of the Chagres Valley provided the anchoring point for the concrete portion of the dam, with a spillway laid in a cut made through the hill. This spillway is half a mile from the locks and easily spotted as you are leaving or approaching Gatun Locks. This spillway controls the height of Gatun Lake and also provides most of the power for the canal.

As with the Gatun Locks, some politicians and the public were apprehensive about the dam's strength during its construction. Just 20 years earlier, the Johnstown Flood disaster in Pennsylvania had claimed 2,200 lives after an earthen dam gave way. The Gatun Dam was huge, over 8,000 feet long and 105 feet high, making it the largest earth dam on record, but the engineers were confident this dam would hold and testified in great detail as to the dam's strengths. Extensive rock 'toes' positioned half a mile apart ran along the front and back edge of the dam. Hydraulic fill (a clay-like material impervious to water) was laid on top and thousands of trainloads of spoil from Culebra Cut were dumped on top of this to bring the final height of the dam to 105 feet above sea level – 20 feet above the normal level of Gatun Lake.

During construction, one U.S. senator wondered if Gatun Dam would be strong enough to bear the water pressure from the wide expanse of Gatun Lake. It was explained to him that water pressure is determined by the height of the water and not the width. Otherwise, it was pointed out, how was it that the dikes in Holland can hold back the Atlantic Ocean.

*Gatun Dam, unprecedented in size when built, created the world's largest man-made lake.*

*(Top) A cruise ship nears the entrance to Bohio Reach.*
*(Above) A view from the ship's bridge shows the close proximity of the shoreline.*
*(Below) Dawn Princess rounds Barro Colorado Island.*

In 1977, the Canal Commission initiated dam inspections under the coordination of the Engineering Division to assure that all three dams – Gatun, Miraflores and Madden – remain in good, safe working condition. Gatun Dam is presently being monitored for the effects of vibrations caused by recent tremors and, so far, the dam shows no sign of instability.

## Gatun Lake

In 1912, upon completion of Gatun Dam, the Chagres River began to slowly fill its valley. It took almost two years for the water level to reach its planned height of 85 feet above sea level, with the new Gatun Lake covering an area of 164 square miles, equal in size to Barbados.

Gatun Lake became the largest man-made lake in the world and it extended from Gatun to the Pedro Miguel Locks – a distance of 32 miles. Dozens of small villages vanished and scores of small islands were created. The world now contains more than 30 man-made lakes larger than Gatun Lake, but it was over 20 years before it had to give up its title.

When the lake first started to form, Canal workers warned local natives of the dangers but many refused to leave their homes and eventually had to be evacuated. In one case, a flood caused a rapid rise and a police launch was sent to a house near Lion Hill. The house was nearly submerged in water and police approached an elderly native and his family resting in a *cayuca* moored to the roof. "Don't you know that the lake is going to cover your house?" asked the anxious police. The old man, unperturbed, replied, "That's the same old story the French told my dad thirty years ago."

Damming the Chagres Valley greatly diminished the cost and effort of excavation north of the Continental Divide and it also tamed the wild "lion" that had been the nemesis of the French. With the dam in place, the Chagres could rage and flood all it wanted, for the additional water merely flowed into Gatun Lake, which might increase a foot or more in height but could easily be regulated at the spillway of the Gatun Dam. In addition to supplying the means for ships to cross the Isthmus, Gatun Lake (and Madden Lake) provide for the electrical needs of the Canal, and drinking water for the cities of Panama and Colon.

To keep a close eye on water levels, ACP installed monitoring stations throughout the lake after the El Nino weather phenomenon in 1998 caused the worst drought in the history of the Canal.

Ensuring adequate water for the canal is essential, and increasing the capacity of the lake by making it deeper is one measure that's been taken in the past. The navigational channel in Gatun Lake has been deepened to reduce draft restrictions and improve water supply, and other measures include legislation defining the boundaries of the watershed to guarantee its conservation.

As your ship transits Gatun Lake, you will likely spot a variety of bird life and possibly a crocodile as you weave past numerous islands. Places of interest include:

**Black Swamp** – This infamous nemesis of pirates trying to cross the Isthmus to Panama City was reported to be bottomless. During construction of the Panama Rail Road a large amount of fill was needed to create a secure rail bed (bottom was finally found at 185 feet below ground surface). Despite

*Looking north to channels leading to Gatun Lake from Tabernilla.*

the best efforts of the rail line, the roadbed kept sinking and required yearly maintenance. The canal goes right over the former Black Swamp just south of Tiger Island.

**Orchid Island** – The most beautiful orchids in the Panama rainforest grew near the top of the largest trees and were difficult to reach. As Gatun Lake rose, however, workers and their wives would row out in small boats to the dying trees and pick off the pretty orchids. Orchids are plentiful on this island.

**Bohio** – Originally known as Bohio Soldado ('Home of the Soldier'), this site was first considered by French and American engineers for building a dam to stop the Chagres River. The French excavated a canal, 25 feet deep and 70 wide, from Gatun to this point and the underlying rock looked promising. However, engineers decided the location at Gatun was better both for the bedrock and because the resulting

*Lush vegetation on islands in Gatun Lake show the dense jungle workers had to deal with.*

lake would be far larger, providing more capacity for controlling the Chagres.

**Barro Colorado Island** – This largest of the lake islands was set aside as a nature reserve by the U.S. Government in 1923 and is an important living laboratory for the Smithsonian Institute of Tropical Research. Almost 400 bird species live here as well as 102 mammal species and 1,316 plant species. Previously only research scientists were allowed on the island, but tour operators now take visitors on day trips along its nature trails.

**Soberania National Park** – This tropical rainforest is a major recreational park covering over 50,000 acres and extending half way across the Isthmus. Among the many hiking trails is a section of the old Las Cruces Trail used in early Spanish times to transport gold and supplies between Panama City and Nombre de Dios and Portobelo. The park is home to numerous species of birds and other wildlife

**Barbacoas Island** – A native Indian word meaning 'bridge',

Barbacoas was an important point in the transit of the Isthmus in the days of the Panama Rail Road. A massive wrought-iron bridge 600 feet in length was erected on stone piers to carry the rail line across the Chagres River at the southwest side of what is now Barbacoas Island. However, during Ferdinand de Lesseps' first visit to Panama in 1879, this bridge was washed out and he and his entourage were forced to cross what was left of the bridge on foot. Although this should have been a clear warning to de Lesseps about the power of the Chagres, he made no mention of this to his investors back in France when he reported on his trip.

**Malachin** – Chinese rail workers, suffering the melancholia effects of malaria, committed suicide here en masse in the mid-19th century.

**Gamboa** – This small town remains an important hub for canal and tug maintenance, and has become a vibrant tourism destination for its nearby rainforest and aerial tram. This is where the Chagres River enters Gatun Lake and you can easily see the rail and highway causeway cross the mighty Chagres near the canal. Two of the world's largest industrial cranes, confiscated from Nazi Germany following World War II, are perched at the edge of the town and attract mechanical engineers from around the world. Just to the south of the Chagres causeway is where a large earth dike was built to divert the river away from the excavation work in Culebra Cut. On a few occasions during the wet season, the river would breach the dike and flood the canal, leaving equipment, steam shovels and rail track under many feet of water. In October 1913, upon completion of the dry excavation at Culebra Cut, President Woodrow Wilson pushed a button in Washington and through a signal relayed by telegraph wire from Washington to Panama, the dike was blown apart and the canal flooded so that dredges could complete the final excavation.

**Madden Dam** – Located on the Chagres River, this dam was constructed in 1935 to further assist in the control of the Chagres and provide additional electrical power for the canal. The large reservoir behind the dam also helps maintain the water level in Gatun Lake during dry season. The dam is 974 feet long and 223 feet high. It was named in honor of Martin B. Madden, a member of the U.S. House of Representatives from Illinois.

*Huge cranes can be seen at Gamboa, which has become a popular ecotourism destination.*

**Canopy Tower** – During the Cold War, the United States Air Force built a three-storey cylindrical tower as part of its intercontinental defense. The tower is now used by the ACP as a communications outpost and a popular eco-lodge. It includes a small museum devoted to the local wildlife and the history of the former military site. The tower has great views over the canal and some of best rainforest in Panama. Canopy Tower is rated by Audubon Magazine as one of the top eco-lodges in the world.

**Summit Botanical Gardens & Zoo** – A few miles beyond Gamboa is this important refuge for the endangered harpy eagle, Panama's national bird. This is one of the largest members of the hawk family, reaching a height of 38 inches. Known by the Aztecs as the winged wolf, the harpy eagle eats macaws and sloths, and

*The infamous Cucaracha Slide on both sides of the canal, kept delaying the Canal's completion.*

was named after the winged monsters of Greek mythology. The botanical gardens were created in 1923 to introduce tropical plants from around the world to Panama and contains some 15,000 plant species.

## Culebra Cut

This nine-mile section, from Gamboa to Pedro Miguel locks, was the main engineering challenge throughout 40 years of construction effort by the French and Americans. Culebra, meaning snake, referred to the Rio Obispo valley north of Gold and Contractor Hills and represented the best pass across the Continental Divide from Gamboa to the Pacific. The actual saddle of the Continental Divide would today be approximately on a line between Gold Hill and Contractors Hill. Water north of this point drained into the Atlantic Ocean and south of this point all water drained into the Pacific Ocean.

Culebra Hill itself is an ancient volcanic core of solid basalt and

the valley soil is an unstable mix of granite, sedimentary rock, shales and many forms of clay which had the tedious ability to stick to everything – especially shovels. The clay when wet, however, would turn into a substance like putty or peanut butter and could flow like a glacier down the slopes and bury months of work in just a few days. The worst of these gravity slides occurred just south of Gold Hill at Cucaracha where, on one occasion in 1907, 500,000 cubic yards slipped into the canal. Miles of track were lost in such slides and steam shovels were buried so deep that only the tips of their cranes were visible. By 1912 Cucaracha had dumped some three million additional cubic yards of material into the canal, all of which had to be removed.

Break slides were even more destructive. These resulted when unstable rock formations lost the lateral support of earth that had been excavated. The first sign would be cracks in the ground along the rim of the cut. What was so unnerving about these slides

*(Above) The depths of Culebra Cut in 1913, where more dynamite was used than in all previous wars of the U.S. combined. (Below) Ships navigate past Gold Hill following the East Culebra Slide in 1915. This view is looking north between Gold Hill and Contractors Hill.*

*The junction of the Chagres River and the canal near Gamboa, viewed from the Gamboa Rainforest Aerial Tram.*

was there was no telling when the next one would occur. It might be weeks, months or even years before an entire slope suddenly collapsed – often in a matter of hours. The worst of these break slides was on the west bank of the cut where some six million cubic yards of earth dropped into the canal during the summer of 1912.

Work along the bottom of the Cut was hell. In the dry season, temperatures were usually in the range of 100 degrees Fahrenheit; in the wet season everything was mud. The noise of steam shovels, trains and blasting was deafening. More dynamite was used during construction of the canal than in all previous wars of the United States combined, and many workers were killed by premature detonations, one of which killed 23 men.

Since the completion of the canal, Culebra Cut has been widened in straight sections from 300 to 500 feet, and further increased to 600 feet in 2002. The cut is also

widely known as Gaillard Cut, named in honor of the Central Division's Chief Engineer, David du Bose Gaillard. In 1913, Gaillard suddenly became incoherent while on the job and, upon returning to New York, died of a brain tumor a few months later.

**Empire** – Situated on the west bank overlooking Culebra Cut, Empire was the location of Central Division headquarters during construction. Every piece of equipment – train cars, steam shovels and even the rock drills – was coordinated with the use of a large map. Schools and most of the housing for the division were located here.

**Culebra** – This was an employee townsite where the main corps of engineers lived during the construction of the canal. At the completion of the canal, Culebra was dismantled and the buildings moved to Ancon.

**Gold Hill** – In the words of Major Sibert, "Gold Hill is a hard trap rock with a volcanic neck extending down to an unknown depth and is there to stay." This hill, the highest point of the eastern side of Culebra Cut, got its name from the assertion of the

French canal company that the hill was full of gold, enough to pay for the total cost of the canal's construction. There was no gold, although cruise passengers can still see streaks of rust along the face of this terraced hill.

**Contractors Hill** – Situated on the west side of Culebra Cut, Contractors Hill got its name from the early days of French excavation when, despite many attempts by numerous contractors who were paid large amounts of money, the hill never seemed to lessen in size. This hill was the high point on the west side of Culebra Cut and was connected to Gold Hill with a saddle-like ridge. Over the

*(Above) Pacific-bound in Culebra Reach, with East Culebra Slide to left and Gold Hill directly ahead. (Below) The Continental Divide.*

years both this hill and Gold Hill have been cut down to minimize slides. Since 1915, about 40 feet has been removed from the top of this hill, which is now about 370 feet above sea level.

**Paraiso** – Originally a native village, this was the site of many slides – one of which fell so suddenly the grass was still intact on top of the slide as it landed on the bottom of the canal

## Pacific Side Locks

**Pedro Miguel Lock** (See Gatun Locks for detail about the lock operations.) – U.S. engineers first thought the Pacific locks would be built in an area near present-day Balboa – adjacent to Sosa Hill. As events transpired it was found that the substrata was not adequate and it was also thought the locks would be vulnerable to enemy ships. So, for both engineering and military reasons, the Pacific locks were moved three miles further north to Miraflores and Pedro Miguel.

Pedro Miguel is about a mile and a half from Miraflores Locks, separated by Miraflores Lake, and is a single lock. It is unique in that the lock lift here is 31 feet as opposed to 28 feet at each step of the Gatun Locks and 27 feet each (without tide consideration) at the two steps at Miraflores. The additional water volume from this lock is discharged over the spillway at Miraflores. The terrain at Pedro Miguel and Miraflores is not

*(Left) A solid core tusk is all that remains of Gold Hill. (Below) The new Centennial Bridge, completed in 2004, is just west of Gold Hill.*

open, like that at Gatun, so during construction a suspended cable way wasn't possible for the pouring of concrete. Pacific Division Engineer Sydney Williamson instead used enormous cantilever cranes, so large they could be seen from miles away, which could move about on tracks inside the locks and were used to pour 2.4 million yards of concrete.

There has been some conjecture whether it was a blunder not to combine all three locks at Miraflores, similar to that at Gatun. But Goethals concluded the bedrock was not adequate for triple locks and the additional concrete needed was too costly. Critics have since said that this has resulted in a bottleneck at this side of the canal, although ACP statistics point to the biggest backups at the Atlantic side.

**Miraflores Lake** – The small depression between Pedro Miguel and Miraflores became an intermediate lake and was planned as

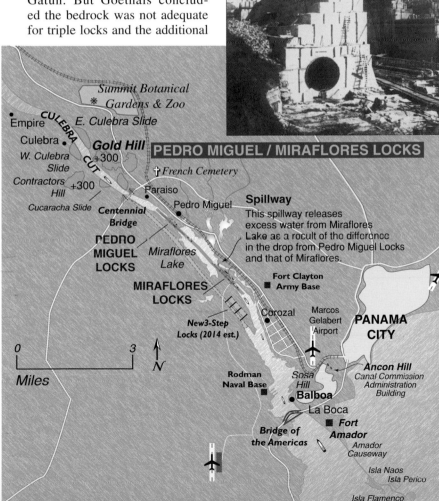

PEDRO MIGUEL / MIRAFLORES LOCKS

Summit Botanical Gardens & Zoo

Empire

CULEBRA CUT

E. Culebra Slide

Culebra

W. Culebra Slide

Gold Hill +300

Contractors Hill +300

Cucaracha Slide

Centennial Bridge

Paraiso

French Cemetery

Pedro Miguel

**Spillway**
This spillway releases excess water from Miraflores Lake as a result of the difference in the drop from Pedro Miguel Locks and that of Miraflores.

PEDRO MIGUEL LOCKS

Miraflores Lake

MIRAFLORES LOCKS

New 3-Step Locks (2014 est.)

Fort Clayton
Army Base

Corozal

Marcos Gelabert Airport

**PANAMA CITY**

Rodman Naval Base

Sosa Hill

Balboa

La Boca

Ancon Hill
Canal Commission Administration Building

Fort Amador

Bridge of the Americas

Amador Causeway

Isla Naos
Isla Perico

Isla Flamenco

0    3

Miles

N

a temporary anchorage. Although ships occasionally do anchor here, almost all traffic continues straight on. A filtration plant is located here, supplying drinking water for the city of Panama. The lake is about a mile and a half long and half a mile wide.

**Miraflores Dam & Spillway** – Located just east of Miraflores Locks, this concrete structure was built in 1914 to control the excess discharge from Pedro Miguel

*(Above) Pedro Miguel Locks.*
*(Below) The Pacific Ocean side of Miraflores Locks has the tallest gates of all the locks.*

Locks and the runoff from the Cocoli River on the west side of the Miraflores Lake. The dam extends from the locks west to the river.

**Miraflores Locks** (See Pedro Miguel and Gatun locks for more detail.) – These southernmost double locks can have the biggest lift of any of the canal locks because of the extreme tidal fluctuations of the Pacific. The maximum lift for these locks can be as much as 65 feet at low water. Miraflores' lower lock gates are the heaviest and largest, built to accommodate the Pacific tides; each gate weighs 745 tons and is 82 feet high. Depending on the state of the tide, this lift can be the largest in the canal (up to about 38 feet) or the least (at about 18 feet). A viewing platform at Miraflores gives visitors a chance to see the locks in action and is especially busy on Sundays. There is a swing bridge at the south end of the locks which was opened in May 1942 and provided cars and trucks with a permanent way to cross the Canal.

**Balboa** – During canal construction some 22 million cubic yards of fill was dumped into a swamp below Ancon Hill, resulting in a reclamation of 676 acres.

This site was actually named La Boca right up to 1909 when a visiting ambassador from Peru suggested to Goethals that he honor the discoverer of the Pacific by renaming the town Balboa, and Goethals promptly complied.

The permanent Administration Building was located at Balboa, and the best buildings from Culebra and Empire were moved around it. Balboa continues to serve as the main fueling and maintenance yard not only for canal vessels but occasionally for cruise ships which may refuel here on cruises from Alaska to the Caribbean.

*Transiting vessels are monitored at the administration building on Ancon Hill near Panama City.*

**Bridge of the Americas** – Almost a mile in length, this bridge provides a highway connection between Panama and Central America. Built in 1962, the bridgedeck is almost 400 feet above the Canal.

**Panama City** – After the destruction of Old Panama in 1671 by Captain Henry Morgan, the Spanish moved their city to a location below Ancon Hill which is surrounded by water on three sides. This small city was almost forgotten by the Spanish in the 18th century when, after repeated pirate attacks on Portobelo, they gave up on their trans-Isthmian route and began shipping gold directly to Spain via Cape Horn. Upon completion of the canal, the city population had reached 30,000 – about what it was at the time of Morgan's visit.

Since 1915 Panama City has grown steadily and its present population of 700,000 resides in an area extending from the Canal

to the old city. Old Panama has very little left from the days of pillage at the hands of Captain Morgan. Most of the city was built over by sprawling residential structures in the 1950s and it wasn't until the mid 1970s that the government protected the ruins by declaring them a protected historic site.

The original city core, Casco Viejo ('old compound') contains some 17th-century Spanish buildings, notably Santo Domingo Church with its famous flat arch. Some French colonial influence is also reflected in the city's architecture, such as the former canal administration building, now housing the Interoceanic Canal Museum. This building faces the famous Plaza de la Independencia which was the scene, on November 3, 1903, of Panama's peaceful revolution and birth as a country.

**Ancon Hill** – During the canal's construction, both the French and Americans located

*Miraflores Spillway controls the water level between Pedro Miguel and Miraflores Locks. (Below) Panama City's modern skyline.*

a hospital for sick workers here. The Panama Canal Authority Administration building now sits atop Ancon Hill (see photo, page 231) at the Pacific entrance to the canal. Ancon Hill is also where rock was quarried and crushed for use in concrete mix for the Pacific locks. Its conspicuous bald top can be seen for miles out at sea.

**Amador Causeway** – This recently developed tourist strip of beaches, hotel resorts and shopping plazas began as a breakwater constructed in 1912 to prevent the canal entrance from filling in with silt. The causeway connects the mainland with four small islands – Culebra, Naos, Perico and Flamenco. The most seaward of the four is Isla Flamenco, location of the **Fort Amador Cruise Port**. Facilities at this terminal include a shopping complex and transportation links to the Panama Rail Road and other area attractions. (See Shore Excursions on page 201.)

A few blocks from the cruise terminal is the new **Bridge of Life Museum**, designed by Frank Gehry and operated in partnership with the Smithsonian Tropical Research Institute. The Smithsonian also operates the Punta Culebra Marine Exhibition Center on Noa Island (which features a touching pool and tropical dry forest trails) as well as a research center on Barro Colorado Island in Gatun Lake.

The United States established Fort Amador (on the mainland) and Fort Grant (encompassing the four islands) to guard the canal's Pacific entrance. In the late 1920s two 14-inch guns with a 30-mile range were mounted on rail carriages and, in the event of an attack, could be quickly moved to either side of the Isthmus. The tracks for moving the guns are still visible on Culebra Island, which was turned into Culebra Point by the causeway's construction.

**Taboga Islands** – Located to the west of the canal's Pacific Ocean entrance, these islands were used as a base by pirates raiding Panama, including Morgan and Drake. During the French attempt to build the canal, workers who contracted malaria or yellow fever were moved to a large sanitarium on the largest of these islands. Today, they are a popular recreational spot for locals and tourists.

**Pearl Islands** – Some ships spend a day in the Gulf of Panama cruising by these islands, one of which (Contadora) was once home to the exiled Shah of Iran in 1979.

*(Above) The Frank Gehry-designed Bridge of Life Museum. (Below) Independence Square in the old part of Panama City.*

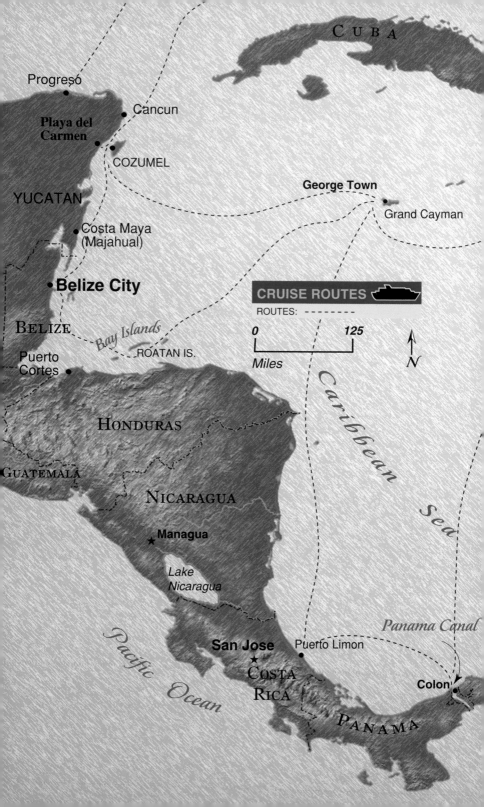

CUBA

Progreso

Cancun

**Playa del Carmen**

COZUMEL

George Town

Grand Cayman

YUCATAN

Costa Maya
(Majahual)

**Belize City**

Bay Islands

ROATAN IS.

BELIZE

Puerto
Cortes

HONDURAS

GUATEMALA

NICARAGUA

Managua ★

Lake
Nicaragua

Caribbean Sea

CRUISE ROUTES

ROUTES: - - - - - - -

0                    125

Miles

N

Panama Canal

Pacific Ocean

San Jose ★

COSTA
RICA

Puerto Limon

Colon

PANAMA

# CENTRAL AMERICA

The dark jungles and misty volcanic peaks of Central America have long fascinated the rest of the world. Hidden waterfalls, exotic birds and fragrant flowers all flourish in the region's tropical rainforests, as do brilliant butterflies, tree frogs, spider monkeys and jaguars.

This mountainous region is a land bridge between North and South America, and it encompasses seven small nations and a variety of ecosystems – from coastal mangroves to cloud-covered summits. It was once part of El Mundo Maya (The Maya World) which thrived for 3,000 years, its territory extending from Mexico's Yucatan peninsula (which includes Belize and northern Guatemala) into El Salvador and Honduras.

The ancient Maya civilization was ahead of its time. Not only did the Maya develop a written language and advanced mathematical and astronomical systems, they left a legacy of monumental architecture and intricate art. When this great civilization suddenly collapsed, its sacred civic centers were mysteriously abandoned and left eerily empty to be consumed by the surrounding jungle.

The Maya did not completely disappear, however, and were living in independent states throughout their region when the Spanish Conquest of the region began with the arrival in 1522 of the conquistador Gonzalez de Avila.

Today the Maya form sizeable communities throughout the region, where women living in mountain villages still weave cloth on backstrap looms, brocading multi-colored yarns into chenille wool or cotton to create eye-catching wraps and shawls. Traditional tunics, called *huipils*, are embroidered with colorful patterns inspired by Maya mythology and reflecting a culture with direct links to antiquity.

*(Below) A Guatemalan weaver heads to market with her wares in Antigua.*

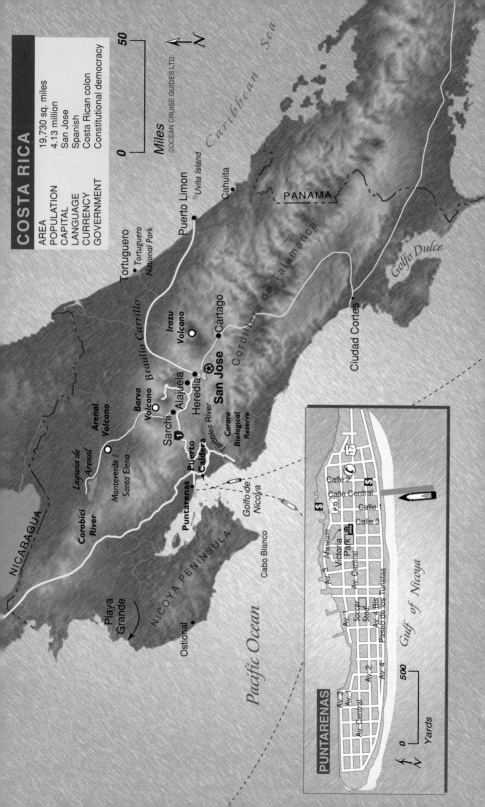

## COSTA RICA

| | |
|---|---|
| AREA | 19,730 sq. miles |
| POPULATION | 4.13 million |
| CAPITAL | San Jose |
| LANGUAGE | Spanish |
| CURRENCY | Costa Rican colon |
| GOVERNMENT | Constitutional democracy |

Miles

0          50

N

©OCEAN CRUISE GUIDES LTD.

Caribbean Sea

PANAMA

Golfo Dulce

Uvita Island

Puerto Limon

Cahuita

Tortuguero
• Tortuguero
National Park

Cordillera de Talamanca

Irazu
Volcano

Ciudad Cortes

Braulio Carrillo

Cartago

San Jose

Barva
Volcano

Alajuela
Heredia

Carara
Biological
Reserve

Arenal
Volcano

Sarchi

Tarcoles River

Puerto
Caldera

Laguna de
Arenal

Monteverde /
Santa Elena

Puntarenas

NICARAGUA

Corobici
River

Golfo de
Nicoya

NICOYA PENINSULA

Cabo Blanco

Playa
Grande

Ostional

Pacific Ocean

Gulf of Nicoya

### PUNTARENAS

N

Yards

0          500

Av. 3
Av. 1
Av. Central
Av. 2
Av. 4

Av. 3
Museum
Av. Central
Soccer
Stad.
Av. 4 Bis
Paseo de los Turistas

Victoria
Park

Calle 2
Calle Central
Calle 1
Calle 3

P.O.

$

$

$

17

# COSTA RICA

Costa Rica may be a tiny country, but it comprises three mountain ranges and supports such an abundance of flora and fauna that nearly one quarter of its total land area is preserved by national parks or private reserves.

The country's natural beauty and protected parkland have made it one of the world's premier eco-tourism destinations supporting an abundant variety of birds and other wildlife. Sea turtles nest on both coastlines, with the largest green turtle rookery in the Caribbean located at Tortuguero National Park. On the Pacific side, Playa Grande on the Nicoya Peninsula is a winter nesting site for the leatherback, while thousands of olive ridley converge on a half-mile of beach at Ostional each fall.

The first ship to cruise past Costa Rica was commanded by Christopher Columbus in 1502. He paused near present-day Puerto Limon, noted the native inhabitants were wearing gold decorations and dubbed the area *costa rica* (rich coast). Spanish colonization began four years later, but the impenetrable jungle and guerrilla attacks by bands of Indians hampered the invasion, as did the region's tropical diseases. Few indigenous people survived the European diseases introduced by colonists, so the Spanish worked the land themselves.

The promise of gold for which Costa Rica was named never materialized, but the country's fertile mountain plateau, where the climate is perenially spring-like, became a prosperous coffee growing region. The majority of Costa Ricans reside in these highlands, many of them living in the modern capital of San Jose or the nearby towns of Alajuela and Heredia, founded in the 1570s and today a center of the coffee and cattle industries.

When the army general Tomas Guardia seized power in 1870, his military regime, although repressive, laid the groundwork for democracy, which has endured to this day. Modern-day Costa Rica provides its 4.8 million cit-

*Costa Ricans are said to be among the happiest people in the world.*

*Common Basilisk Lizard*

*White Heron*

*Great Blue Heron*

*(Above) Northern Jacana*
*(Left) Red-eyed Tree Frog*

*Colorful frogs, reptiles and birds thrive in Costa Rica's rainforests and can be viewed on a variety of excursions, including a boat tour of the Tortuguero Canals – known as Costa Rica's Amazon.*

izens, who are mainly of Spanish descent, with a public health system considered the best in Latin America. The literacy rate is over 90% and although Spanish is the official language, English and French are taught in schools. Voting is compulsory and the president, upon completing a four-year term, cannot be immediately reelected.

Costa Ricans call themselves Ticos, and their unofficial motto is Pura Vida (which means 'pure life' and is pronounced *poo-rah vee-dah*). This popular expression is not only a form of greeting but an affirmation of taking the time to enjoy life and celebrate good fortune.

There are 80 national parks, protected zones, and biological and forest reserves in Costa Rica, and several of these can be visited by ship-organized shore excursion – a recommended way to view a tropical forest, for it's not advisable to hike into the jungle without a knowledgeable naturalist-guide who is able to spot and identify the flora and fauna, and watch out for everyone's safety. It's best to take an eco-tour in the morning when bird and wildlife sightings are more common than later in the day.

## Getting Around

Costa Rica is a small country, and attractions in the interior can be accessed from both its Caribbean ports of **Puerto Limon** and Puerto Moin, and its Pacific ports of **Puntarenas** and nearby **Puerto Caldera**.

**Shopping** – Costa Rica is considered the Bordeaux of coffee-growing countries, and its most famous brand is Cafe Britt, grown and roasted on a plantation near Heredia where visitors can purchase bags (or cases) of fine coffee. Local wooden handicrafts include salad bowls, jewelry boxes and miniature replicas of the colorfully painted oxcarts sold at the Chaverri Oxcart Factory in Sarchi. Costa Rica's official currency is the colon, but U.S. dollars are widely accepted.

**Dining** – The most popular Costa Rican dish is gallo pinto, made with rice and black beans, and Ticos will jokingly explain that for breakfast they eat rice and beans, and for lunch they eat beans and rice. This traditional dish is, however, prepared dozens of different ways and for breakfast is accompanied by eggs and corn tortillas. At lunch, plates of rice and beans also include fried plantains, hearts-of-palm salad, cheese, diced vegetables and a choice of meat, chicken or fish.

*The market at Puerto Limon's cruise port is a good place to buy Costa Rican coffee and local handicrafts.*

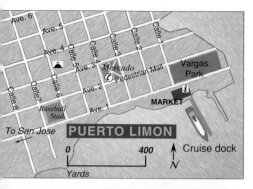

# Puerto Limon

**Puerto Limon**, on the Caribbean coast, is the leading port of Costa Rica from which bananas, cocoa and timber are exported. Although not considered a tourist town, Puerto Limon does have a pleasant waterfront park (Parque Vargas) and an excellent souvenir market at the cruise port where coffee, wood carvings and handcrafted jewellery are sold.

**Shore Excursions** – Local operators offer tours at the visitor center and some sample prices (per person) are: $15 for a one-hour city tour; $25 for a 1.5 hour tour of a banana plantation; $25 for a 1.5 hour boat tour of the Tortuguero Jungle Canals.

## Shore Excursions

*Costa Rica*

Eco-tours dominate the list of excursions, and these include river boat safaris through mangroves to view crocodiles and many varieties of birds. Eco-tours are available to **Monte Verde Cloud Forest** (see page 242), **Rain Forest Aerial Tram** (pg 243), **Tarcoles River**

(pg 244), **La Paz Waterfalls** (pg 244) and **Tortuguero Park** (pg 244), which is famous for its green sea turtles and where bird watching can be enjoyed along the park trails or during boat trips or jungle kayaking on the river. Other active excursions include river tubing and rafting, and zip-line canopy tours.

Cultural excursions include a scenic drive to **San Jose** with a visit to the Opera House and National Museum along with a full-course lunch and a shopping stop at the mountain village of **Sarchi**. Tours to plantations growing coffee, bananas or pineapples are also offered.

Aviarios Del Caribe wildlife sanctuary on the Caribbean coast is where the **Sloth Rescue Center** welcomes visitors to observe up close these cat-sized creatures.

*Rainforest Aerial Tram*

**Beaches** – On the Caribbean side, some beautiful swimming beaches can be found at Cahuita, 27 miles south of Limon, where a long black-sand beach lies at the north end of the village and a white-sand beach lies at the other end within a national park.

## Puntarenas

**Puntarenas** ('sandy point'), on the Pacific coast, is a traditional fishing village situated on a narrow peninsula. Shuttle vans transport passengers to the end of the pier where a few craft stands are situated, but there's not a great deal to see in town and most passengers promptly head to one of the region's nature reserves or to the capital of San Jose, which is a two-hour drive. Red-colored taxis congregate at the pier and fares are approximately $20 to $30 per hour. Most drivers speak limited English and you should agree on a fare before setting out. Sample, round-trip fares (per cab, 1-4 passengers) from Puntarenas: San Jose – $160; Carara Biological Reserve – $90; Sarchi – $100. The fare to Caribbean Village Fiesta Resort (where there is a swimming beach of black volcanic sand) is about $10 each way. The port of **Puerto Caldera** is located 11 miles (18 km) southeast of Puntarenas.

**Beaches** – Many of Costa Rica's beaches consist of black volcanic sand. On the Pacific side, passengers can enjoy a swimming beach and other resort facilities at the Caribbean Village Fiesta Resort, where a day pass is about $40 per person.

## Area Attractions

**San Jose** – Founded in 1738 and the capital of Costa Rica since 1823, San Jose is the cultural center of the country and a transportation hub, connected to both coasts by a railroad and highway. The city's mix of Spanish and North American architecture includes colonial mansions fronted by expansive lawns and gardens. The National Museum is housed in the country's former military headquarters, which were converted into a cultural center when Jose

*(Opposite page) Puerto Limon's cruise port. (Below) The beach at Puntarenas.*

*(Left and middle) The National Theatre in San Juan is Costa Rica's most beautiful building. (Bottom) The colorful carreta is a national symbol of Costa Rica.*

Figueres Ferrer abolished the Army in 1948, and its exhibits include pre-Columbian pottery and artifacts, and colonial furniture and religious art. The Teatro Nacional (National Theatre) is Costa Rica's most beautiful building, designed in the 19th-century neo-classical style with an opulent interior of gold leaf, marble accents and murals.

**Heredia** – The colonial town of Heredia, founded in the 1570s, has retained much of its colonial character. Spanish-style buildings can be seen at Parque Central, north of which is a colonial fortress. East of the park is the 18th-century La Immaculada Concepcion church, which has withstood earthquakes due to its squat design and thick walls. The colonial village of Barva, 1.6 miles north of Heredia, is an historic monument. Also in Heredia is the famous Cafe Britt coffee plantation, where daily tours are held.

**Sarchi** – The oxcart was one of the main means of transportation during colonial times. It became an art form a century ago in the town of Sarchi when a local peasant painted his cart with bright, geometrically patterned colors. These gaily decorated wooden carts,

called *carretas*, are now a national symbol and Sarchi is the place to watch artisans at work, handcrafting multi-colored wooden carts and other ornaments.

**Monteverde Cloud Forest / Santa Elena Reserve** – This biological reserve began as a watershed for the Quaker community of Monteverde and is now one of the country's most popular rainforest hikes. The Monteverde Conservation League, formed in 1985, continues to expand the protected area. In 1988, it launched the International Children's Rainforest project, by which school groups the world over have raised funds to save rainforest lands adjacent to the reserve. Santa Elena Reserve was created in 1989 to relieve some of the visitor pressure on Monteverde.

**Arenal Volcano** – Northeast of Monteverde is Costa Rica's most active volcano, Arenal, its perfect conical shape rising to 5,356 feet (1633 m). It erupted in 1968, killing several dozen people, and continues to discharge red-hot lava, its degree of activity varying from week to week. The nearby Tabacon hotsprings are popular with visitors seeking a quick soak in naturally heated mineral waters.

**Braulio Carrillo National Park** – The Puerto Limon-San Jose highway runs though this park which protects a virgin forest ranging from the Caribbean lowlands to the top of Barva Volcano. The **Rain Forest Aerial Tram** is just outside the park, on a privately owned reserve. This unique attraction – the brainchild of American biologist Donald Perry – whisks visitors over the forest canopy in open tram cars (suspended from a moving steel cable supported by converted ski lift towers) for a unique view of this ecosystem.

**Parque Nacional Volcan Irazu** – The American astronaut Neil Armstrong once described Irazu Volcano as a desolate landscape resembling the surface of the moon. Vapor constantly rises from one of the craters and its cool summit is often shrouded in mist. Irazu is one of Costa Rica's most active volcanoes, destroying Cartago with an eruption in 1723 and blanketing San Jose with ash in 1963. The volcano is 11,260 feet (3,430 m) high and a paved road leads to the summit where, on a clear day, a person can see the Pacific Ocean, the Caribbean Sea and Lake Nicaragua.

*Arenal Volcano*

**Carara Biological Reserve** – This area of lowlands covers 11,750 acres of tropical forest where hiking trails wind beneath a canopy of giant trees. Birds and animals sighted here can include macaws, monkeys, coatis, iguanas and colorful butterflies.

**Tarcoles River** – Located near Carara Biological Reserve, the mouth of the Tarcoles River and its estuaries are home to a large colony of crocodiles and a variety of birds which live among the mangroves and tidal flats. A recommended tour involves boarding a covered Mawamba boat for a cruise along the shoreline while an experienced guide points out various species of bird and the odd crocodile swimming in the river or lying along its banks.

**Rio Corobici** – Costa Rica is filled with rivers spilling through narrow gorges and jungle-clad valleys, and river rafting on the Corobici River in the province of Guanacaste is one way to view the monkeys, parakeets and other birds which live along its banks while you drift and paddle downstream in a large rubber raft.

**Tortuguero** – This park is situated on the Caribbean coast, about 50 miles (80 km) north of Limon, and is an important nesting site for green sea turtles which arrive from July to early October, peaking in late August. The leatherback (February to July) and hawksbill (July to October) also nest here, but in much smaller numbers. The park is also habitat for three species of monkey and over 300 species of birds. Sightings can be made on the park trails or during boat trips on the river, which is home to caimans, crocodiles, basilisk lizards and freshwater turtles.

**La Paz Waterfall Gardens** – Located near Poas Volcano, the grounds contain fern trails, a butterfly observatory, orchid houses, hummingbird gardens and a suspended staircase with platforms for viewing the waterfalls.

*(Above, left) A worker at a banana plantation near Puerto Limon. (Left) A crocodile rests on a mudflat at the mouth of the Tarcoles River.*

# NICARAGUA

The least densely populated of the Central American nations, Nicaragua is a land of outstanding natural beauty, its rivers and lakes once providing a much-coveted trade route between the Atlantic and the Pacific. In fact, Nicaragua was a serious contender for the building of a trans-isthmian canal before the United States eventually decided to take over the failed French project in Panama.

Nicaragua is named for Nicarao, the leader of an indigenous community that inhabited the shores of island-dotted Lake Nicaragua at the time of the Spanish conquest. British and Dutch buccaneers, preying on Spanish treasure ships, would rendezvous in Bluefields Bay on Nicaragua's Mosquito Coast. Named for the region's indigenous inhabitants (the Miskitto) this sultry, swampy coastal belt, about 40 miles wide and never exactly delineated, became a British protectorate in 1678 with Bluefields its capital.

Following Nicaragua's independence from Spain in 1821,

**HONDURAS**

0     50

Miles

N

**NICARAGUA**

| | |
|---|---|
| AREA | 50,193 sq. miles |
| POPULATION | 5.6 million |
| CAPITAL | Managua |
| LANGUAGE | Spanish |
| CURRENCY | Cordoba |
| GOVERNMENT | Presidential republic |

MOSQUITO COAST

San Cristobal Volcano

Leon

*Lake Managua*

Puerto Corinto

**Managua**

Masaya

Granada

Bluefields

*Pacific Ocean*

Concepcion Volcano

Rivas

*Lake Nicaragua*

*Caribbean Sea*

San Juan del Sur

San Juan River

**COSTA RICA**

*The central plaza and cathedral in the Spanish colonial city of Granada.*

the country's politics became polarized between Liberals and Conservatives, centered respectively in the colonial cities of Leon and Granada. A new capital, Managua, was founded in 1855 as a compromise. (An earthquake in 1972 destroyed much of the city.) The Mosquito Coast, after gaining its autonomy from Britain, was forcibly incorporated into Nicaragua in 1894 but its northern part was awarded to Honduras in 1960 after decades of dispute between the two countries.

In 1916 the United States paid Nicaragua $3 million for an option in perpetuity to build a waterway as an adjunct to the Panama Canal. This agreement was terminated in 1970 amid a growing Liberal opposition to U.S. intervention in Nicaragua where the Somoza regime had held power since 1937 and was finally overthrown in 1979 by the Sandinista National Liberation Front. Upon seizing power, the SNLF moved rapidly to the political left and the United States withdrew financial aid, imposed a trade embargo and funded a counter-revolutionary military force. In 1990 a coalition party gained power and a more conciliatory political environment finally prevailed.

The majority of Nicaraguans, who number about 5.6 million and are Spanish-speaking mestizos, live along a volcanic belt lying between the Pacific coast and the country's two large lakes. Lake Managua, the smaller of the two, drains into Lake Nicaragua, which is the largest lake in Central America and drains into the Caribbean Sea via the San Juan River. These two lakes lie in a lowland region, called the

Nicaragua Depression, which was once part of the ocean. When the land lifted, the lakes formed. Several islands and volcanic peaks dot Lake Nicaragua, which contains fish normally found in saltwater, including sharks, which have adapted to fresh water.

**Getting Around** – The cruise ships dock in Puerto Corinto or in **San Juan Del Sur**. The latter is a scenic horseshoe-shaped bay surrounded by mountains where a tranquil fishing village sits at the base of sandstone cliffs. During the California gold rush, this port was the Pacific terminus of Cornelius Vanderbilt's transit route across the isthmus, his customers travelling by steamboat up the San Juan River and by coach from Lake Nicaragua to San Juan Del Sur. Today the port handles export shipments of coffee, sugar and cocoa. It is also a leading holiday resort with its white-sand beaches and warm waters.

**Puerto Corinto** is a small coastal town of about 20,000 inhabitants, its streets lined with quaint shops and lovely churches. The port itself handles large amounts of cargo which arrive by road or rail, and is a convenient staging area for cruise passengers heading to nearby Leon.

Regardless of which port your ship docks at, the easiest way to explore the country is by organized tour.

**Shopping** – Items to look for in Nicaragua include basketry, woven mats and embroidered clothing. Nicaraguans are also noted for their ceramics, wood-

## Shore Excursions

### Nicaragua

Organized tours from San Juan del Sur include scenic drives to Granada for sightseeing and to Masaya for shopping at the famous craft market. A boat cruise among Lake Nicaragua's beautiful islands is also offered, as is a visit to Masaya Volcano National Park. Physically active excursions include a hike up Mombacho Volcano and horseback riding in the Nicaraguan countryside.

Organized tours from Puerto Corinto focus on nearby Leon's historic and cultural attractions, including a visit to the ruins at Leon Viejo and guided tours of the colonial city's art and architecture.

carving, leatherwork and goods made of reptile skin. The crafts market in Masaya is the best place to purchase unique souvenirs. Nicaragua's official currency is the cordoba, but U.S. dollars are widely accepted. Approximate exchange rate: $1 US /CAD = 25 cordobas.

## Area Attractions

**Granada** – Founded in 1523, Granada is scenically situated on the shores of Lake Nicaragua. A showcase of Spanish colonial architecture, the city's churches and convents survived repeated attacks by pirates and other aggressors. Highlights include the Cathedral of Immaculate Conception, the Culture House and the San Francisco Convent, which houses a large collection of pre-Columbian stone sculptures. The city's main plaza sets the stage for music and folk dancing, with a nearby marketplace selling local crafts. Casa de los Leones, adjacent to the square, features lovely gardens.

**Masaya** – Sitting on the edge of a crater lake with Masaya Volcano towering above it, this well-known artisans center features a market selling a huge selection of both local and country-wide handicrafts. Nearby **Volcan Masaya National Park** offers visitors the opportunity to observe an active volcano. A paved road leads from the park entrance to the top of the volcano where steps can be mounted to the summit for a breathtaking view of the entire region and a look inside the volcano's crater, which periodically smokes and

*Visitors can take a close look at Masaya Volcano's smoking crater.*

steams. The Spanish first placed a cross here, believing the volcano was an entrance to hell – which it was in pre-Columbian times for young Indian women who, according to legend, were tossed into the boiling lava at the bottom of the crater to appease their goddess of fire.

**Leon** – Founded in 1524, the original townsite was abandoned in 1610 after nearby Momotombo volcano erupted and caused extensive damage. These ruins, known as Leon Viego, were excavated in 1960 and are a UNESCO World Heritage Site. The rebuilt colonial city of Leon contains fine examples of Spanish colonial architecture, most notably the grand 18th-century Cathedral of the Assumption. A university town of about 200,000 residents, Leon is the country's intellectual center. The famous poet Ruben Dario, the father of modern Spanish literature, is buried in Leon's magnificent cathedral.

# GUATEMALA

There are 33 volcanoes in Guatemala, which means 'House of Fire' in Indian dialect – an apt name for a country that has been plagued throughout its history with volcanic eruptions, floods and earthquakes. Equally turbulent has been the country's politics, beginning with its conquest in 1523 by the brutal Spanish conquistador Pedro de Alvarado, who governed Guatemala with an iron fist until he was killed in 1541 while putting down an Indian uprising in Mexico.

Alvarado's young and ambitious wife, Beatriz de la Cueva, manipulated her own election as her husband's successor, becoming the only woman to hold such a position of power in colonial Spanish America. Her governorship, however, was short-lived. Within weeks of her assuming office, disaster struck when, after several days of earthquakes and relentless rain, a wall of water swept down the slopes of Agua volcano, destroying the capital of Ciudad Vieja at its base and drowning more than a thousand townspeople, including Cueva.

The survivors of this devastating flood built a new capital nearby, naming it Antigua. Dominated by three volcanoes, including Agua, the capital thrived despite being continually subjected to volcanic eruptions, floods and earthquakes. As the capital of Spanish Guatemala, it became one of the richest cities in the New World and by the 18th century, Antigua was a center of the arts and learning with a university, churches, convents, monasteries, public buildings and private residences all built in an opulent style. The end came in 1773 when Antigua was leveled by two earthquakes. This time the capital was moved to a highland plain supposedly free of seismic disturbances. Named Guatemala City, it too was hit by earthquakes in 1917 and 1918, but was completely rebuilt.

Guatemala's repressive dicta-

*Antigua's Cathedral of San Jose.*

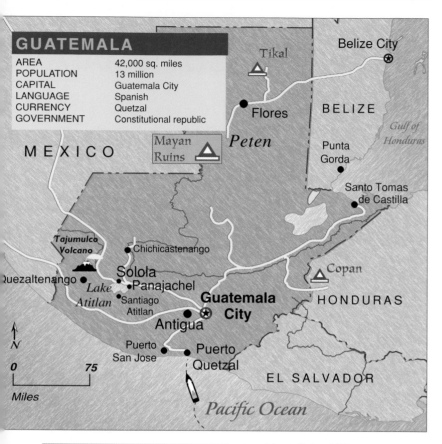

## GUATEMALA

AREA            42,000 sq. miles
POPULATION      13 million
CAPITAL         Guatemala City
LANGUAGE        Spanish
CURRENCY        Quetzal
GOVERNMENT      Constitutional republic

## Shore Excursions

*Guatemala*

For passengers docking in Puerto Quetzal, full-day tours to Antigua include a scenic drive and exploring on foot the city's historic core. Some excursions to Antigua include a stop at a coffee plantation or at a highland village. Other tours feature a boat ride on Lake Atitlan and visiting a village in the highlands where Maya weavers practice their age-old craft. Santo Tomas de Castilla on the Caribbean coast provides access to Tikal's famous temples.

torships of the 19th century were followed by volatility and violence in the 20th century as the country see-sawed back and forth between economic reform and reaction. Ruled by the military and plagued with ongoing terrorism by both the political right and left until a peace treaty was signed in 1996, the country was also hit by a devastating earthquake (7.6 on the Richter scale) in 1976 which killed close to 23,000 people. Most of the country's population, which is evenly divided between Maya Indians and mestizos, lives in the southern highlands where a rugged range of mountains includes the inactive volcano Tajumulco, the highest point in Central America at 13,816 feet (4,211 m).

The northern half of the country is covered by a vast tropical forest, called El Peten, where the magnificent temples of Tikal, the largest and possibly oldest of the Maya cities, rise above the surrounding jungle. Tikal was abandoned by about 900 AD, but Guatemala's modern Maya continue their distinctive mode of life in the highlands between Chichicastenango (an ancient trading center) and Quezaltenango, where the capital of the ancient Maya-Quiche kingdom once stood. The Quiche (*kee-chay*) was the most important group of ancient southern Maya, having attained a high degree of learning at the time of the Spanish conquest, and is today the largest of Guatemala's contemporary Indian groups, numbering about 300,000. More than 20 Amerindian languages, including Quiche, are still spoken by 40% of Guatemalans (who number 13 million), while the remaining 60% speak Spanish. Courses in Spanish have become very popular with foreign visitors.

Cruise ships visiting Guatemala's west coast pull into **Puerto Quetzal**, situated east of Puerto San Jose, which was the country's major Pacific port from the mid-1800s until well into the 20th century, when it was supplanted by the more modern Puerto Quetzal. Guatemala's chief Caribbean port, **Santo Tomas de Castilla,** was built in the 1960s by the Guatemalan government to replace Puerto

Barrios, a few miles to the north, which was controlled by foreign commercial interests.

Major attractions are located a considerable distance from the cruise port, so ship-organized shore excursions are recommended for Guatemala.

**Shopping** – Mayan craftsmanship includes elaborate weavings, decorative stitching and ceremonial masks, which can be bought at markets in Chichicastenango, Panajachel

*Guatemalan crafstmanship.*

*(Above) The preserved Spanish colonial architecture of Antigua. (Below) Volcanic peaks surround the deep waters of Lake Atitlan.*

and Antigua. The official currency is the quetzal (named after the national bird, the Resplendent Quetzal), but U.S. dollars are widely accepted. Approximate exchange rate: $1 US / CAD = 7.5 quetzals.

## Area Attractions

**Antigua** – Founded in 1542 and now a United Nations World Heritage Site, Antigua is one of the loveliest colonial towns in Central America. In addition to several beautiful churches, the town's central plaza (Plaza de Armas) is fronted by the Palace of the Captains General with the coat of arms of Spain's King Charles III displayed over the portal. The Cathedral of San Jose

features an original ornate facade and tiers of intact arches, while the enormous San Francisco Church, destroyed in 1773 and reconstructed in 1960, contains many fine frescoes, paintings and statues. One of the city's most famous buildings is La Merced Church, which is richly decorated with lacy white stonework.

**Lake Atitlan** – This high-altitude lake, its sparkling waters surrounded by volcanic peaks, is a flooded caldera in which the water reaches depths exceeding 1,000 feet. Panajachel is the gateway to the lake, which is best toured by boat for views of waterfalls cascading down high cliffs and visits to traditional lakeside villages whose inhabitants descend from various Mayan tribes. At the village of Santiago Atitlan, Mayan women can be seen weaving on looms outside their thatch-roof houses which line the main street leading from the lake to the local church. The nearby town of Solola holds a traditional Mayan market on Tuesdays and Fridays which is second only to the marketplace in the mountain village of Chichicastenango.

**Chichicastenango** (often shortened to Chichi) – Situated in the heart of the highlands, this ancient trading town became a spiritual center for the Quiche following the Spanish conquest. The Spanish called the town Santo Tomas and founded a Dominican monastery in 1542. It was here that the famous Popul-Vuh manuscript of Maya-Quiche mythology was discovered. This sacred document, in which the Quiche recorded their history, mythology and other subjects, was destroyed by Alvarado but rewritten in Spanish shortly after the conquest by a converted Quiche. Chichi is today considered quaint and charming, its maze of winding streets surrounding the main plaza which is the scene of one of the most colorful town markets in Central America.

**Tikal** – Built during the Classic Period (AD 300-900) deep in the jungle of El Peten, this famous archeological site is the largest (500 acres) and possibly the oldest of the Mayan cities. A United Nations World Heritage Site and part of a national park, Tikal

*A Maya woman sells flowers at the market in Chichicastenango.*

stands on limestone hills surrounded by swamps and lush tropical vegetation, its nine groups of courts, plazas, pyramids and temples interconnected with bridges and causeways. These ruins were once a hub of the Mayan world, where traders would bring fish and shells from the Caribbean and Pacific, and jade and obsidian (a volcanic glass) from the mountains. At its height in the 8th century, Tikal was home to 100,000 people before falling into decline at the end of the 9th century. When the Spaniards marched past Tikal in 1525, they did not see the abandoned city concealed behind the tropical foliage, and not until 1848 was this site discovered.

Situated an hour's drive from the airstrip at Flores, Tikal is surrounded by 222 square miles of rainforest and is an impressive sight as the Great Plaza comes

into view, its two facing temples rising above the treeline. Temple of the Grand Jaguar (Temple I) contains the tomb of one of Tikal's greatest rulers, and a replica of this elaborate tomb can be viewed in the Tikal Museum near the Visitors Center. Temple of the Masks (Temple II) stands opposite, and Temple IV, standing at the end of causeway leading from the Great Plaza, is the site's tallest structure at 229 feet. It's a Tikal ritual to climb the wooden stairs leading to the base of this temple's roof comb for a sweeping view of distant temples poking through the green canopy of the jungle.

**Copan** – Rivaling the ruins of Tikal in Guatemala are those of Copan, just across the border in Honduras. Although smaller in size than some of the other great Maya sites, Copan's monuments were the most artistically embellished, the profusion of carved images providing archaeologists with clues to the society's nobility and royal succession. Dotting the Great Plaza are tall stelae carved with depiction's of Copan's rulers, and the site's famous Hieroglyphic Stairway is comprised of 63 steps covered with nearly 2,000 glyphs recording the history of the royal house of Copan. The site also contains the Temple of the Inscriptions, its walls covered in superb relief, and the second-largest ball court in Central America.

*The famous Maya site of Tikal.*

# BELIZE/ ROATAN ISLAND

The tiny country of Belize, squeezed between Guatemala and the Caribbean Sea, was part of the Maya civilization before the arrival of Europeans. The Spanish paid the region little notice, but British buccaneers preying on Spain's treasure ships began hiding out in the white-sand cays that dot the coast. When British settlers from Jamaica started colonizing the area, several battles ensued between Spain and England until a decisive defeat of the Spanish at St. George's Cay in 1798 settled the matter. Known as British Honduras until gaining independence in 1981, Belize had been claimed by Guatemala since 1821 as part of its inheritance from Spain. Finally, in 1991, Guatemala officially recognized Belize's sovereignty.

Belize City, devastated by three hurricanes in the last century, was the country's capital until 1970 and it remains the commercial center and major port for Belize, the only Central American country with English its official language, although Spanish is widely spoken along with Creole and Maya. The Belize dollar is worth 50¢ US, and American currency is accepted almost everywhere. The city is situated at the mouth of the Belize River and has retained the air of a British colonial port with its canals, wooden houses and fishing boats. Offshore the cays (low islands) are sheltered by the longest unbroken reef in the Western Hemisphere. Dive and snorkel excursions can be taken to several of these cays where the underwater attractions include Shark Ray Alley, which is part of Hol Chan Marine Reserve and an area where southern stingrays and nurse sharks congregate.

In addition to dive trips and fishing charters, shore excursions can be taken from Belize City to the nearby Mayan ruins, such as the sprawling site of Altun Ha. There, amid hundreds of mounds, archaeologists discovered the Green Tomb, so named for its stash of jade treasures that included a carved head representing the Mayan sun god, now

*Belize's extensive offshore reef is second in size only to Australia's Great Barrier Reef.*

one of Belize's national symbols. Nearby Lamani, still occupied when Spanish conquistadores sailed up the New River, is an immense site of some 700 struc-

## Shore Excursions
*Belize*

Escorted shore excursions include snorkeling, scuba diving, cave tubing, kayaking, canoeing and reef bottom fishing. Land-based options include traversing jungle trails by bicycle, 4X4 or jungle buggy. Horseback riding and canopy tours are also offered, as are tours to several Mayan sites. Belize City tours often include a visit to the Belize Zoo or Baboon Sanctuary. Golfers can enjoy a round at Caye Chapel Golf Resort's 18-hole course.

tures standing on high ground that is now home to howler monkeys. An excursion to Lamani still requires a boat trip up the river, past mangroves, crocodiles basking on the banks, and a variety of birds and tropical flowers.

In between these two Mayan sites is the Crooked Tree Wildlife Sanctuary, its guided tours touted as one of Belize's best nature experiences. Established by the Belize Audubon Society in 1984, the sanctuary is habitat to a wealth of bird life, It encompasses the fishing and farming village of Crooked Tree; a lagoon upon which boat trips can be taken; and a system of trails, observation towers and an elevated boardwalk. South of Belize City is the 98,000-acre Cockscomb Basin Wildlife Sanctuary, where the world's highest concentrated population of big cats roam, including the puma, gaguarondi and jaguar, the latter numbering about 200 of the world's remaining 15,000 jaguars.

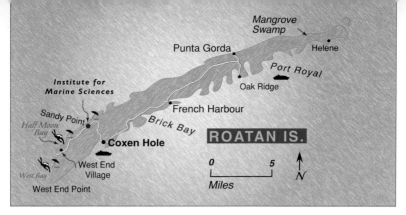

# Roatan Island

The sultry Bay Islands, lying off the coast of Honduras, were once a 17th century hideout for the Welsh pirate Henry Morgan who established his base at Port Royal on Roatan Island, the largest of the three main islands making up this archipelago. Today, Roatan Island is a popular tourist resort of powdery white beaches and clear turquoise water protected by a reef that surrounds the island. Seaside towns hug the coastline of this long, narrow island, home to about 15,000 seafaring inhabitants who are as likely to hop into a boat as a car to get somewhere on the island. Taxis, however, are plentiful and visiting cruise passengers – who are tendered ashore at Coxen Hole – should agree on a fare before setting out (riding *colectivo* is the cheapest way to go, which means the driver can pick up more fares along the way). English is the main language on Roatan.

The best beaches are at the island's western end, about five miles from Coxen Hole. West Bay Beach is considered the island's most beautiful, with good snorkeling and diving along the protected reef, especially in the Blue Channel. Half Moon Bay is also good for snorkeling, and semi-submersible glass-bottomed boat tours operate out of both bays. Anthony's Key Resort, which offers scuba lessons and escorted boat dives, also owns and operates the Roatan Institute of Marine Sciences, where visitors can swim with dolphins who reside in a natural lagoon and are trained in the open ocean. Other excursions include a forest canopy ride along cables leading from a mountain ridge into Gumbalimba Park where the tropical forest is home to monkeys and a variety of birds.

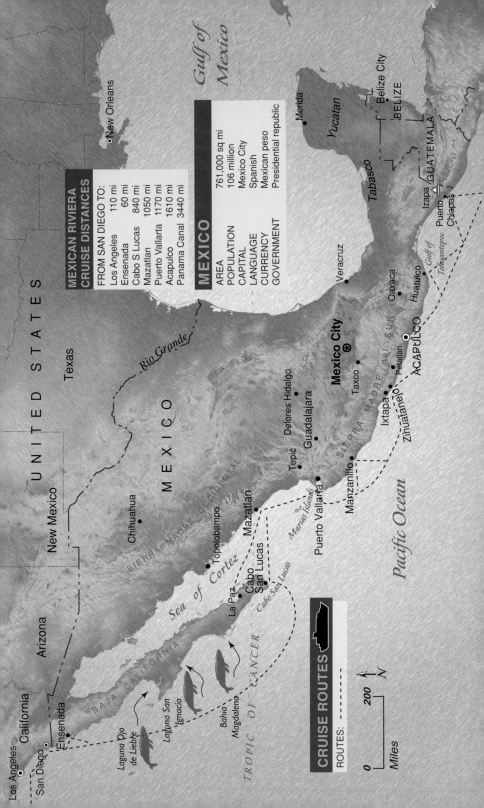

**Gulf of Mexico**

New Orleans

Belize City

BELIZE

Merida

*Yucatan*

GUATEMALA

Izapa

Puerto
Chiapas

*Tabasco*

Gulf of
Tehuantepec

Veracruz

Oaxaca

Huatulco

**MEXICAN RIVIERA
CRUISE DISTANCES**

FROM SAN DIEGO TO:
Los Angeles   110 mi
Ensenada   60 mi
Cabo S Lucas   840 mi
Mazatlan   1050 mi
Puerto Vallarta   1170 mi
Acapulco   1610 mi
Panama Canal   3440 mi

**MEXICO**

AREA   761,000 sq mi
POPULATION   106 million
CAPITAL   Mexico City
LANGUAGE   Spanish
CURRENCY   Mexican peso
GOVERNMENT   Presidential republic

**Mexico City**

Taxco

**ACAPULCO**

Petatlan

Ixtapa

Zihuatanejo

SIERRA MADRE del SUR

Manzanillo

Delores Hidalgo

Guadalajara

Tepic

Marias Islands

Puerto Vallarta

**U N I T E D   S T A T E S**

Texas

New Mexico

Arizona

California

Los Angeles

San Diego

Ensenada

Rio Grande

**M E X I C O**

Chihuahua

SIERRA MADRE OCCIDENTAL

Topolobampo

Mazatlan

Cabo San Lucas

Cabo San Lucas

La Paz

Sea of Cortez

B A J A   C A L I F O R N I A

Laguna Ojo
de Liebre

Laguna San
Ignacio

Bahia
Magdalena

T R O P I C   O F   C A N C E R

*Pacific Ocean*

**CRUISE ROUTES**

ROUTES: ----

N

0   200

*Miles*

# MEXICAN RIVIERA

Washed by the Pacific Ocean and called the Mexican Riviera, this thousand-mile-long stretch of rocky headlands and dazzling beaches is dotted with resorts rivaling the best the world has to offer. Acapulco led the way when discovered by the post-war jet-set crowd, followed by Puerto Vallarta – forever immortalized as the love nest of Richard Burton and Elizabeth Taylor when John Huston filmed *The Night of the Iguana* there in 1963. Since then other sleepy fishing villages have been transformed into world-class beach resorts and alluring ports of calls.

## Mexico's Past & Present

Centuries before Spanish conquistadores landed on Mexico's beach-lined shores, the country's tropical lowlands and temperate highlands supported ancient civilizations of advanced artistry and social organization. The Aztecs were the last of these to hold power in Mexico, their magnificent capital of Tenochtitlan razed by the Spanish conquistador Hernando Cortez in 1521 after he defeated the last Aztec emperor, Montezuma II. A new capital – Mexico City – was built on this site and is today a growing metropolis with a population approaching 20 million.

Mexico, with a population of 109,000,000, is the world's largest Spanish-speaking nation, and the country's colonial past is evi-

*Mexico's Pacific ports of call include the scenic fishing village of Zihuatanejo.*

dent everywhere – the overhanging grilled balconies, the arcaded courtyards, the colorful fiestas. Cities and towns each contain a central square (*zocalo*) overlooked by a church or cathedral, and Roman Catholicism is the dominant religion, encompassing 97% of the population, the great majority being of mixed Spanish and Native American descent. Yet, a sizeable minority is pure Indian and speaks only Indian tongues, most notably Nahuatl – a language descended from the Aztec and spoken by about one million Mexicans. Folk art such as weaving, pottery making and silver work have flourished since the beginning of Mexico's long history, and the country's indigenous foods, such as chili peppers and cornmeal, form the basis of authentic Mexican cuisine.

The land is rich in minerals, and the mountains of the Sierra Madre ranges dominate the landscape. Only 20% of Mexico's total land area is arable, with river water used to irrigate crops. Petroleum reserves are Mexico's single greatest asset, but its other important source of foreign exchange is tourism. The natural beauty of the land, especially the seaside resorts, has made Mexico a popular tourist destination, as has the country's rich cultural heritage. As far back as 1300 BC, the Olmec peoples inhabited the coastal states of modern-day Veracruz and Tabasco. Food was grown on the fertile flood plain and huge pieces of basalt, weighing as much as 40 tons, were floated on rafts to riverine settlements where skilled sculptors carved colossal human heads out of the volcanic rock. The Olmec influenced other Mesoamerican civilizations, most notably the Maya.

At the time of the Spanish conquest, the Pacific coast was dotted with villages whose inhabitants farmed the land and fished

*Traditional dance costumes*
*reflect the Spanish influence.*

## Day of the Dead

The pre-Lenten Carnival celebrations held throughout Mexico are well known for their exuberant festivities, but one of the country's most-anticipated religious festivals is the Day of the Dead (*Dia de los Muertos*), held on November 1 and 2, when plazas are elaborately decorated and families hold nocturnal, candle-lit picnics at the gravesides of loved ones. This celebration of souls follows weeks of preparation, which includes making decorative candles and special dishes of food to place at household altars. Thousands of sugar skulls and papier mache skeletons are handcrafted for the event, its rituals rooted in the Aztec belief in the afterlife. Celebrations commence with the tolling of church bells on the night of October 31, heralding the arrival of the spirits.

*The ancient Olmec peoples carved colossal heads out of basalt rock.*

*(Above) Manila galleons were a target for pirates off the Mexican coast. (Below) A cannon on display at Fort San Diego in Acapulco.*

local waters. They excelled in colorful beadwork, and their social activities included a form of *ulama* – the ball game for which the Maya built stone playing courts.

Acapulco became an important port for Spanish ships sailing between the Philippines and Mexico, their holds loaded with exquisite items made of porcelain, ivory, jade and silk, all carefully wrapped in bales to survive their sea voyage across the Pacific. Loaded with silver from Peru, the Manila galleons that departed Acapulco would pick up the prevailing northeast trade winds to the south and ride these to the Philippines. It was a relatively easy three-month voyage compared to the return trip, which covered 8,000 miles, took about six months and entailed crossing the stormy North Pacific to Cape Mendocino, near San Francisco, where the ships sailed down the coast to Acapulco.

The sturdy Manila galleons, built of teak, were so heavily sheathed as to be impervious to cannon shot. Pirates attacking these galleons as they were about to make port in Acapulco would often run out of ammunition trying to hole one of these vessels, which were also armed for defence and difficult to board from another ship. Those who did succeed in capturing a Spanish treasure ship were instantly wealthy. In November 1587, after six hours of hard fight-

# BULLFIGHTING

Bullfighting was brought by the Spanish to Mexico, where the first bullfights were held in town plazas. The modern bullfight, held in a large outdoor arena called the *plaza de toros*, unfolds in three ritualistic parts. First, toreros wave capes at the bull and mounted picadors thrust at it with lances. The next stage involves banderillos who, while on the run, poke short barbed sticks into the bull's withers. Finally the matador, holding a small cape and a sword, makes daring passes at the bull who eventually stops charging and succumbs to the matador's dominance. When the bull strikes a stationary stance, with its four feet square on the ground and its head hung low, this is the moment when, according to ritual, the matador must shove his sword into the bull's heart. Fighting bulls are specially bred, and successful matadors are highly paid and admired for their skill and courage.

ing, the English privateer Thomas Cavendish captured the treasure-filled *Santa Maria* off the coast of Baja California, and in 1708 the British privateer Woods Rogers intercepted a Spanish galleon heading to Acapulco, its cargo of silks, bullion and precious stones worth a fortune. To protect its Manila galleons, which sailed the Acapulco-Philippines route from 1565 to 1815, Spain built San Diego Fort overlooking the harbor in Acapulco. But the main enemy was scurvy, an ever-present threat to crew and passengers on the long sea voyage, the most horrific example being that of the *San Jose* which was sighted near Acapulco in June 1657, nine months after leaving Manila. When a boarding party reached the ship, which was sailing closehauled under shortened sail, corpses littered the decks. All on board had died of scurvy or starvation.

Whenever a Manila galleon pulled into port at Acapulco, there was great rejoicing. The news spread quickly to Mexico City, where church bells rang and prayers of thanksgiving were offered before residents hurried to Acapulco and its galleon trade fair. Many a fine house in Mexico City became furnished with superbly crafted Chinese wares. The bulk of the ships' precious cargo, however, was hauled by pack animals over the Sierra Madre mountains to Veracruz for shipment to Spain, along with vast quantities of silver mined in Central Mexico.

The Spanish governed the viceroyalty of New Spain, as Mexico was then called, with an iron fist.

The *encomienda* system of land ownership was forced upon the natives, who were 'granted' land by the Spanish crown, for which they paid tribute and provided services to the local conquistador in return for military protection and instruction in the Christian faith.

This oppressive system of forced labor met with great resistance and the Spanish had difficulty establishing control. Eventually a society evolved, consisting of three distinct classes – Spanish, Native American and Mestizo (mixed Spanish and Native American). Members of the privileged Spanish class differentiated between those who were born in Spain and those, considered inferior, who were born in America and called criollos (creoles).

Various priests and missionaries tried to help the Native Americans by petitioning the Spanish government for reforms, but the status quo prevailed until the start of the 19th century when a revolutionary fervor gripped Europe and spread to Spanish America. On September 16, 1810, a Creole priest and social activist named Hidalgo Y Costilla, serving in the parish of Dolores, launched Mexico's revolution when he boldly issued the Grito de Dolores (Cry of Dolores) in the village square, a decree calling for racial equality and redistribution of land. He quickly raised an immense army of Native Americans, which was soon joined by radical creoles. After some initial victories against the royalist forces, Hidalgo's ill-organized army was crushed and their leader executed. But the independence movement continued under new leadership, and in September 1821 Spain accepted Mexican independence.

Vestiges of Spanish colonialism remained, however, and amid the ongoing corruption and social disparity there were frequent turnovers of dictatorial governments. In the 1840s, a dispute with Texas led to an all-out war with the United States, in which Mexico lost 40 per cent of its territory. In 1864, following a civil war, Mexico sought foreign aid from France's Napoleon III, who installed the Hapsburg prince Maxmilian to oversee his new colonial empire, which top-

*A carriage built during the brief reign of the Hapsburg prince Maxmilian is on display at Fort San Diego in Acapulco.*

# TEQUILA

The national drink of Mexico, tequila is made by redistilling mescal which is a colorless liquor distilled from the fleshy leaves of the maguey plant. Maguey is a Mexican name for the American aloe, also referred to as an agave plant. Mexico's agave plants were plagued by a fungus in 1997 which, combined with overharvesting to meet a growing demand for tequila, has drastically diminished its population. The agave plant cannot be quickly replenished, for it needs at least eight years to mature. The Aztecs revered mescal as a gift of the gods but it wasn't until 1795, in the town of Tequila, that the Spanish applied a distillation process to mescal which produced a potent drink they called *vino de mezcal* and became known as tequila. To fully enjoy tequila, aficionados recommend licking some salt off the hand and squeezing some lime juice on the tongue before taking a shot. The worm in the bottom of the tequila bottle comes from the agave plant and is added as a sign of quality.

pled within three years. A century later, despite revolutionary reforms and the establishment of democratic institutions, Mexico was still struggling with widespread poverty and corruption. It was not until the election of Vicente Fox to the presidency in the year 2000 that decades of authoritarian one-party rule were finally ended.

## Travel Tips

**Currency** – The unit of currency is the Mexican peso, but American currency is widely accepted. ATM machines are found throughout most major resort areas and these accept cards with Cirrus, Plus and NYCE systems. The Mexican peso is worth approximately 10¢ US or CAD, and $1 US or CAD = 10 pesos.

**Dining** – Tex-Mex fast-food cooking has little to do with traditional Mexican cuisine, its regional dishes based on native recipes that have been modified by Spanish, French and Italian cooking styles. Examples of authentic Mexican foods are *ceviche* (raw seafood marinated in lime juice, chili peppers, tomatoes, onion and cilantro) and *mole* (a rich, slowly simmered sauce made of chili and various ingredients such as tomatoes, bananas, raisins, sesame seeds and onions). *Mole* is used to flavor chicken and meats, which are often served in *tamales* – cornmeal steamed in a corn husk. Traditional Mexican bread is baked in small, torpedo-shaped loaves called *bolillos*.

**Shopping** – Mexican handicrafts are among the finest in the world and most coastal resorts have shops and open-air markets selling crafts from all over Mexico, includ-

ing Taxco silver jewelry and black pottery from Oaxaca. The assortment of ceramics, tiles, pottery, copperware, glassware and whimsical hand-painted wooden animals is impressive. Quality leather goods include wallets, belts, sandals and cowboy boots, while hand-woven products range from baskets, rugs and hammocks to embroidered blouses, fine beaded tapestries and colorful woolen shawls called *serapes*. Gold and silver filigree (intricate ornamental work) is another Mexican specialty, creating exquisite ear-

*(Above) Decorative plates on display in an Acapulco shop window. (Below) A brass band greets ship passengers arriving in Acapulco.*

rings, necklaces and bracelets. When buying expensive jewelry, it's prudent to do so at reputable stores recommended by the cruise lines or shops that have been recommended online from cruise forums. Flea markets and street vendors can offer little or no guarantee of quality. Most

Mexican ports have an open-air artisans' market where tourists can barter for local handicrafts and souvenirs. The larger ports also have a municipal market where the locals shop for food and other items.

**Taxis** – Available at all ports of call, taxis are unmetered and a fare should be agreed upon before hiring a driver. US dollars are widely accepted.

HOLLYWOOD SOUTH

From the 1940s to the 1970s, Mexico was a favored location of Hollywood film directors who were attracted to the varied terrain of jungle-clad mountains and semi-arid plains, the latter used as backdrops for dozens of westerns. Then, for two decades, Mexico fell off the movie-making map as other countries competed for Hollywood's business and Mexico's reputation for corruption kept film producers away. That situation changed with the establishment in 1995 of Mexico's National Film Commission, which promotes Mexican locations and the reliability of Mexico's American-trained film crews. Hollywood producers have rediscovered Mexico and movies shot here include *Blow* in Acapulco and *Pearl Harbor* in Baja California, along with scenes for *Titanic, Troy* and *Quantum of Solace*. Mismaloya Bay, shown here, is where scenes from *The Night of the Iguana* were filmed in 1963.

## Puerto Chiapas

Puerto Chiapas is new cruise port that opened in 2006. It is located in Mexico's southernmost state of Chiapas and is about a 30-minute drive from **Tapachula's** city center. A city of about 200,000 people, Tapachula is comprised of a diversity of ethnic groups (including Germans who settled in Chiapas during the coffee boom) and its metropolitan area encompasses several suburbs, including the residential area of Playa Linda near Puerto Chiapas (formerly called Puerto Madero).

The **cruise terminal** has extensive visitor facilities, including a swimming pool and a selection of shops selling local crafts. Folk dancing and marimba music are performed in the main 'palapa'. **Taxis** can be hired at the cruise terminal.

## Local Attractions

Local attractions include nearby **Playa Linda** (a 15-minute drive) where several resorts line the beach and offer palapa rentals and access to their swimming pools and restaurants.

Escorted excursions include exploring a mangrove forest and observing the exotic bird life. White-water rafting, horseback riding, jeep rides and jungle hikes are also offered. Boat trips are offered in spectacular **Sumidero Canyon**, which is a short plane ride from the cruise port. Coffee tours feature a visit to a German hacienda. Tours to the city of Tapachula feature Miguel Hidalgo Central Park and the Archaeological Museum.

Archaeological sites in Chiapas include **Izapa**, situated on the eastern outskirts of Tapachula at the base of Tacana volcano. This large site of earth mounds and stone platforms possibly dates as far back as 1500 BC. It is most famous for its abundance of carved stelae and stone monuments depicting a variety of animals, winged objects, long-lipped gods (similar to Maya

*(Above, left) The famous Maya ruins at Palenque. (Left) Puerto Chiapas cruise terminal.*

art) and swirling clouds (as in Olmec art).

The famous Maya ruins at **Palenque** – a UNESCO World Heritage Site – can be visited on an aerial excursion from Puerto Chiapas. The ruins, although a medium-sized site, contain some of the finest art and architecture the Maya produced. The great Maya ruler Pacal the Great (615 to 683 AD) oversaw the rebuilding of Palenque following attacks by rival states, and his funerary monument is called the Temple of Inscriptions for the lengthy text it contains.

Another famous Chiapas landmark is the colonial **Cathedral of San Cristobal de Las Casas**. Originally founded by Bartolome de Las Casas in 1545, the present structure dates from the 1700s. Its brightly colored baroque facade has been restored to its original state, highlighting its intricate iconography and statuary. In 1994, the cathedral was the scene of a hunger strike by its controversial bishop, Samuel Ruiz Garcia, in support of the Maya's indigenous rights. Public negotiations were held in the cathedral between Mexican officials and Maya rebels, and armed confrontations have since eased.

*(Above, right) Cathedral of San Cristobal de Las Casas. (Right) Sumidero Canyon National Park is one of Mexico's most stunning natural attractions.*

# Huatulco

Until the early 1980s, the small fishing village of Santa Cruz, set on the edge of the Gulf of Tehuantepec between mountains and sea, was surrounded by jungle. Today it's surrounded by resort development, but of a unique nature. Situated on one of nine beach-ringed bays lying along 20 tropical miles of pristine coastline, Santa Cruz is now part of the Mexican government's first eco-tourism resort, called Huatulco (*wa-tool-ko*). Features of this ecologically sensitive plan include strict building codes that specify the architectural styles of new hotels, their heights limited to six storeys. To preserve the natural allure of this jungle paradise, the government's master project has designated 70% of this 50,000-acre area be held as ecological reserves. Although the entire resort will not be complet-

*Passengers visiting Huatulco are tendered ashore to Santa Cruz.*

ed until 2020, several bays now have resort and visitor facilities, including a marina and 18-hole golf course. For the time being, however, golden beaches and countless coves far outnumber Huatulco's sprinkling of luxury resorts.

## Getting Around

The cruise ships anchor off Santa Cruz and tender passengers ashore to the local marina where sightseeing boats await and taxis are available. Huatulco's original fishing village, Santa Cruz (Holy Cross) has two waterfront plazas, each surrounded by shops and an artisans marketplace. Boat trips depart from the local marina on tours of the Nine Bays of Huatulco, including El Organo Bay with its natural rock formation in the side of a cliff, dubbed 'stone face'.

**Beaches** – There are 36 beaches lining the bays of Huatulco,  the closest being Playa Entrega in Santa Cruz and those in adjacent Chahue

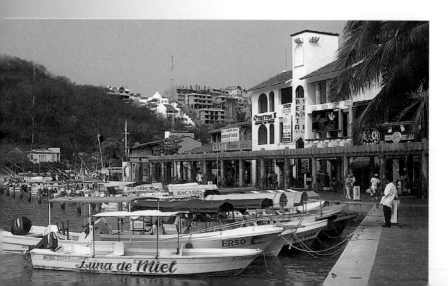

*(Top) A pristine ocean beach.*
*(Right) A local sells beach*
*snacks. (Bottom) La Crucecita.*

Bay, which offer pleasant swimming in a moderate surf. Other popular beaches include those of Tangolunda Bay where the Sheraton and other luxury resorts allow visitors access to their facilities for a small fee. A public beach (Tangolunda Beach Park) is situated on the bay's eastern shore and provides changing facilities, showers and toilets. Quieter beaches are found at Bahia Conejos (the bay just beyond Tangolunda) or in the opposite direction, past Santa Cruz, at Cacaluta Bay.

**Dive & Snorkel Sites** – Local waters provide opportunities to see such reef inhabitants as angelfish, parrotfish and other tropical species, as well as sea turtles. Good snorkeling can be enjoyed in the clear waters off Playa Entrega and off Playa Maguey.

**Shopping** – Santa Cruz offers a small selection of shops while La Crucecita features a bustling market and plenty of shops bordering the central plaza. Look for handcrafted items from the interior town of Oaxaca, its artisans'works among the best in Mexico, including hand-wrought gold and silver filigree, black pottery, hand-woven rugs and shawls, and *alebrijes* (whimsical hand-painted wooden animals).

## Local Attractions

**Tangolunda Bay** – The bay's Zapotec name means 'place where the gods live' and its five beaches are now home to seven luxury low-rise resorts, including a Club Med which is the largest of its kind in the Western Hemisphere, as well as an 18-hole golf course, a shopping area and several restaurants.

**La Crucecita** – A mile inland from Santa Cruz is a fascinating faux village, built in 1986 to resemble an authentic colonial settlement with a central plaza, bandstand, art deco cathedral and municipal market.

**Copalita River** – The trails along the banks of this river afford the perfect opportunity for tropical birding and wildlife viewing. The region's 200+ bird species include the egret, falcon, parrot and hummingbird, while land animals include the iguana and armadillo.

**Finca de Pacifico** – High in the hills behind Huatulco, this 120-hectare coffee plantation is an organic operation producing a rich, aromatic coffee which can be sampled in the hacienda restaurant.

**Oaxaca** – A hundred miles inland from Huatulco is the state capital of Oaxaca (pronounced *waha-ka*), one of Mexico's most historic cities. Founded by the Aztecs in 1486 in a valley surrounded by low mountains, Oaxaca was taken by the Spanish in 1522 and is today a small commercial and tourist center noted for its colonial churches and beautiful gardens, as well as its thriving artistic community.

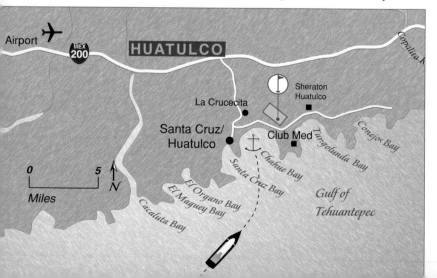

# Acapulco

The world once came to Acapulco. An international playground attracting the rich and famous to its beautiful crescent-shaped bay and sizzling nightlife, Acapulco became Mexico's premier beach resort in the 1960s. John and Jackie Kennedy honeymooned here in a private villa in 1953, but it wasn't until direct international air service to Acapulco began in 1964 that this scenic resort, strung like a necklace at the base of the Sierra Madre mountains, was embraced by the international jet set.

Hollywood film stars and European aristocrats arrived in their ready-to-wear Pucci designs, ready to party into the night as the setting sun turned the bay a burnt orange and the twinkling lights of hillside villas cast a magical glow on the gentle surf below. Those who flocked to Acapulco included the dashing Florentine fashion designer Emilio Pucci. His comfortable yet chic lines of summer clothes were often inspired by native motifs, including dresses designed in bold Aztec prints, and they were the perfect 'resort wear' favored by the glamorous starlets who frequented Acapulco.

As the first and still the most popular resort in Mexico, Acapulco has it all, although some would say it has too much. Too many hotels lining its famous beaches, too many taxi drivers vying for fares, too many pedlars trying to sell their wares. Yet this cosmopolitan city of 2 million residents continues to draw 3.5 million visitors annually and, to regain some of its lost allure, Acapulco began a beautification program in 1994, improving its public areas, cleaning its beaches, renovating several hotels and building new ones beyond Acapulco Bay.

The magic of Acapulco is easy to understand when experienced from the deck of a cruise ship. A pre-dawn arrival is best, when the city surrounding Acapulco Bay is a display of sparkling lights, and approaching cruise ships are often escorted by dolphins into the Boca Grand, the mouth of the bay. Late evening departures are equally magical, as the ship slips its moorings and draws away from the bay's glittering shoreline while passengers dance to the ship's band on the upper decks.

## Getting Around

The cruise ships tie up beneath the ramparts of El Fuerte de San Diego, the Spanish-built fort that once protected the port from pirates. Taxi drivers congregate outside the cruise terminal, but

only the specially licenced drivers are allowed into the building and it's one of these you should hire if you're planning to explore the town by taxi. Fares are posted inside the terminal and a dispatcher is on hand to answer questions. Sample fares one-way from the terminal, are: Cliff Divers – $8; Papagayo Park – $6; Las Brisas – $15; Fairmont Acapulco Princess Hotel – $25.

Many sights are within walking distance, such as the streets of Old Acapulco, the fort, and the beaches which stretch eastward from the cruise terminal. Just be prepared to walk a gauntlet of eager cabbies on the street immediately outside the terminal entrance.

**Shopping** – Several excellent shops selling handmade jewelry and silverware are located inside the cruise terminal. Little Margarita's provides free transportation to its main store – Joyeria Margarita – in Old Acapulco, which offers

*A view of the Acapulco cruise terminal from nearby beaches.*

an array of leather goods, handmade jewelry, dolls, T-shirts and unique arts and crafts. B&B also has a larger store, called the B&B Marketplace and Factory, located in Papagayo Park – within walking distance or a 10-minute taxi ride – where visitors can enjoy free margaritas while shopping for handcrafted jewelry and Mexican handicrafts. Plaza Taxco, located near La Quebrada, contains an extensive selection of gold, silver and gemstone jewelry where designers can create a customized piece of jewelry upon request.

**Beaches** – The curved shoreline of Acapulco Bay extends for more than four miles and is lined with beaches.

Easiest to reach are those just east of the ship terminal. Playa Tamarindo, Playa Hornos and Playa Hornitos are where fishermen haul in their catch and locals like to swim in the moderate waves or enjoy a game of soccer on the beach. An umbrella and two chairs can be rented for 5 pesos. Further along, where the hotel zone begins, La Condesa beach is popular for its

amenities and watersports. West of the cruise terminal, on the far side of the peninsula, are several smaller beaches, including Playa Caleta, which is also popular with the locals.

**Golf Courses** – One of Mexico's finest courses, designed by Robert Trent Jones, Jr., is found at the Fairmont Pierre Marques resort on the east side of Acapulco Bay. The nearby Fairmont Acapulco Princess also has an 18-hole course, as does the Mayan Palace.

## Local Attractions

The **Zocalo 1** – Old Acapulco's central plaza, this tree-shaded square is a gathering place for locals and is overlooked by Nuestra Senora de la Soledad, the city's unusual-looking cathedral of stark design with Byzantine towers. The most pleasant route for reaching the square is along the waterfront, where a tiled walkway winds past a cluster

*Pleasant walkways lead west from the cruise terminal, past shops and waterfront views.*

### Shore Excursions

*Acapulco*

City tours feature visits to Fort San Diego and the Chapel of Peace, usually with a stop at La Quebrada to watch the breathtaking cliff diving. Historic walking tours are also offered, as are shopping trips, beach getaways and excursions featuring the preparation of Mexican cuisine. High-energy excursions include ATV off-road adventures, horseback riding, helmet diving and deepsea fishing. Golfing is available at the Mayan Palace Golf Course or the Fairmont Pierre Marquez Golf Club. Out-of-town excursions include a scenic drive through the Sierra Madre to the silver city of Taxco. The Papagayo River's spectacular gorges can be experienced on river rafting excursions or jet boat rides.

of boutiques selling Mexican handicrafts. White, wrought-iron benches flank the promenade as it leads to a central fountain, at which you turn right and head into the center of Old Acapulco where the zocalo is located.

**La Quebrada 2** – No visit to Acapulco is complete without watching the spectacular cliff diving at La Quebrada. The men who perform these heartstopping swan dives and pike somersaults have spent years training for their 136-foot plunges down the face of a jagged granite cliff into a narrow gorge where the water is only 12 feet deep. The six divers pray at a small shrine before climbing to a rock ledge called La Punta where, poised on the edge, they wait – in pairs – until just the right moment, timing their dives to coincide with an approaching wave as it washes into the gorge below.

The walk to La Quebrada takes about 15 minutes from the cathedral. Follow Lopez Mateos (the road to the left when facing the church entrance) which ends at the top of a very steep hill. By taxi (much less strenuous) it's about a 10-minute ride from the terminal. The daily show times are 1:00 p.m., 7:15 p.m., 8:30 p.m., 9:30 p.m. and 10:30 p.m. The view is best from the upper area beside the ticket booth. Admission fee is $2.00.

**Fuerte de San Diego 3** – For a hands-on look at the history of Mexico's Pacific coast, Fort San Diego is well worth a visit. Built in 1783, replacing the original structure (1615) which was destroyed

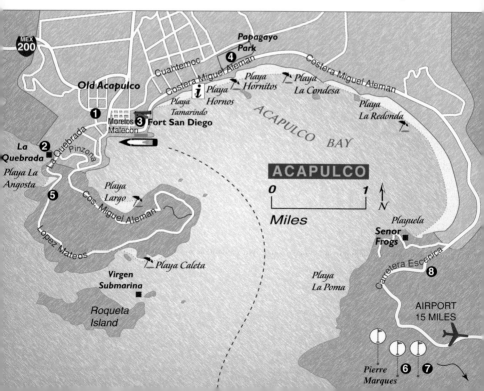

by an earthquake in 1776, this pentagon-shaped fortress was designed using advanced military engineering concepts of the period. Defensible on all flanks and surrounded by a dry moat, the fort could hold up to 2,000 troops and stock enough provisions and ammunition for a year-long siege. The fort was attacked by revolutionary forces in 1810, withstanding repeated attacks and a two-year siege before it was taken. In 1986 the fort became the Acapulco Historical Museum, its vaulted rooms (entered off the central courtyard) now housing Spanish colonial exhibits. These include The Manila Galleon Room, the Pacific Piracy Room and The East Trade Room, with treasures from the Orient on display. Reaching the fort entails crossing busy Costera Miguel and climbing up a few flights of steps to the entrance. The entrance fee is $4.00 and opening hours are 10 a.m. to 6:40 p.m., Tuesday through Sunday.

**Papagayo Park 4** – This 52-acre municipal park is filled with attractions, including a botanical garden, a replica of a Manila galleon and B&B Marketplace and Factory where tours allow you to see designers crafting pieces of gold and silver into beautiful jewelry.

Several of Acapulco's famous resorts are attractions in themselves, where visitors can stroll the grounds and public areas, and pause to enjoy a refreshment. **Los Flamingos 5**, an art deco-style hotel built in the 1930s overlooking the Pacific, was the former hideaway of movie legend John Wayne and his Hollywood cronies. Also in this old town area is the former home of the artist Diego Rivera, one of his tile murals gracing the house's facade. At the other end of the bay is the world-famous **Fairmont Acapulco Princess Hotel 6** which is shaped like an Aztec pyramid, and the **Mayan Palace 7**, built in the shape of a Mayan temple and featuring lovely gardens. **Las Brisas 8**, on a hillside overlooking Acapulco Bay, is considered one of the world's finest resort hotels, its individual casitas each featuring a private pool. A stunning view of Acapulco Bay can be enjoyed here at the Chapel of Peace, erected as a memorial to two children who perished in a plane crash.

*The entrance to Fort San Diego.*

# ACAPULCO

*(Above) A soccer game unfolds on Playa Hornos. (Below) Fishing skiffs dot the sands of Playa Tamarindo. (Opposite) Spectators gather at La Quebrada to watch Acapulco's famous cliff divers perform their heartstopping swan dives into the shallow waters of a narrow gorge.*

## Zihuatanejo

One of the Mexican Riviera's most relaxing ports of call, the fishing village of Zihuatanejo (*zee-wah-tah-nay-ho*) is situated at the base of mountains on a sheltered bay ringed with beaches. The tidy village is easily explored on foot with time left to lounge on a local beach or visit nearby Ixtapa, a planned tourist resort where high-rise hotels line a 2.5-mile stretch of spectacular beach. Stone carvings and stelae have been unearthed in the area, indicating an indigenous civilization dating back to antiquity whose nobility used Zihuatenejo as a sanctuary. In more recent history, Zihuatenejo was an isolated fishing port when, in the 1970s, the Mexican government developed neighboring Ixtapa into a world-class tourist resort.

### Shore Excursions

*Zihuatanejo*

Motorcoach tours to Ixtapa, countryside tours and a visit to Petatlan are all offered, as is a walking tour of Zihuatenejo. Golf is available at Club De Golf Marina Ixtapa. Other excursions include jungle horseback riding, kayaking and snorkeling at Las Gatas Beach, and sailing around the bay with a stop for swimming and snorkeling

*A cruise ship lies at anchor in Zihuatanejo Bay.*

### Getting Around

The ships anchor in Zihuatanejo Bay and tender passengers ashore to the municipal pier. Ixtapa is four miles away by highway; public mini-buses run between Zihuatenejo and Ixtapa, and taxis are plentiful and reasonably priced. Sample **taxi fares** (per person, one-way) from Zihuatenejo are: **La Madera**

Beach – $1.50; **La Ropa Beach** – $2.00; **Ixtapa** – $4.00 **Playa Linda** – $5.00

The water taxi to **Las Gatas Beach**, which departs from Zihuatanejo's municipal pier, is $5 round-trip per person and departs every 30 minutes.

**Shopping** – Zihuatanejo's artisans are widely known for their bright ceramics and carved  wooden fish and masks. The vendors here are less aggressive than those in the larger ports, so this is the place to leisurely browse for local crafts. The tourist flea market is a short walk from the pier along Avenue 5 day Mayo. The town's main street is Avenida Cuauhtemoc, where shops carry such noteworthy items as handmade pottery and silver jewelry from the mountainside town of Taxco, a famous center of silversmithing since colonial times.

**Zihuatanejo Beaches:**

**Playa Principal** – Good for people-watching, this municipal beach beside the

*Playa La Ropa*

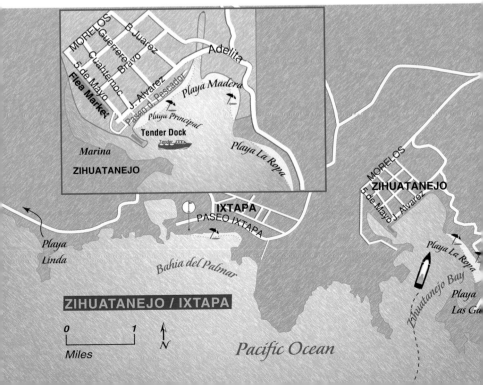

pier is busy with local fishermen and families.

**Playa La Madera** – Once used for loading fine hardwoods (hence its name which is Spanish for wood) this swimming beach of fine sand and gentle surf is overlooked by some hillside hotels.

**Playa La Ropa** – Lying at the base of a cliff in the center of the bay, this is the town's longest beach and, although popular with surfers, has an uncrowded feel due to its length. Ask your taxi driver to drop you off at La Perla restaurant and arrange for a pick-up time.

**Playa Las Gatas** – Reached by a 10-minute water taxi ride from the pier, this beach is recommended for snorkeling, with equipment rentals available. A stone wall parallels the beach, constructed as a shark barricade by a Purepecha king so his family could safely bathe here. Over time the stone barrier has become encrusted with coral and attracts an abundance of marine life.

**Ixtapa Beaches:**

**Playa Del Palmar Beach** – Ixtapa's main beach and lined with hotels, it can be accessed by public path at either end. Open to the Pacific, this stunning stretch of sand is washed by a continuous surf.

**Playa Linda** – This tranquil beach, and adjacent Quieta Beach, are ideal for swimming. The pier

*(Top to bottom) Paseo del Pescador; Zihuatanejo's hillside villas; La Ropa Beach.*

*Ixtapa's impressive beach.*

at Playa Linda provides water taxi service to tiny Isla Ixtapa which offers picturesque beaches, good snorkeling, and scuba diving on its ocean side.

**Snorkel & Scuba Sites** – Excellent snorkeling can be enjoyed at Las Gatas Beach in Zihuatanejo, and at Isla Ixtapa (off Playa Linda).

## Local Attractions

**Paseo del Pescador** – This beachfront road leads from the municipal pier past a pleasing assortment of shops and seafood restaurants, and provides lovely views of the bay and the ship at anchor. A tourist office and archeological museum are also found along this street.

**Petatlan** – Located in the coastal foothills east of Zihuatanejo, this place of pilgrimage is famous among Mexicans for its local church where miracles have been linked to the patron saint, Father Jesus of Petatlan.

# Manzanillo

Mexico's largest shipping port and home to the Mexican navy, Manzanillo is relatively small as a tourist resort. The hotel zone is a few miles from the dock area, and here you will find the beaches made famous in the movie *10* – a romantic comedy starring Bo Derek and Dudley Moore, filmed at Las Hadas resort in 1979.

The Moorish-style Las Hadas Golf Resort & Marina is situated on Peninsula de Santiago, overlooking Manzanillo Bay – which is over five miles long. The resort began as a private residence built by a Bolivian millionaire in the 1960s and evolved into a world-class resort with an 18-hole golf course and other amenities.

Watersports in Manzanillo include sportfishing, jet skiing, kayaking, snorkeling and scuba diving. Other excursions include hiking along the winding shoreline or into the hills for stunning views of Manzanillo Bay. Driving tours to mountain villages and jungle waterfalls are also available.

## Puerto Vallarta

*Puerto Vallarta's waterfront.*

A person could be forgiven for thinking that Puerto Vallarta was a Hollywood creation. Legendary motion picture director John Huston had already shot *The Treasure of Sierra Madre* in Mexico when he brought a star-studded cast to Puerto Vallarta in 1963 to film *The Night of the Iguana*. Ava Gardner and Richard Burton played the film's leading roles, but Elizabeth Taylor provided the off-screen drama when, still married to Eddie Fisher, she accompanied Burton to Puerto Vallarta. Their scandalous love affair drew reporters to the seaside town, who were immediately enamored of this exotic hideaway nestled at the base of the Sierra Madre mountains. Whitewashed buildings with red tile roofs lined the cobblestone

streets, bougainvillea spilled from wrought iron balconies, and the waterfront Hotel Oceana provided sweeping views of a sapphire blue sea.

Puerto Vallarta overlooks Banderas Bay (Bay of Flags), named by a Spanish conquistador in 1541. Sailing ships dropped anchor here when making long voyages along the coast, but it wasn't until 1851 that a townsite (called Puerto de Penas) was established as a port for shipping silver and supplying salt to silver mines on Rio Cuale.

In 1918 the village became a municipality of the state of Jalisco and its name was changed to Puerto Vallarta in honor of the state's governor. The bay's shoreline is 25 miles long, and from October through April this wide bay is frequented by humpback whales, who spend their winter breeding season in tropical waters.

Puerto Vallarta (population 175,000) is one of Mexico's most popular resorts, receiving 1.5 million visitors a year as well as an influx of retirees to its waterfront condominiums. Yet, the original town center has retained its Old Mexico character, and bylaws are in place to preserve this ambiance – new houses must be painted white and parking lots paved with cobblestone. Some say the place has become too prettified, yet a stroll along the back streets reveals a Mexican colonial town that's as authentic as the brilliant blue bay it overlooks.

## Getting Around

The ship docks about three miles north of the town center, next to Playa Del Oro. Taxi cars and vans are available outside the terminal gate. Taxi vans transport groups of passengers between the cruise terminal and

*Richard Burton and Elizabeth Taylor (right) stayed at the Hotel Oceana (below) on their first visit to Puerto Vallarta.*

## Shore Excursions

*Puerto Vallarta*

The excursions offered in Puerto Vallarta are extensive. They include sailing, snorkeling, scuba diving, beach visits and encounters with dolphins and sea lions. Driving/walking tours feature city highlights and coastal resorts. Some travel into the foothills to visit haciendas and traditional Mexican villages. Off-road mountain biking, jeep safaris and ATV expeditions are also offered, as are horseback trail riding and jungle canopy adventures. Golf can be arranged at El Tigre's 18 hole championship course.

town center for $2 per person. To return to the ship from town, take a yellow Nissan taxi for $5 per carload. Other fares, per car, one-way: Gringo Gulch $6; Playa de los Muertos $6; Mismaloya Beach $15.

**Shopping** – Items to look for in Puerto Vallarta include glassware, pottery, stoneware and fine beaded tapestries. Shops selling quality jewelry and leather goods face the malecon (waterfront promenade), while the flea market (on the north side of the Cuale River) is a good place to barter for local handicrafts. For fine Mexican Indian art, the Galeria Indigena on Juarez Street (a block south of the main square) features ceremonial masks, Aztec-style etchings and bead-and-yarn art by the local Huichols. Seven blocks north of the town square, at Juarez and Leona Vicario, is Mexico's first and largest jade workshop and gallery (called Jades Maya Gallery) where archaeological reproductions are on display and jewelry and other gifts can be purchased.

**Beaches** – The beaches begin on either side of the cruise port, where hotels line the waterfront. In the town itself, the most popular beach is Playa de los Muertos (Beach of the Dead) where another strip of hotels is situated. Watersports are available here and on adjacent Playa de Olas Altas (High Waves Beach). A gay beach is situated on a small section of

*(Above) Mismaloya Bay.*
*(Right) Los Arcos.*

Muertos Beach near its southern end. South of town is the beautiful crescent beach of Mismaloya. Further south along the coast are secluded beaches accessible only by sea, such as the one at Las Caletas, John Huston's former hideaway (see page 289), and the twin beaches of Las Animas and Quimixto.

**Snorkel & Dive Sites** – For both snorkeling and diving, Los Arcos National Underwater Park contains a cluster of rock islands, some hollowed out in places by wave action, which provide a habitat for tropical and subtropical fish, marine mammals and sea birds. Islas Marietas is one of the area's best dive sites, featuring reefs and underwater caverns, and is an hour-long boat ride from town. Las Caletas also offers good snorkeling opportunities.

**Golf** – Marina Vallarta Golf Course is an 18-hole 6,500-yard championship course dotted with lakes, ponds and lagoons. Although designed as a private golf club, it is open to cruise passengers who can book a package through the ship's shore excursion office.

## Local Sights

**Malecon** – The Old Town of Puerto Vallarta is pleasant for strolling, especially along the beach-fronted *malecon* (seawall) which is dotted with benches and sculptures. Opposite the Seahorse Statue, at the foot of Calle Galeana, stands the Hotel Oceana

*(Above) Cathedral of Our Lady of Guadalupe. (Below) The Night of the Iguana Restaurant overlooking Mismaloya Bay.*

(where Burton and Taylor stayed) and which now houses Tequila's Restaurant & Bar. A few blocks south along the malecon is the Old Town's central square, with some shaded benches and a statue of Don Ignacio Luis Vallarta.

**Cathedral of Our Lady of Guadalupe** – Rising above the town square is the landmark steeple of the Cathedral of Our Lady of Guadalupe (1906), which is topped with a huge replica of the crown worn by the empress Carlotta, whose husband Maximilian was emperor of Mexico from 1864-67. Part of this crown toppled during an earthquake in October 1995.

**Gringo Gulch** – Narrow streets behind the cathedral lead up the hillside to the wealthy Zaragoza neighborhood, better known as Gringo Gulch. Richard Burton and Elizabeth Taylor each owned a villa here with beautiful views of the bay and their residences were joined by a footbridge spanning the street in between. Now a bed & breakfast hideaway called Casa Kimberley, these two villas house the Taylor-Burton Museum (Zaragoza 445) which is filled with original furniture and mementos. Visitors can gain admission ($6.00) by ringing the door bell.

**Isla Cuale** – This island lies in the middle of the Cuale River, which divides Old Vallarta from the town's Romantic Zone where a bohemian atmosphere can be enjoyed at the many sidewalk cafes and beachside bars. A museum, boutiques and restaurants are located on the lushly overgrown river island.

*(Above and right) Las Caletas.*

**Playa Mismaloya** – The coastal drive south of town to Mismaloya winds past luxury hotels and homes overlooking the bay, including a villa owned by Steven Spielberg. Lying off-shore are the rounded rock islets of Los Arcos, and just beyond is Mismaloya Bay where scenes from *The Night of the Iguana* were filmed. A modern resort now stands at one end of the crescent beach and at the opposite end, atop a rugged hillside, is The Night of the Iguana restaurant where palm-fringed views of the beach and bay can be enjoyed from the outdoor patio.

**Las Caletas** – A visit to this tranquil retreat is available as an all-inclusive day-long excursion involving a scenic 45-minute boat trip each way. A relaxing day is spent at this isolated cove where visitors can lounge on the palm-fringed beach, snorkel or kayak in the clear water, and enjoy a buffet lunch featuring local cuisine. The grounds contain a range of facilities in the tile-roofed pavilions and palapa-style beach huts, including a restaurant, complimentary bar and John Huston's Museum with a small collection of the movie director's memorabilia on display. In describing his Mexican hideaway, Huston said, "Las Caletas faces the sea and its back is to the jungle so for this reason one thinks of it as an island."

# Mazatlan

The heart of a port city is the dock area, and cruise passengers arriving at Mazatlan are provided with a close-up view of its industrial heart. As the sun rises over Isla Chivos and the ship slips past the stone breakwaters into the harbor, early risers can watch from the ship's rail the waterfront activities of docked freighters and moored fishing vessels. A city of some half-million residents, Mazatlan is a major cargo port, and its fishing fleet nets large quantities of shrimp and tuna, while marlin, swordfish and dorado are also plentiful.

First inhabited by nomadic tribes who fished and hunted, Mazatlan derives its name from a Nahuatl word meaning 'place of deer'. The Spanish conquistador Don Nuno Beltran de Guzman landed here in 1531 and called his newly founded settlement 'The Islands of Mazatlan' for the three offshore islands that were a natural landmark and navigational aid for Spanish merchant ships. Mazatlan flourished as a colonial port once gold and silver deposits were discovered nearby in the Sierra Madre mountains. Today the city hosts a growing number of tourists lured by the beautiful beaches and superb sportsfishing.

## Getting Around

The ship docks at the commercial dock where complimentary trams whisk passengers to and from the terminal, which contains telephones, restrooms and a handful of shops. Outside is a flea market and taxis. The fare, per taxi (up to four people) to the Golden Zone (where the beachfront hotels are located) is about $10. For a drive

*A dawn arrival (left) at Mazatlan's harbor (opposite).*

along the *malecon*, with stops at scenic outlooks and a visit to Plaza Machado to view the cathedral before returning to the port, a reasonable fare is $12 to $15 per taxi. Small open-air vehicles (similar to golf carts) called *pulmonia*, are available for hire on the street outside the terminal gates.

**Shopping** – The shops are concentrated in the Golden Zone (tourist zone), between Rodolfo Loaiza and Avenue Cameron Sabalo. Items to look for include Huichol beadwork and embroidery, and the Mexican fire opal – a bright red translucent stone.

**Beaches** – Mazatlan's beaches begin in the Old Town with the surfing beach of Playa Olas Altas (Beach of Tall Waves) and Playa Norte where the locals swim.

Next is the Golden Zone, the city's tourist area, where waterfront resorts and restaurants overlook Playa Las Gariotas. A lovely stretch of sand lies in front of Los Sabalos Resort at the south end of the Zone. Another popular section of beach with watersports rentals stretches past the Royal Villas Resort. Offshore lie three islands (named Bird, Deer and Goat). Deer Island (the middle one) is an ecological reserve offering good swimming and snorkeling, and can be visited by water taxis available at several hotels, including one that departs from the beach next to the El Cid Mega Resort.

**Sportfishing** – The marlin and sailfish caught off Mazatlan routinely break records, and the local swordfish, caught in March, are considered one of sportfishing's most challenging catches. The sportfishing docks are located in a bay southwest of the cruise ship dock.

**Golf** – An area of lagoons beside the Golden Zone has been transformed into an upscale residential community of custom-built homes and a nine-hole golf course designed for the El Cid Golf & Country Club by Lee Trevino.

## Local Attractions

**El Faro** – Mazatlan's most prominent landmark and the world's second-tallest natural lighthouse (after Gibraltar), El Faro stands atop a 500-foot hill near the entrance to the port. It takes about half an hour to hike from its base to the top for sweeping views of the city and surrounding area.

**The Malecon** – This waterfront promenade, backed by Icebox Hill, runs for 13 miles along the edge of the bay and provides vistas of Mazatlan's ruggedly beautiful coastline. Public art graces the wide walkway, one of the largest sculptures being Fisherman's Monument. At Cliff Divers Park a diving platform has been built on a large rock outcropping from which a trained diver takes the plunge for the benefit of tourist groups. On the landward side of the *malecon* is haunted Devil's Cave where a murder once took place, its entrance sealed by a locked, wrought-iron gate.

**Plaza Machado** – The city's Moorish-style cathedral, built in 1856, overlooks the central

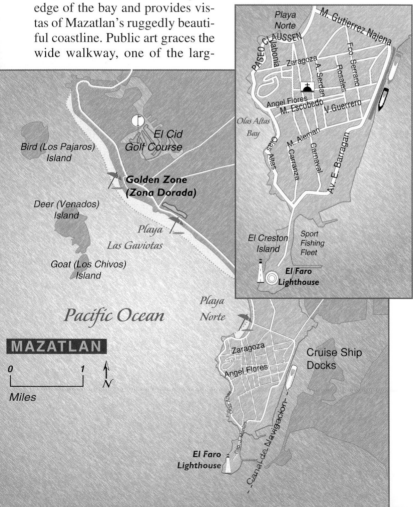

*A lighthouse stands atop El Faro in Mazatlan.*

square where locals gather to peddle their wares or enjoy the shade of its ornate gazebo, built during the regime of Porfirio Diaz (1876-1911) who admired the lavish splendor of French Second Empire architecture, a style introduced to Mexico during the brief (1864-67) reign of Emperor Maximilian. Nearby is the open-air public market where fresh fish, produce and local crafts are sold. Two blocks south of the plaza is the 19th century Angela Peralta Theatre, recently restored to its original grandeur.

**Aztec Theater** – Situated in the Golden Zone, this open-air theater presents daily shows of Mexican folkloric dancing and a daredevil routine by the Papantla Flyers who reenact a Totonac Indian ritual called The Dance of Those Who Fly. The show also features costumed dancers performing festive numbers, including the Mexican Hat Dance.

---

Shore Excursions

*Mazatlan*

The excursions offered in Mazatlan include a tour of the old downtown combined with shopping in the Golden Zone and a show at the Aztec Theater that features the Papantla Flyers. A walking tour of Old Mazatlan is also offered, as is a hike up to El Faro lighthouse. Horseback riding at a hacienda or canopy zip lining at a plantation are also offered, as is golf at El Cid Golf Resort. Mexican cuisine is featured in several excursions, and the Pacifico Brewery tour spotlights Mexico's popular beer. Other excursions include kayaking around Cactus Island. Beach getaways include a boat ride to Stone Island where birdwatching can also be enjoyed.

*(Above) Mazatlan's moorish-style cathedral at Plaza Machado. (Left) The Papantla Flyers. (Below left) Dancers perform at the Aztec Theater.*

**Sierra Madre Mining Towns** – Several colonial towns are located a short distance into the foothills of the Sierra Madre Occidental. The nearest is Concordia, 28 miles from Mazatlan, which was founded in 1565 and is noteworthy for its 17th-century stone church and local crafts, including handmade pottery and furniture. Farther afield, 15.5 miles from Concordia, is the town of Copola where the 16th century Church of San Jose overlooks the town's cobblestone streets and colonial houses.

## Cabo San Lucas & Sea of Cortez

Known as 'the other Mexico', Baja California is distinctly different from the rest of Mexico. An extension of the California coast, the Baja peninsula – the longest in the world – was formed millions of years ago when seismic activity along the San Andreas Fault created a depression in the earth's surface and sea water flooded in, creating the Gulf of California – also called the Sea of Cortez.

The peninsula's long, craggy coastlines were first explored in the 1530s by Spaniards, who named it Baja (Lower) California. This arid region of scrub-covered mountains lacked gold or silver deposits, so it was left to missionaries to colonize. The first Jesuit mission was established in 1697 at Loreto, on the Baja's east coast, and was the first of a chain of Spanish missions established along the length of the Californias.

In the mid-1700s, the Franciscans, followed by the Dominicans, continued the mission work begun by the Jesuits. However, diseases introduced by the Spanish were decimating the Indians whose numbers plummeted, and the missions were eventually abandoned.

American troops marched on La Paz and San Jose del Cabo during the Mexican War, but the Baja remained with Mexico when a peace treaty was signed and Alto (Upper) California was ceded to the United States.

The Baja's semi-isolation and sparse population have made it a paradise for naturalists who come to study the region's indigenous plants, animals and marine life. The Sea of Cortez deepens from north to south, and nutrient-rich upwellings from the sea floor support a wealth of marine life, including sponge and oyster beds, as well as some 800 species of reef fish. John Steinbeck, the Nobel-winning American writer from California, accompanied the marine biologist Edward Rickets on a collecting expedition to the area, after which they co-wrote *The Log from the Sea of Cortez* (1951).

At the southern tip of the Baja peninsula, where the Sea of Cortez meets the Pacific Ocean, the waters off Cabo San Lucas contain underwater cliffs where

***Land's End, Baja California***

*Humpback Whale*

## Whalewatching

The outer coast of Baja California is one of the best places in the world to sight gray whales. Each fall, an estimated 11,000 to 15,000 gray whales migrate south from their feeding grounds in the Beaufort Sea to the Baja's warm-water lagoons where the females give birth and nurse their young from January to early April.

Another migratory whale that frequents Mexico's warm waters is the Pacific humpback, which arrives from its summer feeding grounds in Alaska for a winter of mating or birthing calves that were conceived during the previous year's breeding season. While rival male humpbacks confront one another with tail smacking, the nursing mothers are uninterested in these antics for they are busy taking care of their newborns.

depths drop off to 1200 feet. One submarine canyon, discovered in 1960, was filmed by Jacques Cousteau for its unique spectacle of sand cascading over its edge into an abyss of darkness. Cousteau's son Jean-Michel, continuing his late father's cause of preserving the earth's oceans, has spoken out about the deteriorating conditions in the Sea of Cortez, where the deepwater coral has been depleted and overfishing by Asian trawlers, licensed to longline for shark and squid but apparently are also scooping up other species, is slowly clearing out what has long been regarded as the world's greatest fish trap.

Visitors eager to experience the Baja's famous sportfishing and pristine beaches arrive in ever-increasing numbers by air and by land, along the Transpeninsular Highway which was completed in the late 1960s. The best arrival, however, is by sea – as the Mexican sun rises above the Sea of Cortez and casts its glow on the granite sentinels at Land's End. This timeless sight is the reward for rising early and being at the ship's rail when the anchor goes down in the bay of Cabo San Lucas.

## Cabo San Lucas

On a November day in 1587, the English privateer Thomas Cavendish pulled into the bay of Cabo San Lucas where he disembarked 190 crew and passengers from the *Santa Maria*, a treasure-filled Spanish galleon he had captured off the coast of Baja California. After transferring the gold and other treasures onto his two small ships, Cavendish burned the *Santa Maria* to her

*(Above) El Arco, the massive sea arch at Land's End. (Below) Lovers Beach. (Opposite page) Bay of Cabo San Lucas viewed from Giorgio's Restaurant.*

waterline, and departed. At that time, the southern tip of Baja California was a desolate wilderness of rocky headlands and hostile natives, and it was with some urgency that the Spanish crew

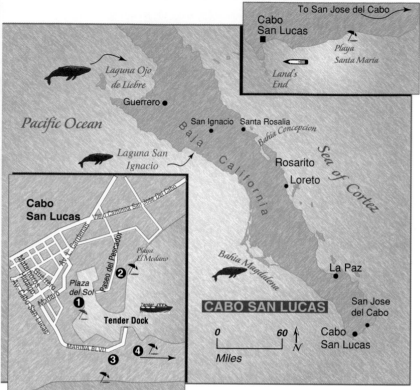

salvaged their ship's burned-out hulk and sailed her to safety across the Sea of Cortez.

Today's half-million annual visitors to Cabo San Lucas are in no hurry to leave, for the stark scenery is among the world's most dramatic. At Land's End, where the Pacific Ocean meets the Sea of Cortez, the pounding surf has carved rocky pinnacles that stand like silent sentinels in the swirling wash. Granite cliffs guard secluded beaches, and all day long the azure blue bay buzzes with sightseeing boats and sailing craft, including parasailers soaring high above the spectacular sea stacks off Land's End.

## Getting Around

The seaside resorts of Cabo San Lucas and nearby San Jose del Cabo are referred to as Los Cabos (The Capes) and their atmosphere is part Mexico, part California. Luxury hotels and golf courses overlook the beaches that dot nearly 20 miles of coastline between the two capes, and the U.S. dollar is the preferred currency. Cabo San Lucas is a booming tourist town while San Jose del Cabo offers the more languid pace of a Spanish colonial village.

Passengers are tendered ashore to the marina at Cabo San Lucas where dozens of docks accom-

*(Above) Pelicans perched on rocks are often seen during a glass-bottom boat ride to Land's End (below).*

modate the many tour boats providing excursions from the waterfront, including glass-bottom boat rides to El Arco ($7-$8) (45 minutes round trip) which also serve as water taxis to Lovers Beach. The town can be reached on foot, along the waterfront, in about 15 minutes. Taxis are located near the tender pier, behind the flea market, and are usually eight-seater vans. A taxi ride into town costs about $3 per person. Other fares, per person, are: Playa Medano ($3 – $4); Palapa Beach Club ($2-$3).

**Shopping** – A flea market selling Mexican crafts is located near the tender pier, while the town's jewelry shops are situated on or near Marina Boulevard.

**Beaches** – Closest to the tender pier is the excellent beach in front of **Plaza Las Glorias Hotel 1**. **Medano Beach 2**, where watersports equipment can be rented, stretches east along

## Shore Excursions

### Cabo San Lucas

A variety of boating excursions are offered, including those to Land's End and whalewatching expeditions (January through March). Snorkeling, scuba diving, sportfishing, sailing and kayaking excursions are all available, as are snuba and helmet diving. Beach getaways and dolphin encounters are also offered. Land-based excursions include zip-lining, horseback riding, four-wheel drive adventures and nature walks. Golf on a championship course is also available.

the bay from the marina and is backed by several hotels and beachfront restaurants. **Palapa Beach Club 3** at Hotel Finisterra provides access to a Pacific beach which is fine for sunbathing and strolling, but not swimming due to its strong currents. **Playa del Amour 4 (Lovers Beach)**, reached by water taxi, is a stunning swath of pristine white sand lying at the base of cliffs near Land's End. Swimming and snorkeling are popular here on the Gulf side of the beach but not the Pacific side where strong currents can be treacherous.

**Dive & Snorkel Sites** – The rocky foreshore and clear waters off Cabo San Lucas are an ideal environment for tropical fish, as well as starfish, sea fans and sponges. Pelican Rock Cove and Lovers Beach at Land's End offer good snorkeling, as does Playa Santa Maria which lies 8 miles east of Cabo San Lucas (accessible by road or by boat) and is considered the area's best snorkeling beach. Snorkel gear can be rented in town. One of the area's best dive sites is Playa Barco Varada (Shipwreck Beach), located 5.5 miles west of San Jose del Cabo, where a sunken tuna boat lies in depths of 80 feet (27 m). The submarine trench in Cabo San Lucas Bay also attracts an abundance of tropical and sub-tropical species of fish.

*(Left) A parasail soars above Lovers Beach. (Below) A ship's tender returns from the marina at Cabo San Lucas.*

*The dawn came quickly now, a wash, a glow, a lightness, and then an explosion of fire as the sun arose out of the Gulf. A passage from John Steinbeck's parable, The Pearl (1948), set in Baja California Sur.*

**Golf** – There are five championship golf courses in Los Cabos, all with ocean views. For more information, consult with the ship's shore excursion manager.

## Local Attractions

**El Arco** – This massive sea arch at Land's End has become the symbol of Cabo San Lucas. It can be viewed up close by glass-bottom boats that depart regularly from the marina; the trip is also an opportunity to view the underwater life, as well as pelicans perched on rocks and the resident sea lion colony.

**San Jose del Cabo** – An Old Mexico atmosphere endures in this colonial town, its main street a wide pedestrian boulevard lined with lovely gardens and interesting boutiques, galleries and restaurants. The town's Spanish colonial architecture includes a handsome Municipal Palace, mission church and tree-lined plaza.

*Sportfishing for marlin and sailfish is popular in Cabo San Lucas and the Sea of Cortez.*

## Sea of Cortez

**La Paz** – With a population of 200,000, La Paz (meaning 'peace') is the largest city and capital of the state of Baja California Sur, which comprises the southern half of the Baja peninsula. Situated at the head of a bay and first settled in 1811, La Paz was famous for its pearl fishing – evocatively described in Steinbeck's parable *The Pearl* – until disease destroyed the oyster beds in the middle of the 20th century. The palm-lined *malecon* provides lovely views of sailboats at anchor and the waterfront square is a popular gathering place for locals as the sun sets over the bay. Plaza Constitucion, the city's central plaza, is graced with a 19th-century cathedral (Cathedral de Nuestra Senora de la Paz) and the Palacio del Gobierno.

The port of La Paz is located on the Pichilingue peninsula, which forms the bay's eastern shore and is lined with beautiful beaches. The unspoilt islands of Espiritu Santo and Partida, the latter a seal sanctuary, can be visited by boat from La Paz and are popular with divers. These two islands are protected by UNESCO as biospheres and the beach at Ensenada Grande on Isla Partida is considered one of the most beautiful in Mexico.

**Loreto** – The region's oldest permanent settlement, Loreto was founded by Jesuit missionaries in 1697. This quiet town of 12,000 residents has been hard hit in the past by hurricanes and earthquakes, but the mission church has been beautifully restored, its cloisters containing a museum recounting the local histories of the three religious orders – Jesuit, Franciscan, Dominican – which colonized the region when it was part of New Spain.

Nearby **Isla Corondos** offers superb swimming beaches and snorkeling, as does Bahia de la Concepcion, about 40 miles north of Loreto, where crystal-clear waters and breathtaking beaches lie at the base of stark cliffs.

**Santa Rosalia** – Unlike the Baja's mission settlements, Santa Rosalia was strictly a company

*A 19th-century cathedral overlooks La Paz's central plaza.*

*La Paz's beachfront promenade.*

town, built in 1868 by French interests on the slopes of a mountain containing rich deposits of copper ore. The streets are lined with weatherboard houses – company officials lived on the upper slopes and the workers were housed below on the lower slopes. The French colonial style is seen in overhanging fretwork balconies and the town's cast-iron church, designed by a contemporary of Gustave Eiffel and exhibited in Paris before being shipped to Santa Rosalia in 1895.

Inland from Santa Rosalia is the oasis town of **San Ignacio**, situated atop an underground supply of fresh water, its shady central plaza graced with colonial buildings such as the mission church, built by the Dominicans in 1786 to replace an earlier one built of adobe by the Jesuits. Nearby is Sierra de San Francisco, where archaeologists have discovered caves containing pre-historic wall paintings.

**Topolobampo** – This former shrimping town is a port of access for the train ride through Mexico's spectacular Copper Canyon. The Chihuahua-al-Pacifico Railroad is a breathtaking stretch of tracks that weaves through the rugged mountains of the Sierra Madre, straddling dozens of deep gorges and plunging through 86 tunnels. The Copper Canyon is a system of six canyons which, in its entirety, is larger than the Grand Canyon. Topolobampo, scenically set on a bay surrounded by hills, was a fishing port before PEMEX (Mexico's state-owned petroleum company) built a local oil-storage complex and the shrimp disappeared.

## Ensenada

*(Above) A landward view of Ensenada. (Below and opposite page) Art galleries, shops and restaurants line both sides of Avenida Lopez        Mateos.*

This Pacific port is located just 70 miles south of the U.S. border. Its cruise terminal has two berths to accommodate arriving cruise ships, each berth with its own market village selling Mexican handicrafts and liquor. Larger ships anchor off and tender their passengers ashore. The town center is within walking distance or a 5-minute drive from the cruise docks; shuttle vans charge a couple of dollars per person and drop you off near the **shopping** streets. An outdoor crafts market selling excellent Mexican handicrafts is at the junction of Avenida Lopez Mateos and Avenida Macheros.

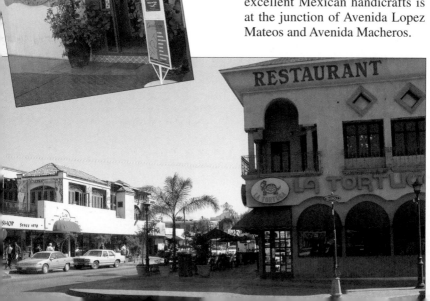

Other attractions in Ensenada include the Regional History Museum, housed in the town's former jailhouse and displaying interesting exhibits and archival photographs. The Museum of History is housed in a white waterfront complex that was once the Riviera del Pacifico casino – frequented by Hollywood stars such as Myrna Loy and Lana Turner.

The local fish market at the harbor entrance provides an intriguing glimpse at the Baja's cooperative distribution of seafood where small fishboat operators bring their catch to market. For fine views of the town, head up to El Mirador atop Chapultepec Hill.

**Estero Beach**, located six miles south of town, is one of Ensenada's most popular stretches of sand. The Estero Beach Resort has a restaurant and beach facilities, and this seaside resort also features a small museum dedicated to folk art and ancient artifacts.

Out-of-town excursions include a visit to **La Bufadora** blowholes. Local operators charge $15 per adult ($12 per child) for a 1.5 hour tour which includes time at a beach and an authentic market. La Bufadora can also be visited on a ship-organized excursion.

Other excursions include a visit to Bodegas De Santo Tomas winery and a tour of Ensenada's wine country.

From late December to the end of March (when gray whales have migrated to local waters), Ensenada boat operators work with the Ensenada Science Museum to offer guided whale-watching excursions.

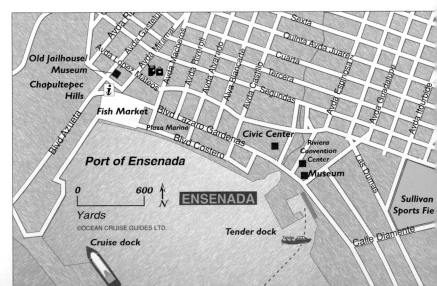

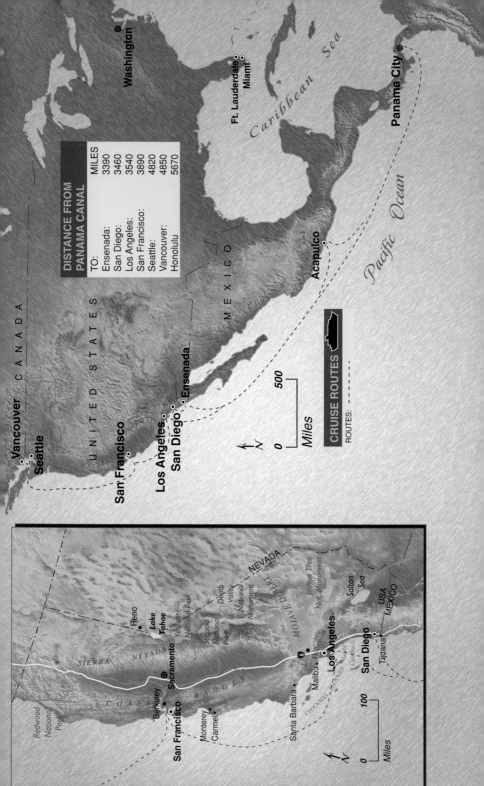

**DISTANCE FROM PANAMA CANAL**

| TO: | MILES |
| --- | --- |
| Ensenada: | 3390 |
| San Diego: | 3460 |
| Los Angeles: | 3540 |
| San Francisco: | 3890 |
| Seattle: | 4820 |
| Vancouver: | 4850 |
| Honolulu | 5670 |

CRUISE ROUTES

ROUTES: - - - - -

Pacific Ocean

Caribbean Sea

CANADA

UNITED STATES

MEXICO

Washington

Vancouver
Seattle

San Francisco

Los Angeles
San Diego
Ensenada

Acapulco

Ft. Lauderdale
Miami

Panama City

N

Miles

0        500

*Inset map:*

Redwood National Park

SIERRA NEVADA

Reno

*Lake Tahoe*

Yosemite National Park

COAST RANGES

Sacramento

Berkeley
San Francisco

Monterey
Carmel

Santa Barbara

Sequoia National Park

Death Valley National Monument

NEVADA

Joshua Tree Nat. Monument

MOJAVE DESERT

Salton Sea

Malibu
Hollywood
Los Angeles

Channel Islands

San Diego
Tijuana

USA
MEXICO

N

Miles

0        100

# WEST COAST PORTS

California is America's third largest state in land area but second to none in terms of natural wonders. The state's northernmost coastal region is home to huge cathedral-like redwood forests containing some of the world's tallest trees, over 300 feet tall. In stark contrast is arid Death Valley, the lowest point in the Americas, where some of the world's hottest temperatures have been recorded.

A hundred miles northwest of Death Valley, in the glacier-scoured valleys and mountains of Yosemite National Park, is North America's highest waterfall, Yosemite Falls. And in Sequoia National Park, the giant pines are as impressive as the jagged peaks of the High Sierras, among them Mount Whitney, highest mountain in the U.S. outside Alaska.

Yet it's the Pacific beaches of coastal California that most often come to mind when people think of life in the Golden State – those beaches of wavewashed sand and rugged headlands where seals lounge on rock outcroppings while movie stars lounge on the decks of their beach houses.

With a population approaching 40 million, California is the most populous state in the U.S and its highly diversified economy is the eighth largest in the world. A land of plenty, California has long attracted immigrants – from other states and other nations – whose pursuit of the American dream fueled the growth of cities and beach communities now lining the west coast.

In 1850, when California entered the Union, it was the region's fertile soil and long growing season that supported a thriving agricultural economy. Today, despite being hit hard by the recession of 2008-2009, California remains a global leader in the digital economy, biotechnology, and the aerospace and entertainment industries. Its famous tourist attractions continue to attract visitors by the millions and its coastal cities – San Diego, Los Angeles and San Francisco – are base ports and/or ports of call for ships plying the Panama Canal or heading to the Mexican Riviera.

# San Diego

Few cities seem to be as perfectly situated as San Diego. Its sub-tropical climate is ideal for enjoying the city's beaches, and the excellent natural harbor (at the downtown's doorstep) makes San Diego a cruise port of undisputed appeal. The second-largest metropolis in California with a population approaching 3 million, this city that attracts artists and retirees is also home to a third of the U.S. Navy's Pacific Fleet.

San Diego became an important naval base during World War I, and other branches of the military soon established bases in the area, their presence giving rise to a booming aerospace industry.

Shipbuilding is another important industry in San Diego, and yachting is a popular pastime. In 1987, the San Diego Yacht Club won the America's Cup for the United States and successfully defended the Cup in 1992. The first sailing ship to pull into San Diego Bay was commanded by Portuguese-born Juan Rodriguez Cabrillo, who landed at Point Loma in 1542 and claimed what he saw on behalf of Spain. In 1769, San Diego became the first Spanish settlement in Alto (Upper) California and, like the rest of California, eventually joined the United States. However, the city's Spanish past and close proximity to Mexico remain part of the cultural vitality of this Pacific port.

**Getting Around** – San Diego International Airport (also known as Lindbergh Field) is a 10-minute drive from the downtown cruise ship terminal on San Diego Bay. The main cruise facility is at B Street, with an auxiliary terminal adjacent to it on Broadway. Parking isn't available at the cruise piers; for a list of nearby parking lot operators, visit www.sandiego-

*Aerial view of San Diego Bay and San Diego-Coronado Bridge.*

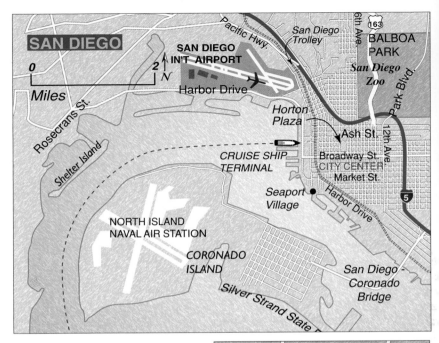

cruiseport.com.

The city's extensive trolley system is an ideal way to tour the downtown and the historic **Old Town**. (One- to four-day trolley passes can be purchased at The Transit Store, 102 Broadway.) Attractions on the downtown harborfront include the Arthur Erickson-designed **Convention Center** with its glass-enclosed lobby and landscaped outdoor plazas and terraces. **Coronado Island**, which is located across the harbor from downtown, can be reached via the San Diego-Coronado Bridge or by ferry.

Upscale **hotels** in San Diego include the Manchester Grand Hyatt with its spectacular water-front location beside Seaport Village. Hyatt properties are also located at Mission Bay and La Jolla. The US Grant – a heritage property – is a city landmark

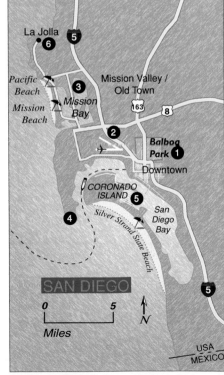

and part of the Starwood Luxury Collection. The W San Diego, at 421 West B. Street, is topped with a roof bar. The famous Hotel Del Coronado is located across the bay on Coronado Island.

**Shopping & Dining – Seaport Village**, located next door to the Convention Center, is a large waterfront complex of shopping, dining and entertainment (and is also a good place to observe the U.S. Navy's Pacific Fleet of cruisers, carriers and destroyers docked across the bay at Coronado Island).

The architecturally acclaimed **Horton Plaza** features six open-air levels of upscale shops and restaurants. Its construction in the 1980s began the downtown's revitalization. Adjacent to the Plaza is the historic **Gaslamp Quarter** where shops, galleries and restaurants are housed in restored, Victorian buildings.

**Beaches** – The sandy beaches of Coronado Island are popular, as is the family-oriented Silver Strand State Beach (situated on the long sandbar joining Coronado with the mainland). More beaches lie north of downtown in the seaside communities of Pacific Beach, Mission Beach and La Jolla.

**Golf** – There are numerous municipal courses in the San Diego area, including the oceanside Torrey Pines Golf Course in La Jolla where the annual Buick Invitational is played each February. Tee times at public courses can be obtained from the concierge at your hotel.

## Local Attractions

**Balboa Park 1** – This beautifully landscaped park covers 1,200 acres and is home to the world-famous **San Diego Zoo**, itself designed as a 100-acre tropical garden. The zoo houses 800 different species, including rare giant pandas on long-term loan from China, and can be toured on foot or by taking a three-mile guided bus tour. Other attractions in Balboa Park are a fine art gallery and over a dozen museums, including the **San Diego Aerospace Museum**. Much of

*San Diego's B Street Terminal*

the Park's architecture dates from the Panama-California Exposition of 1915 and the California Pacific International Exposition of 1935, and includes the Old Globe Theater, the California Tower with its working 100-bell carillon and the Spiracles Organ Pavilion, which features concerts on Sunday afternoons. The free Balboa Park Tram runs daily.

**Old Town 2** – This was the heart of San Diego when it was part of Mexico. Many of the Spanish-style colonial buildings around the Old Town Square were built between 1820 and 1869, and are now part of a state historical park.

**Mission Bay Park 3** – Mission Bay beach community is home to a huge public aquatic park stretching along 17 miles of oceanfront beaches and containing designated areas for various outdoor sports. Mission Bay is also home to **SeaWorld San Diego**, a marine park featuring trained killer whales and dolphins, as well as manatees, penguins and beluga whales.

**Cabrillo National Monument – 4** Situated on Point Loma, this monument marks the site where Spanish conquistadors, led by Juan Rodriguez Cabrillo, landed in 1542. This rocky point provides a panoramic view of San Diego Bay, and is also an ideal spot to watch for migrating gray whales.

**Coronado 5** – The centerpiece of this bayside beach community is the illustrious **Hotel Del Coronado**. Built in 1888, this landmark building of turrets, cupolas and verandahs was featured in Billy Wilder's classic film *Some Like It Hot*. A seven-storey tower and poolside complex have been added to the original Victorian structure, and the hotel features shops, restaurants and other resort amenities. There are other hotels and charming cottages in the vicinity, and the village itself features a large central park and the popular Ferry Landing Marketplace.

**La Jolla 6** (*le hoi ye*) – A 20-minute drive from downtown San Diego, this upscale resort is well known for its beautiful ocean beaches, sea-washed caves and abundance of tidal pools. Situated here is the **Scripps Institution of Oceanography and Birch Aquarium** where an outdoor tidepool exhibit introduces visitors to the shore life that can be seen in La Jolla Cove. Just south of La Jolla Cove, along the waterfront, is the **Museum of Contemporary Art**.

## Los Angeles

America's motion picture industry began at a California race track in the 1860s when a gifted English eccentric named Eadweard Muybridge set up a row of cameras with shutters tripped by wires and successfully took the first serial photographs of a horse running. New York studios soon began screening short films, but when Thomas Edison tried to monopolize the industry in 1909 by claiming patents on certain technical elements, a number of independent producers moved their studios to southern California where they could flee to Mexico if faced with legal injunctions. In a few short years, Hollywood became the movie capital of America, if not the world.

Today, Los Angeles is home to countless studios in the motion picture, television, radio and recording fields, and the allure of Hollywood endures, the city's landmark buildings and beaches having appeared in countless films and television shows over the years. Los Angeles is the second largest American city in both population and area, is one of the nation's busiest ports, and is a leading producer of a huge range of goods, but in the public consciousness it is first and foremost the home of Hollywood.

Back in the 18th century, America's future entertainment capital was a cattle-ranching center and capital of the Spanish colonial province Alto California. Founded in 1781 as The Town of Our Lady the Queen of the Angels of Porciuncula, the settlement was captured by U.S. forces in 1846. Los Angeles enjoyed steady growth following the completion of two intercontinental railroads and the discovery of oil in the late 1800s. The opening of the Panama Canal in 1914 spurred the growth of its port, and the city boomed during World War II, when thousands of African-Americans arrived to fill factory jobs. Growth continued after the war, and the expanding city absorbed surrounding communities. The influx of immi-

grants of various ethnic backgrounds, including Hispanics and Asians, created a cosmopolitan and sprawling metropolis that now encompasses five counties and over 15 million people.

**Getting Around** – Los Angeles Harbor, situated in San Pedro Bay, is one of the world's great man-made harbors, built with breakwaters, channels, piers and wharves. Downtown Los Angeles is 21 miles due north of Los Angeles Harbor, and Hollywood is 7 miles northwest of downtown. Los Angeles International Airport is located about 20 miles from Los Angeles Harbor – approximately 30 minutes ($50) by taxi. The cruise lines offer airport transfers which can be combined with motorcoach tours of L.A.

**Shopping & Dining** – Beverly Hills' three-block stretch of **Rodeo Drive** between Santa Monica and Wilshire Boulevard is L.A.'s most famous shopping strip. In addition to the specialty stores and fashion boutiques on Rodeo Drive and surrounding streets, department stores in the vicinity include Neiman-Marcus, Barneys New York and Saks Fifth Avenue, all located on Wilshire Boulevard. **The Grove Shopping Center** (next door to the historic L.A.Farmers Market) is an outdoor boutique mall, its cobblestoned square and dancing fountain providing a European ambiance. A vintage trolley connects The Grove and Farmers Market. Other shopping venues include the seaside community of **Santa Monica**, its pedestrian-only 3rd

Street Promenade lined with boutiques and restaurants.

**Beaches** – The reclusive, and exclusive, resort area of **Malibu** is where many of the show business stars own homes along a beach escarpment overlooking Santa Monica Bay. **Santa Monica**, south of Malibu, has three miles of oceanfront beach. Its famous pier, with its 46-horse carousel, was built in 1906 and has appeared in numerous films, including *The Sting*. The main attraction at **Venice City Beach** is the mile-and-a-half boardwalk, dotted with street entertainers and bustling with cyclists and rollerbladers. South of the beach is Marina Del Rey, an enormous man-made marina.

## Local Attractions

**Downtown Los Angeles** – The city's original Spanish settlement is preserved by **El Pueblo de Los Angeles Historic Park 1**. On the north side is Olvera Street, a Mexican street market originally called El Paseo de Los Angeles (Walk of the Angels). Facing the park's east side is Union Station, built in 1939 in the Spanish-mission style and featured in numerous Hollywood films, including *The Way We Were*.

Two blocks south of the park is the **Civic Center 2**, where City Hall (which served as Clark Kent's *Daily Planet* in TV's old Superman series) provides panoramic views from its tower. Also in the vicinity is the stunning post-modern **Cathedral of Our Lady of the Angels**, built with no right angles and costing $190 million upon its completion in 2002.

Grand Avenue, a pedestrian promenade, connects the cathedral with the new **Walt Disney Concert Hall**, designed by Frank Gehry. Other landmark buildings in downtown L.A. include the beaux-arts **Biltmore Hotel** on Grand Avenue (which hosted the Academy Awards in the 1930s) and the post-modern **Westin Bonaventure Hotel** on Figueroa Street, its five shimmering cylinders sheathed in mirrored glass. Red Line's guided tours of downtown L.A. and its historic theaters depart from the Victorian-era **Bradbury Building** (on Broadway) which has appeared in numerous films, including *Chinatown* and *Blade Runner.*

**Wilshire Boulevard** is a main thoroughfare which runs for 16 miles from downtown L.A. to Santa Monica Bay. Major attractions along Wilshire include the renowned **Los Angeles County Museum of Art 3**, with its huge collection of art from ancient times to present. The museum is housed in a large complex situated in a park it shares with the prehistoric La Brea Tar Pits, where fossils extracted from oil upwellings are displayed in an adjacent museum.

A few blocks north, at 3rd Street and Fairfax Avenue, is the famous open-air **Farmers Market 4**, a hub for locals and tourists with over 100 stalls and 20 restaurants. Next door is **The Grove Shopping Center** (see Shopping section).

**Hollywood & Beverly Hills** – The heart of Hollywood is the intersection of **Vine Street** and **Hollywood Boulevard**, overlooked by the Capitol Records Tower, which resembles a stack of 45s. Stretching west along Hollywood Boulevard is the **Walk of Fame** – a mile of sidewalk where the names of legendary entertainers are embossed in brass. About halfway along the Walk of Fame, beside the **Hollywood & Highland Center** 5, is the **Kodak Theatre** – where the annual Academy Awards ceremony has been held since 2002. Next door is **Mann's Chinese Theatre** (formerly Grauman's) where many a motion picture premiere has been held.

*Handprints of the stars car be seen at Mann's Chinese Theatre.*

Nestled in the hills north of Hollywood Boulevard is the **Hollywood Bowl** 6, an amphitheater where summer evening concerts are held. Nearby **Griffith Park** 7, containing a zoo and planetarium, is one of the largest urban parks in the world, occupying land donated in 1896 by a mining tycoon. Scenes from the TV series *Bonanza* and the James Dean film *Rebel Without a Cause* were shot here.

Just north of Hollywood, on the edge of the San Fernando Valley, is **Universal Studios Hollywood** 8 where visitors are transported around a 420-acre theme park and introduced to the movie art of special effects, including an encounter with King Kong and aliens armed with death rays. The Valley is home to most of the major film and television studios, and tours are available at Warner Bros. Studios and NBC Television Studios.

West of Hollywood is **Beverly Hills**, an exclusive residential area where many of the stars reside in hedge-hidden mansions. The **Beverly Hills Trolley** provides street tours of local landmarks and the former homes of celebrities.

The pastel-pink **Beverly Hills Hotel** 9 on Sunset Boulevard was built in 1912 and was, for decades, the place where movie producers would cut deals in the Polo Lounge. The neo-Gothic **Greystone Mansion** 10 on Doheny Road (a setting for scenes in *The Witches of Eastwick*) was built by a wealthy oilman in 1927. Now owned by the city of Beverly Hills, its manicured grounds are open to visitors.

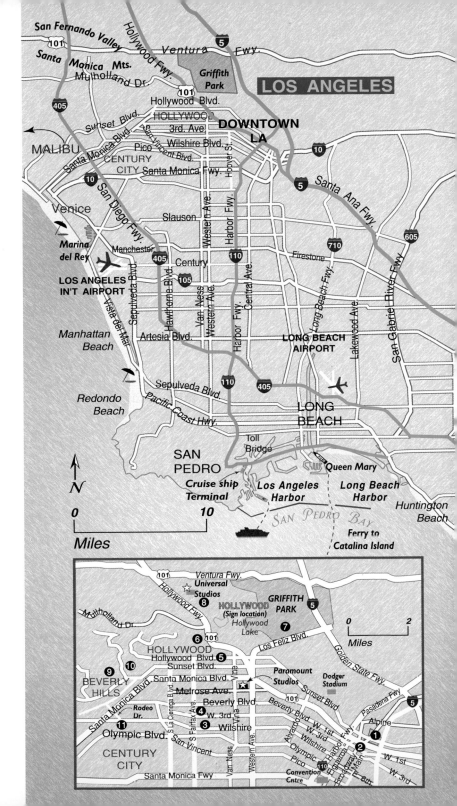

The **Regent Beverly Wilshire** **11**, at the south end of Rodeo Drive, is another landmark hotel, its Wilshire wing built in 1928. Scenes for the hit movie *Pretty Woman* were shot in the presidential suite. The nearby **Beverly Hilton** opened in 1955 and has hosted the Golden Globe Awards in its International Ballroom since 1961.

On Hollywood Boulevard, across the street from Mann's Chinese Theatre, is the **Hollywood Roosevelt Hotel**, built in the 1920s to house movie stars shooting on location. Hollywood's first Oscars were presented, in 1929, at this historic hotel, which was built in the Spanish Revival style and was once home to Marilyn Monroe.

Another L.A. attraction is the **Getty Center**, located on a hill in Brentwood overlooking Bel-

Air with views (on a clear day) of the entire Los Angeles basin and the Pacific Ocean. Four major art collections (including Greek and Roman antiquities) are housed in the campus's five pavilions.

**Long Beach** – About 5 miles east of the cruise port is Long Beach, where the former Cunard liner the *Queen Mary* has been permanently docked since 1967. Part hotel, part tourist attraction, the 80,000-ton luxury liner was built in the 1930s and her art deco interior included enough wood paneling, cut glass and silver-plated handrails to impress the most privileged wealthy. Daily tours of the ship are available to the public, and there are several restaurants and shops on board. Ferry service connects Long Beach with the charming port town of **Avalon** on Catalina Island, lying 22 miles offshore.

Ships calling at **Catalina Island** offer numerous shore excursions, including a walk-

*A meeting of the Queen Marys took place at Long Beach Harbor.*

ing tour of the Avalon Casino, built in the Mediterranean style in 1929 by William Wrigley and housing an array of art deco memorabilia. Scenic driving tours wind along the waterfront and up into the hilly interior to such points of interest as a botanical garden, nature reserve and bald eagle habitat. Kayaking, snorkeling, glass-bottom boat tours and coastal exploring by boat or inflatable raft are also offered, as is a a 9-hole round of golf at the oldest course in California.

**Orange County** – Tourist attractions include **Knott's Berry Farm** with its replica of an early California Gold Rush Town, and **Disneyland**, the huge amusement park that has been the centerpiece of Anaheim (Orange County's tourist hub) since opening in 1955. Beautiful beaches line the coast of Orange County, including **Huntington Beach** with its broad white-sand beaches, and **Newport Beach** where an island-dotted harbor is home to hundreds of yachts. Other popular beach communities are **Laguna Beach**, its hillside homes popular with artists, and **Dana Point**, one of southern California's top surfing destinations and named for Richard Henry Dana, author of *Two Years Before the Mast* in which he describes the local harbor as it was more than a century ago. **San Juan Capistrano** is home to a famous Spanish mission, founded in 1776. For decades swallows would arrive in mid-March at the mission from their winter home in Argentina.

## San Francisco

The city by the bay began in 1776 as a Spanish mission called San Francisco de Asis. The nearby presidio overlooked Golden Gate at the entrance to San Francisco Bay and was called Yerba Buena when claimed by an American naval force in 1846. It remained a quiet village until gold was discovered inland and gold seekers converged by steamship on this sleepy port, the local population ballooning from 800 to 25,000 in the space of two years. The waterfront was dubbed the Barbary Coast for its seedy activities, and a period of lawlessness prevailed until vigilantes were organized to keep the peace.

San Francisco eventually became a major commercial port and financial hub. Then, in the mid-20th century, this scenic city was discovered by the counterculture, attracting first the beatniks of the 1950s, then the hippie generation of the 1960s. The city also has a large gay population, and its reputation for social tolerance remains part of its appeal. It is also one of the most beautiful in the world. Visitors come to ride those vintage cable cars up and down streets lined with Victorian townhouses, and to gaze from hilltops across San Francisco Bay, where fog often obscures all but the uppermost spans of the famous Golden Gate Bridge.

*(Left) The Powell-Hyde cable car provides hillside views of San Francisco Bay and Alcatraz Island. (Below) Alcatraz Island, a former prison, is now a popular tourist attraction run by the National Park Service.*

**Getting Around** – The cruise ships dock at historic Pier 35 or at the new Pier 27 (which served as the start and finish line for the 2013 America's Cup). Within walking distance are numerous attractions. A waterfront promenade called Herb Caen Way runs alongside The Embarcadero from Fisherman's Wharf to the Bay Bridge. Vintage **street cars** also run along The Embarcadero and Market Street, and can be boarded outside the cruise terminal.

The **cable cars**, which fill up quickly in the summer months, can be caught at the turnaround stations or at various stops along the way. They are hauled by cables that are in constant motion beneath the street and the car's gripman operates a device beneath the car that grabs onto the cable. Union Square, North

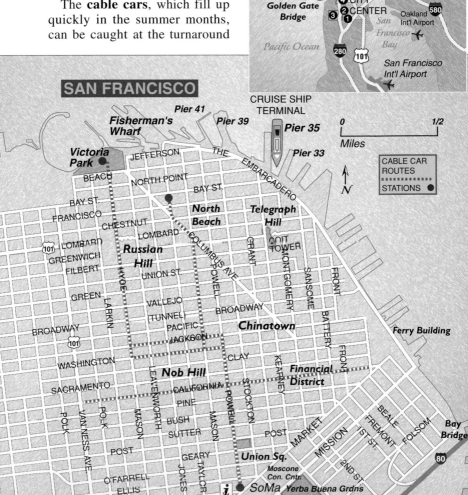

Beach, Nob Hill, Chinatown and SoMa can all be reached by cable car, while other areas of interest, such as Haight Ashbury, Golden Gate Park and Presidio can be reached by city buses, street cars or taxi.

In addition to ship-organized shore excursions, numerous tour operators offer city tours and scenic drives, including full-day trips north to California's wine country and south to the Monterey Peninsula. **Alcatraz Island** can be accessed by passenger ferry from Pier 41.

A taxi from the airport to downtown costs about $35, and the minibus shuttle is $11. Luxury **hotels** on Nob Hill include The Fairmont (at Mason and California Streets) and The Ritz-Carlton (Stockton Street at California). The Four Seasons is in the Yerba Buena district, two blocks from Union Square, and the Mandarin Oriental on Sansome Street provides breathtaking views from its upper floors.

**Shopping & Dining** – The retail area around **Union Square** and **Market Street** is the city's best-known shopping enclave, containing premier department stores such as Saks Fifth Avenue and Macy's, and international fashion houses. Maiden Lane, on the east side of Union Square, is lined with boutiques, and more shops are housed in the San Francisco Shopping Centre.

Few cities eclipse San Francisco in terms of eclectic restaurants and fine dining. Superb French cuisine is served at La Folie in Russian Hill, and a cocktail with a view can be enjoyed in the Fairmont's rooftop Crown Room.

**The Embarcadero**, the city's original working waterfront, was revitalized following the 1989 collapse of the elevated Embarcadero Freeway during an earthquake. Today, at its southeast end, lies one of San Francisco's most stylish areas to dine and shop. Its focal

*Golden Gate – the most famous suspension bridge in the world.*

point is the beautifully restored beaux-arts Ferry Building (at the foot of Market Street along The Embarcadero), which now houses specialty food shops and upscale ethnic restaurants.

## Local Attractions

**Fisherman's Wharf** encompasses the waterfront between Pier 39 and the Municipal Pier, and includes adjacent Victorian Park where the ship-shaped National Maritime Museum is located. A panoply of restaurants, shops, street performers, foodstands and fishboat docks, this waterfront area's most-visited attraction (one of the top three in California) is **Pier 39**, where broad boardwalks dotted with benches create a village-like atmosphere for this colorful complex of specialty shops and restaurants. Sea lions congregate on adjacent K Dock, and boat trips depart every hour from Pier 41 for **Alcatraz Island**. 'The Rock' was once a notorious high-security prison housing the likes of Al Capone, 'Machine Gun' Kelly and Robert 'The Birdman' Stroud, and is now a tourist attraction drawing over a million visitors annually.

**North Beach**, an Italian section of excellent eateries and delicatessens, became an enclave for beatniks in the mid-1950s where famous hangouts included Lawrence Ferlinghetti's City Lights Bookstore at 261 Columbus and the Hungry I, where Lenny Bruce honed his stand-up comedy. The **Coit Tower** on **Telegraph Hill** was built in 1933 with a bequest from an eccentric named Lillie Hitchcock Coit and its public elevator whisks visitors to the top of this 210-foot column for spectacular views of the city.

**Russian Hill** is home to Lombard Street, said to be the most crooked street in the world, while **Nob Hill** is the home of millionaires. **Chinatown** is a 24-block area of residential and commercial streets, its attractions including the dragon-crested gate at Grant Avenue and Bush Street, several temples and dozens of exotic food stalls.

South of Market Street is **SoMa**, where the San Francisco Museum of Modern Art, Sony's Metreon family entertainment complex and numerous galleries surround Yerba Buena Gardens. **Mission District ■** is named for Mission Dolores, a Spanish mission established in 1782 and originally called San Francisco de Asis. **Haight Ashbury ■** is where the 'flower children' of the 1960s hung out, and nearby **Golden Gate National Recreation Area ■** contains two natural history museums, an aquarium, planetarium and **Presidio Park ■** – a former US Army base and site of the original Spanish fort, built in 1776. Film director **George Lucas** was chosen to build the **Letterman Digital Arts Center** on the site of the Letterman Army Hospital, and this 23-acre wooded campus (17 acres of which are public park) is home to Lucasfilm, Industrial Light & Magic and LucasArts. The lobby of Building B is open to the public and contains a gallery of **Star Wars** memorabilia.

# Seattle

The city of Seattle enjoys a superb setting on the shores of Elliott Bay. The cruise ships dock at Pier 66 (at the foot of Bell Street) and at Pier 91 (about a 20-minute drive from downtown). Long-term parking ($12-$14 per day) is available at both terminals and can be prepaid online at www.rpnw.com. Seattle's Sea-Tac Airport is about a 30-minute drive to downtown and taxi fares range from $25 - $40.

Seattle's waterfront is serviced by vintage trolleys which travel up and down Alaskan Way. They stop at various pier attractions, then carry on to Pioneer Square and the International District. Seattle trolley tours can be boarded at the waterfront or downtown booths for a one-hour narrated loop tour of the city's attractions, with on/off privileges at each stop.

The downtown Metro buses in the core area – between Battery Street and South Jackson Street, and between Sixth Avenue and Alaskan Way – are free from 6 a.m. to 7 p.m. A high-speed monorail whisks passengers between Westlake Center and the Seattle Center. Pier 66 is within walking distance of the Space Needle (20 minutes along Broad Street) and Pike Place Market (10 to 15 minutes). The stairs of Pike Place Hillclimb connect the market with the waterfront below.

Shopping can be enjoyed on Fifth Avenue at Westlake Center, Nordstrom and Rainier Square.

Ship-organized **shore excursions** include narrated driving tours of the city with walking stops at the Space Needle, Experience Music Project and/or Pike Place Market. A boat cruise from Lake Union along the Ship Canal and through the Chittenden Locks is sometimes included. Also offered are driving tours to out-of-town attractions such as the Future of Flight & Boeing Factory Tour at Paine Field Airport in Everett (north of Seattle) and a culinary tour of Woodinville's wineries.

Seattle attractions begin at the waterfront where the **Olympic Sculpture Park** (beside Pier 70) is an open green space for displaying public art. The **Seattle Imax Dome Theater** is located on historic Pier 59, next to the **Seattle Aquarium.** The Bell Street Pier (Pier 66) is where **Odyssey, The Maritime Discovery Centre** is located. A public rooftop deck, with telescopes, is a good spot to enjoy the harbor views.

Perched on a bluff overlooking the waterfront is the century-old **Pike Place Market** 🚩 at the foot of Pike and Pine streets. The cobblestone streets here are lined with food stalls and restaurants.

Four blocks up from the Pike Place Market, at Pine and 5th Avenue, is the Westlake Center monorail terminal where you can embark on a two-minute monorail ride to Seattle Center and the famous **Space Needle** 🚩, built for the 1962 World's Fair, its observation deck providing 360-degree views of the city and nearby Cascade Mountains. The Space Needle is part of the 74-acre **Seattle Center** which encompasses a theater, opera house

(McCaw Hall), children's museum and Pacific Science Center (the U.S. Science Pavilion at the 1962 World's Fair). Near the base of the Space Needle is the **Experience Music Project**, an interactive rock'n'roll museum, and the **Science Fiction Museum and Hall of Fame**, brainchild of sci-fi fan Paul Allen. Other downtown attractions are the **Seattle Art Museum 3**, the restored brick buildings of **Pioneer Square 4**, **CenturyLink Field** (the Seahawks Football Stadium) and adjacent **Safeco Field 5**, home to the Seattle Mariners baseball club. Walking tours of both the stadium and the ballpark are available. Due east is the **International District 6**, filled with Asian restaurants, bazaars and exotic shops.

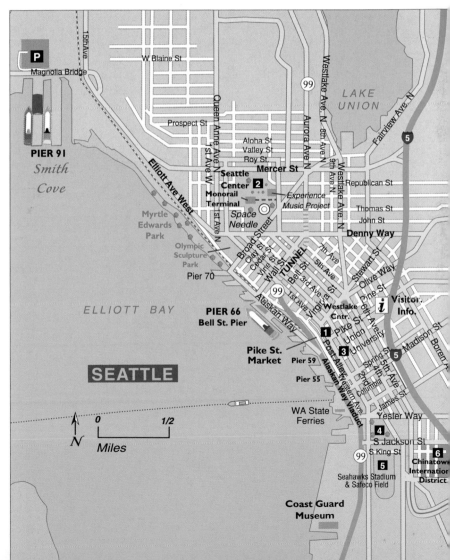

## Vancouver

Considered Canada's most scenic city, Vancouver is the northernmost port of call on Panama Canal repositioning cruises. The ships dock in the heart of downtown at **Canada Place**, a landmark complex crowned with white sails, or at **Ballantyne Pier**, a refurbished heritage facility situated a short taxi ride from the downtown core.

For a panoramic overview of the city, visit **The Lookout!** , downtown Vancouver's highest viewpoint atop the Harbour Centre Tower, a few blocks east of Canada Place. Some prominent buildings to look for: **Hotel Vancouver** **2** on Georgia Street (a grand railway hotel); **Marine**

*An aerial view of downtown Vancouver's cruise port.*

**Building** **3** on Burrard Street (Vancouver's finest example of art deco architecture); **Library Square** **4** on Georgia Street (a coliseum-like structure housing Vancouver's main library as well as shops and restaurants); **Law Courts** **5** at Robson Square (a long, low building with a sloped glass roof and streaming waterfalls designed by Vancouver architect Arthur Erickson) and **Vancouver Art Gallery** **6** (a former court house built in the beaux-arts style).

**Gastown**, a short stroll from Canada Place, was Vancouver's original townsite, founded in 1867 by a smooth-talking saloon keeper named John 'Gassy Jack' Deighton. Its western entrance is marked by **The Landing** **7** – a refurbished heritage complex of shops and restaurants. Water Street, lined with shops and

restaurants, leads past the working steam clock to **Maple Tree Square** ⑧ where Gassy Jack's saloon once stood.

**Robson Street**, Vancouver's premier shopping street, leads from Robson Square to the **West End**. Here attractions include **English Bay Beach**, where waterfront restaurants overlook the beach and bay. At adjacent **Sunset Beach** a passenger ferry can be taken across False Creek to **Granville Island** ⑨. This popular venue features a public market, boutiques, pubs and restaurants.

Also in the West End is famous **Stanley Park**, containing 1,000 acres of forest and trails. Among the park's many attractions are a rose garden, totem pole display, aquarium and several restaurants.

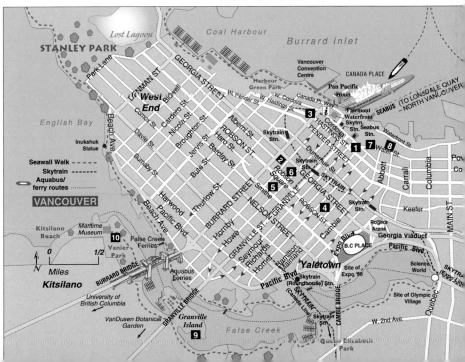

*Azamara Journey (2007)*
*708 passengers, 30,000 tons*

**AZAMARA CLUB CRUISES** , founded in 2007 and owned by Royal Caribbean Cruises Ltd., operates medium-sized boutique ships offering a country-club atmosphere. These finely appointed ships are ideal for seasoned cruisers seeking out-of-the ordinary destinations and frequent overnight stays at ports of call.
(www.azamaracruises.com)

*Carnival Liberty (2005)*
*2,974 passengers, 110,000 tons*

**CARNIVAL CRUISE LINES**: The 'Fun Ships' of this contemporary cruise line are family-friendly and attract a high number of first-time cruisers. The ships feature brightly colored, theme-based interiors and provide excellent facilities for children and teens. Carnival offers the occasional trans-canal cruise between Flordia and Los Angeles (Long Beach). Roundtrip cruises to Baja Mexico and the Mexican Riviera are available from Los Angeles. Officers are Italian; service staff is international.
(www.carnivalcruises.com)

*Summit (2001)*
*1,950 passengers, 91,000 tons*

**CELEBRITY CRUISES**: Founded in 1990 as an offshoot of the Greek line Chandris Inc., Celebrity Cruises is now owned by Royal Caribbean Cruises Ltd. A premium cruise line, Celebrity is noted for its sophisticated service, gourmet cuisine and stylish ships appointed with modern art. The children's programs are excellent and family staterooms are available on most ships. Celebrity offers transcanal cruises between Fort Lauderdale or Miami and San Diego. Officers are Greek and service staff are international.
(www.celebritycruises.com)

**CRYSTAL CRUISES**: Owned by NYK of Japan, this luxury line's Panama Canal itineraries feature tailor-made shore excursions to suit individual preferences. Crystal's mid-sized ships are finely appointed with spacious interiors and almost all outside cabins. Transcanal itineraries depart from New York or Miami on the Atlantic side and from San Francisco, Los Angeles, San Diego or Costa Rica on the Pacific side. Officers are Scandinavian and service staff are international.
(www.crystalcruises.com)

*Crystal Serenity (2003)*
*1,080 passengers, 68,000 tons*

**CUNARD LINE:** This prestigious British line (now owned by Carnival Corporation) began operations in 1840 when Sir Samuel Cunard's fleet of four ships began carrying mail between Liverpool, Halifax and Boston. Cunard's classic ocean liners – *Queen Mary 2, Queen Elizabeth* and *Queen Victoria* – are modern ships offering traditional elegance and British ambiance. Officers are British; service staff is international.
(www.cunard.com)

*Queen Victoria (2007)*
*2,014 passengers, 90,000 tons*

**HOLLAND AMERICA LINE**: This Seattle-based premium cruise line, known for its gracious and attentive service, commands a loyal following. The company's classic blue-hulled ships feature teak promenade decks (which are a real treat to stroll in the morning), spacious staterooms (most with a bathtub) and fine art and antiques displayed throughout the public areas. The newer, larger ships of HAL's fleet feature children's facilities and are ideal for multi-generational family groups.

*Westerdam (2006)*
*1,848 passengers, 85,000 tons*

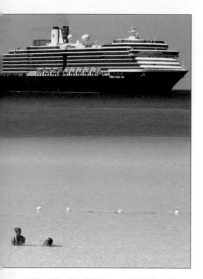

*HAL's 82,000-ton Zuiderdam anchored off Half Moon Cay.*

Holland America offers a selection of transcanal cruises between Fort Lauderdale on the Atlantic side and San Diego, Seattle or Vancouver on the Pacific side.

Partial transits are offered on 10- and 11-day roundtrip cruises from Fort Lauderdale and often feature a port call at the company's private Bahamian island, Half Moon Cay.

HAL also offers round-trip Mexican Riviera and Sea of Cortez cruises out of San Diego.

Officers are Dutch and service staff are Indonesian and Filipino.

(www.hollandamerica.com)

*MSC Musica ( 2006)*
*2,550 passengers, 89,000 tons*

**MSC ITALIAN CRUISES**: This Italian line features ships that are traditional in design and appeal to experienced cruisers. Officers and service staff are mostly Italian.

(www.mscitaliancruises.com)

*Norwegian Jewel (2005)*
*2,400 passengers, 92,000 tons*

**NORWEGIAN CRUISE LINE**: This innovative company was one of the first lines to invent modern cruising with trips from Miami to the Bahamas in the mid-1960s. A contemporary line with a casual atmosphere, extensive children's facilities and unstructured dining, NCL appeals to active couples and families. The line is also known for its excellent entertainment, notably Broadway musicals. NCL's transcanal cruises run between Miami and Los Angeles, on 13- to 17-day itineraries. Officers are Norwegian and service staff are international.

(www.ncl.com)

**OCEANIA CRUISES**: This upper-premium line's mid-sized ships carry 684 passengers in style, offering gourmet cuisine and attentive service in a country-club casual atmosphere. Full transits are available between Miami and Los Angeles. Officers and service staff are international. (www.oceaniacruises.com)

*Regatta (1998)*
*684 passengers, 30,000 tons*

**PRINCESS CRUISES**: Well known for its role in *The Love Boat* television show in the 1970s, this premium line is based outside Los Angeles. Princess ships feature a high percentage of staterooms with private verandahs, and the public areas are tastefully appointed with wood paneling and Italian marble. Princess ships appeal to a wide range of passengers, from retired couples to young families, and offer spacious playrooms, teen centers, fitness and spa facilities, and flexible dining options. The Coral Princess and Island Princess, each with more than 700 balcony staterooms, were designed specifically to cruise the canal.

*Grand Princess (1998)*
*2,600 passengers, 109,000 tons*

Princess offers full transits of the canal on a variety of 14- to 20-day cruises between Fort Lauderdale and Los Angeles, San Francisco and Vancouver A full day at Fuerte Amador (near Panama City) is featured on most full transits of the canal, providing Princess passengers with a two-day canal experience.

Partial transits are offered on 11-day roundtrip cruises from Fort Lauderdale.

*Diamond Princess (2003)*
*2,674 passengers, 113,000 tons*

Mexican Riviera itineraries include 7-day roundtrip cruises from Los Angeles, and 10-day roundtrip cruises from San Francisco. Officers and service staff are international. (www. princess.com)

*Seven Seas Navigator (1999)*
*490 passengers, 30,000 tons*

*Radiance of the Seas (2001)*
*2,112 passengers, 90,000 tons*

*Seabourn Spirit (1989)*
*208 passengers, 10,000 tons*

**REGENT SEVEN SEAS**: This luxury line offers small-ship intimacy, spaciousness and fine cuisine. Accommodations are all-suite, all balcony, and the cruise fare is all inclusive, including shore excursions. Officers are European and service staff are international. (www.rssc.com)

**ROYAL CARIBBEAN INTERNATIONAL**: This Miami-based cruise line operates a large fleet of contemporary ships in the Caribbean. These modern megaships offer impressive public areas such as a multi-deck atrium with glass elevators and a glass-wrapped observation lounge located on the highest deck to provide passengers with panoramic views of the passing scenery. RCI has introduced onboard activities not normally associated with cruising, such as rock climbing (with a wall constructed on the back of the funnel). Family staterooms, well-equipped playrooms and teen centers make these ships ideal for passengers with children.

RCI offers a few full transits of the canal between Fort Lauderdale and San Diego. Officers are Scandinavian; service staff are international. (www.royalcaribbean.com)

**SEABOURN CRUISE LINE**: Widely considered the ultimate in luxury cruising, Seabourn offers nothing but the finest cuisine, spacious and elegant accommodations, and white-glove service. The fleet's mega-yachts each carry 208 passengers, with the newer ships accommodating 450 passengers in ocean view suites, 90% of which have a private verandah. Seabourn combines interesting itineraries with unique shore excursions. Officers are Norwegian. (www.seabourn.com)

**SILVERSEA**: Consistently rated the Number One Small Ship Cruise Line by *Conde Nast Traveler*, this six-star luxury line features oceanview suites and European styling on its all-inclusive ships. Transcanal cruises run between Fort Lauderdale and Los Angeles or San Francisco.
(www.silversea.com)

*Silver Whisper (2001)*
*382 passengers, 28,250 tons*

**WINDSTAR CRUISES**: This is a premium line of high-tech sailing ships, each accommodating about 150 passengers (except Wind Surf which carries 312 passengers). Noted for their fine cuisine and good service, Windstar ships appeal to people seeking luxury in a casual setting along with a bit of sailing adventure. The line offers several transits of the Canal on seven-day cruises between Costa Rica's Pacific port of Puerto Caldera and Panama's Caribbean port of Colon.
(www.windstarcruises.com)

*Wind Spirit (1988)*
*140 passengers, 6,000 tons*

OTHER CRUISE LINES
Small-ship expedition cruises are offered on several lines specializing in adventure travel. These include:
**LINDBLAD EXPEDITIONS**: This company was founded in 1979 by Sven Lindblad, son of Swedish-born Lars Linblad who pioneered adventure expeditions in the 1950s and became known by many as the father of eco-tourism. Lindblad Expeditions partners with National Geographic to offer cruises covering Costa Rica and the Panama Canal.
(www.expeditions.com/wild)
**UN-CRUISE ADVENTURES**: Formerly American Safari Cruises and headquartered in Seattle, this company offers island-hopping itineraries in Mexico's Sea of Cortes.
(www.un-cruise.com)

ENT

**PHOTO AND ILLUSTRATION CREDITS:**

Michael DeFreitas, 5, 51, 90, 91b, 93a, 93b, 95a, 95b, 96 (inset), 97 (all), 99, 100, 145, 148, 153, 159, 173, 177, 182a, 186, 187, 226, 232b, 233, 240a+b, 256, 307, 314

Judi Lees, 21b, 21c, 29, 87a, 87b, 234, 246, 248, 249, 251a, 251b, 252a, 252b, 253, 254, 271a, 271b, 271c

Additional Photography:

2, 23c, 270, Martin Gerretsen

3, 55, 57, 70, 80, 81, 85, 209b, 213, 224, 231, Panama Canal Authority

8, 32, 217, Holland America Line

19a, 107 (inset), Jim Ferrier

27, 37b, 218, 220, 228b, Princess Cruises

31, Royal Caribbean International,

13, 46, NOAA

47, 311, 317, Circa Art

50a, 50b, Mary Evans Picture Library

54, Otis, F.N. (from The Illustrated History of the Panama Railroad)

43, 58, 63, 65, 72, 74, 75, 76, 77, 206, 207, 209a, 215, 224, 225, 229, Library of Congress

79, Bettman Archives

92a, Buddy Mays / Corbis

82, 92b, Underwood & Underwood

20c, 84, 198, 201a+b, Colon 2000 (Aventuras 2000)

101, Oliver Henriquez

102, Dave Matilla, NMFS

103, Tom Brakefield / Corbis

104, George Rhodes

111, Port of Miami

122, Port Everglades

142, Raymond Norris-Jones

143, Johnnie Black

149, Gordon Persson

150, Grant Kelly

243, Jos Lloyd

261a, Tomas Castelazo, Museo de la Ciudad, Leon, Mexico

263, Tourist Office of Spain

265, Stan Shebs

268a, 268b, 269a, 269b, Puerto Chiapas

296a, John Hyde / Alaska Stock

303, Luyten

310, Dale Frost / Port of San Diego

316, Cunard Line

320, Rich Niewiroski, Jr.
324, Port of Vancouver

Other photography by Anne Vipond.

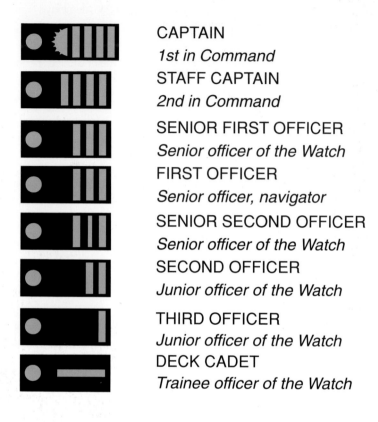

**CAPTAIN**
*1st in Command*
**STAFF CAPTAIN**
*2nd in Command*
**SENIOR FIRST OFFICER**
*Senior officer of the Watch*
**FIRST OFFICER**
*Senior officer, navigator*
**SENIOR SECOND OFFICER**
*Senior officer of the Watch*
**SECOND OFFICER**
*Junior officer of the Watch*
**THIRD OFFICER**
*Junior officer of the Watch*
**DECK CADET**
*Trainee officer of the Watch*

*To distinguish officers on board your ship, the above striping, as displayed on the officer's sleeve or epaulet, will indicate rank.*

917.2870405 P187 2014              ROB
Panama Canal by cruise ship.


ROBINSON
02/15